NISSAN / DATSUN

=NISSAN/DATSUN=

A HISTORY OF NISSAN MOTOR
CORPORATION IN U.S.A.
1960–1980

JOHN B. RAE

McGRAW-HILL BOOK COMPANY

New York   St. Louis   San Francisco   Auckland   Bogotá
Hamburg   Johannesburg   London   Madrid   Mexico
Montreal   New Delhi   Panama   Paris   São Paulo
Singapore   Sydney   Tokyo   Toronto

Library of Congress Cataloging in Publication Data

Rae, John Bell, date
  Nissan/Datsun, a history of Nissan Motor Corporation in
U.S.A., 1960–1980.

  Includes index.
  1. Nissan Motor Corporation in U.S.A.   2. Datsun
automobile.   3. Corporations, Japanese—United States.
I. Title.
HD9710.U54N557   338.7'6292'0973   81-8367
ISBN 0-07-051112-8   AACR2

 234567890   DODO   898765432

ISBN 0-07-051112-8

*The editors for this book were William A. Sabin and Christine M. Ulwick,
the designer was Naomi Auerbach, and the production
supervisor was Thomas G. Kowalczyk. It was set in Palatino
by University Graphics, Inc.
Printed and bound by R. R. Donnelley & Sons.*

CONTENTS

7037764

14 RACING, RALLIES, AND SPORTS CARS   251

The NMC-USA Start · The Competition Department · The Datsun Competition Record · The Z-Cars

15 ADMINISTRATIVE ORGANIZATION   269

Finance · Corporate Administration · Personnel · Legal · External Relations · Community Relations

16 PAST TO FUTURE   283

Twenty Years of Growth · A Changing Automobile Market · The Datsun Prospect

PREFACE

Nissan Motor Corporation in U.S.A. (NMC-USA) is an American company, incorporated under the laws of the state of California for the primary purpose of importing, distributing, and selling motor vehicles, specifically cars and trucks made by the sole stockholder, Nissan Motor Company, Ltd., of Japan. Consequently NMC-USA can be regarded as a representative of an expanding class of American business organizations, that is, concerns that are engaged in importing manufactured goods into the United States and are owned by the manufacturers of those goods. Such firms have become an integral part of the American economy; therefore the record of the founding of one of them and its growth during its first twenty years is of some historical importance.

The study of NMC-USA's first twenty years necessarily goes beyond the ordinary scope of a company history, because in the Nissan structure the relations between the parent company in Japan and the subsidiary in the United States occur in the area of international trade, with all its attendant complexities. This could have been a source of serious difficulty in writing the history, but it was not because Nissan people on both sides of the Pacific have steered me through these problems by their wholehearted cooperation.

When the arrangements were made for me to write this book,

the only stipulations, other than details of length and scheduling, were that it should be of sufficient scholarly merit to be acceptable in college classrooms, and that it should describe the growth of NMC-USA against the background of the whole import car industry. I have tried to meet these standards and at the same time produce a book whose appeal would be general rather than limited to students of business history.

In carrying out this assignment I am indebted to those who freely and willingly provided assistance. A Steering Committee of NMC-USA executives has guided the production of the history: Hiroyuki Yoshii, Vice President, Administration; Robert O. Link, Senior Vice President; Robert B. Kent, Vice President, Marketing Services; John L. Bukaty, Senior Administrative Advisor; John R. Gladen, Director, Market Planning (Mr. Gladen left the company at the end of 1980); John C. McDonnell, National Public Relations Manager; Richard E. Aldrich, National Manager, Corporate Administration. All have been unfailingly helpful and supportive. They have provided information and advice and they have read the manuscript thoroughly and corrected my mistakes.

Two people have been especially helpful to me. One is Mr. Aldrich, the coordinator of the project. He has taken care of the administrative details and has helped me in more ways than I can properly acknowledge. The other is Moon Kim, Corporate Librarian. He did the preliminary planning for this book. As my research assistant, he has made a vital contribution to this history. He has been indefatigable in collecting and organizing materials, including much essential information that I would have been unaware of otherwise, and he arranged and scheduled the interviews. Without his help the book would have taken longer to complete and would not have been of the same quality.

I am indebted to many others in the company. Those who were interviewed are listed in the section on Sources; I regret that I cannot acknowledge all of them as fully as they deserve. Presidents Majima and Arakawa have given their full support to this work, and their predecessors, former President Yutaka

Katayama and former Executive Vice President Soichi Kawazoe have contributed in many ways besides their recorded interviews. Mr. Kawazoe provided a copy of the relevant chapter of his memoirs, other notes, and a number of the pictures that appear in this book. Timothy J. Conley, of the company's legal staff, has read the manuscript, steered me clear of pitfalls, and offered much useful comment. Michael A. Cornelius, General Counsel, has also been generous in giving his time to discuss various problems on which I sought his advice.

I am very grateful to Gunnel V. Vacha for being a constant and always willing resource when I was looking for information. Kaye S. Park of the Import Department secured the information that went into the Introduction and enlightened me on the working of the import and distribution system. Martin Schwager and Melvin J. Wexler of the Market Research Department have responded more than generously to my requests for data. The results are, I hope, made amply clear in the text. Marty McLaughlin and Pamela Matulavage contributed to locating suitable illustrations, and Dennis Fujita provided data on the growth of company staff. Reid Briggs, in addition to his informative interview, took time, along with his associate Joseph Toy, to provide useful information about the company's antitrust suit.

When I went to Japan I was given the same cordial cooperation as I encountered at NMC-USA. I am obligated to so many people that I hesitate to single out specific individuals, but I must acknowledge especially in Nissan Motor Co., Ltd., Shoji Kato, Business Management Manager, Export Department, North America; Sanii Kanazawa of the same department; and Noriko Haneda and Chieko Takayanagi of the International Division. In addition, the Business Research Department of Nissan Motor Co., Ltd., has read the manuscript and I wish to thank Haruhiko Nishiyama, General Manager, and his staff for their service in keeping the record straight.

Professor Koichi Shimokawa of the faculty of business administration, Hosei University, Japan's leading historian of the automotive industry, was my principal host during this visit and devoted much time and effort to ensuring that it was profitable and enjoyable. He has also read the manuscript and his advice and suggestions have been of inestimable assistance.

Further thanks are owed to Toshitaka Enomoto and Takeshi Ando of NMC-USA for assistance in innumerable ways. I have had willing cooperation from everyone that I have encountered in the NMC-USA organization; if I have inadvertently left anyone off my list who should be there, I apologize.

Finally, I owe more than I can express to Mary P. Dunton, who has patiently typed and retyped the manuscript and in the process made very useful suggestions, and to Elsie Yee, who assisted in transcribing the tapes of the interviews. My daughter Helen zealously typed my drafts and my wife Florence assisted in compiling the index, as she has become accustomed to doing.

John B. Rae

NISSAN / DATSUN

INTRODUCTION

The car would not have attracted any special attention as it came together on the assembly line in the big Oppama plant of Nissan Motor Company, Ltd. It was one of some 2.3 million cars that Nissan would build in 1976, and also one of 1.25 million Datsuns that would be exported. The assembly line workers would have known that it was going to be an export car because the steering wheel and controls were placed for driving where "keep to the right" was the rule, instead of "keep to the left" as in Japan; that simply meant it might go anywhere in the world, except maybe Great Britain and a few other places. There was nothing special about it to mark it as the two-millionth Datsun that would be sold in the United States. It came off the line as a cocoa-brown 210 Datsun hatchback, serial number HLB210-167304, engine number 299376, and got its final inspection and approval—rigorous inspection, no mere formality—on March 8, 1976. Then it was taken to the Hommoku Wharf in neighboring Yokohama, 38 acres of storage and shipping facilities built by Nissan exclusively to handle its export of motor vehicles.

At that point the brown hatchback had already been the object of a considerable amount of paperwork, not all by itself of course. Sometime earlier, maybe three months, the Nissan Export Department had advised Gary Holland, Import Director for Nissan Motor Corporation in U.S.A. (NMC-USA), what the estimated production for March 1976 would be. Holland, in return, placed an order in the middle of January, itemizing what he wanted in terms of two- or four-door models; automatic or manual transmissions; preference in body styles and colors. This order was developed through the use of computer calculations based on market projections, dealer requests, previous sales records, and a solid core of experience.

Next, the Nissan Export Department informed him how many vehicles could actually be shipped in March; this depended mainly on the quantity of shipping available and the routes for which the vessels were chartered. Then it became the responsibility of NMC's top sales management to decide what went where, and out of all of this HLB210-167304 found itself with a sticker on its windshield reading "SDN," which meant that it would go to Seattle and from there to Denver.

Cars in transit have to be kept moving; it costs too much to have them sitting on a dock. So on March 14, HLB210-167304 was in the hold of the freighter *Jalanta*, pulling out of Yokohama to head across the Pacific with 1320 Datsuns aboard. The *Jalanta* was under charter to the Nissan Motor Car Carrier Company, Ltd., but it was not one of the company-operated ships specially designed and built for carrying motor vehicles. They have ramps so that the cargo can be driven on and off, but with Nissan's export business mushrooming, these ships have to be supplemented with conventional lift on/lift off freighters such as *Jalanta*. It takes a lot of tonnage to transport 1.25 million motor vehicles all over the world.

At this stage of its journey, HLB210-167304 was officially in the custody of the Marubeni America Corporation. This is a customary, although not necessarily universal, arrangement in Japan's international trade, whereby one of the great trading corporations, an institution unique to Japan, acts as the legal importer and handles the technicalities of shipping and clearing goods through customs. In this case, Marubeni had given valuable help to Nissan in introducing the Datsun to the United States and the association continued.

The voyage across the Pacific was uneventful and the *Jalanta* docked in Seattle after a ten-day trip. The cargo had been properly stowed so that the brown hatchback and practically all the others arrived in excellent condition. It had not always been so. In the early days, before Hommoku Wharf and the Nissan Motor Car Carrier Company, it was not unusual for ships to come in with one-third of the cars damaged by poor stowage, dirty holds, or seawater leaking through loose hatches. But those days were over. The hatchback was hoisted on to the dock ready to go. It had to go through customs first, of course. Then it was turned over to the Auto Processing Company, Seattle port agent for NMC-USA. It was thoroughly checked over and put on the lot with other cars destined for Denver—this was determined not just by the windshield sticker but by the copy of the *Jalanta*'s manifest given by Marubeni to the port agent. There was no hit-or-miss parking here; everything was neatly in order by model and color.

So presently, the brown hatchback was loaded onto a Burlington Northern rail car, which was hauled to the classification yard and there attached to a long freight train that headed eastward over the Cascades. Eventually the rail car went to Billings, Montana, then south across Wyoming, through Cheyenne and into Denver. There HLB210-167304 became the responsibility of the Denver Regional Office of NMC-USA, which gave it another thorough check and then assigned it, as determined by the Equitable Distribution System, to Arapahoe Datsun at 6260 South Broadway, in neighboring Littleton, Colorado.

Lloyd Tyson, the manager of Arapahoe Datsun, had the option of accepting or rejecting the car, and he accepted it. The assignment was made by computer through the Equitable Distribution System, based on availability of cars, marketing guides, and average sales for each dealer. This produced the allocation of HLB210-167304 to Arapahoe Datsun by the Vehicle

Distributor for the Denver Region of NMC-USA, and once it was accepted, the computer prepared the bill of lading and the "Monroney Label." This is the window sticker itemizing the total suggested price for the vehicle that we can see on all new automobiles. It is required by a law named for its sponsor, United States Senator "Mike" Monroney of Oklahoma.

The brown hatchback was now in the last part of its long trip. It was moved to the staging area of the Denver Region's warehouse, and there a truck belonging to the Convoy Company, which does the road hauls for the Denver Region, picked it up and delivered it to Arapahoe Datsun. No one had placed a specific order with Mr. Tyson for a cocoa-brown 210 hatchback, the way domestic cars are frequently ordered. This is seldom done with import cars because it would add further complications to an already elaborate process. Thus, like most Datsuns, HLB210-167304 went into the showroom, where it stayed just three weeks. On May 13, Mr. P. Auriemma, then of 2930 West Cornell, in a nearby section of Denver, bought it. So the brown hatchback reached the end of its journey. It had come a long way—at least 7000 miles—and it had been looked after by a variety of people. None of them knew, nor did the dealer or the buyer, that HLB210-167304 was, as accurately as it is possible to determine, the two-millionth vehicle to be sold by Nissan Motor Corporation in U.S.A. At that point, the company had been in business for fifteen and a half years and Datsun cars had been on the U.S. market for just over seventeen years. The sale of HLB210-167304 thus marks a major achievement. The rest of this book attempts to explain how it was done.

1

THE PRELIMINARY STEPS

Los Angeles, California, January 9 to 19, 1958. The automobile sections of the southern California press were featuring the Imported Motor Car Show then being held at the Shrine Exposition Hall in Los Angeles; in its edition for Sunday, January 12, the *Los Angeles Times* gave first place to this item:

> Two newcomers, the Toyopet and Datsun, manufactured in Japan, are making their premiere at the Shrine. This marks the first time American buyers will have the opportunity to inspect the cars which have been favorites in the Land of the Rising Sun. And although both models have proved popular in South American and Asiatic countries, their unveiling at the Imported Motor Car Show marks the initial Japanese automotive industry's bid to compete for Southland customer dollars.

The writer's reaction, if he had been able to foresee how successful that bid would eventually be, makes an interesting speculation. At that time, few Americans knew anything about Japanese automobiles or their makers; even the *Times* correspondent missed the highly newsworthy fact that Japan's two largest motor vehicle manufacturers had chosen simultaneously to carry their vigorous rivalry into the United States market.

This decision represents a landmark stage in the growth of the Japanese automotive industry. In the light of what has happened since, it seems incredible that *total* Japanese motor vehicle production surpassed 100,000 for the first time in 1956. (The figure excludes trucks and three-wheel cars, which then constituted a substantial part of Japanese automotive output.) Until this time the Japanese industry had been small-scale and, in general, technically inferior to both the American and European automotive industries. This situation was the consequence of a somewhat late start (commercial manufacturing of motor vehicles in Japan began about 1910), a home market severely limited by lack of sufficient purchasing power to support quantity production, and generally poor roads. Purchasing power began to increase with the rapid recovery of the Japanese economy after the Occupation authorities turned industry completely back to its owners, but the building of a modern road system in Japan was not really accomplished until the 1960s.

The Early Years

The origin of the Datsun name and the Nissan Motor Company can be traced back to 1911, when Masujuro Hashimoto founded the Kwaishinsha Motor Car Works.[1] What appears to have been his first car, a small 10-horsepower passenger automobile, was exhibited in 1914 and received an award. Hashimoto's backers were three businessmen named Den, Aoyama, and Takeuchi, and the car took its name from their initials: D A T. This company ran into financial trouble and was reorganized in 1918 as the Kwaishinsha Company, Ltd., which produced a small, sports-type two-seater that became the "son of DAT," or Datson. However, the English letter combination S-O-N as pronounced in Japanese sounds like an expression for losing money, and it seems to have been important to have a name for the car that could be spelled in English. At any rate the difficulty was resolved by changing "son" to "sun," which has a good connotation in both English and Japanese.

Production remained very limited, and after the disastrous earthquake of 1923, which destroyed many of Japan's automobile factories, the DAT firm found it necessary to merge with the Jitsuyo Jidosha Seizo (Practical Automobile Manufacturing) Company as the DAT Jidosha Seizo Company, Ltd. The merger was effective in 1926. The combined company was still small, but in 1932 it introduced a new Datsun line, a small car with a 500cc engine, which marked the beginning of regular, continuous production of motor vehicles carrying the Datsun name. The year 1932 was gloomy throughout the world, but for the Japanese automotive industry as a whole, it was the beginning of a period of growth (see Table 1.1). Throughout the 1920s the development of the industry remained slow, although the destruction of rail transport facilities in the 1923 earthquake stimulated reliance on motor vehicles. General Motors (1927)

TABLE 1.1   *Japanese Motor Vehicle Production and Exports, 1930–1945   (Four-Wheel Vehicles Only)*

Year	Production (fiscal year, April–March)	Exports (calendar year)
1930	458	—
1931	436	—
1932	880	—
1933	1,681	—
1934	2,787	349
1935	5,089	1,361
1936	12,186	3,998
1937	18,055	3,413
1938	24,388	2,118
1939	34,514	7,064
1940	46,041	4,915
1941	46,498	2,210
1942	37,188	1,180
1943	25,879	1,599
1944	21,762	213
1945	6,726	—

SOURCE: Nissan Motor Co., Ltd.

and Ford (1925) both established assembly plants in Japan and these accounted for the largest part of the country's output of motor vehicles during this decade.

The 1930s brought a change. The effect of the worldwide depression was to stimulate in Japan, as elsewhere, a desire for greater economic self-sufficiency. In addition, the Japanese military, faced with heavier commitments in East Asia, was interested in greater output of highway vehicles, especially trucks; there was an understandable feeling that a product this important to national welfare and security should come from domestic rather than foreign or foreign-owned sources. Legislation in 1936 was directed at excluding foreign firms and encouraging domestic automotive manufacturers to strengthen themselves by merger. With this encouragement, Japanese motor vehicle production—four wheel vehicles, excluding three-wheelers and motorcycles—climbed from just under 1700 units in 1933 to almost 47,000 in 1941, predominantly trucks. Passenger car production started to rise but was curtailed by government-imposed restrictions in 1938 because of shortages of materials resulting from the spread of hostilities in China. This development was the work of small companies such as Nissan, Toyota, and Isuzu. The big Zaibatsu—Mitsui, Mitsubishi, Sumitomo—were still reluctant to enter what they considered a risky business despite the government support.[2] Automobile manufacturing was left to smaller organizations, such as Nissan, that were willing to accept the challenge.

An output of 47,000 vehicles a year was still minuscule in comparison with that of the United States and prewar Western Europe, but the stimulus of growth was strong enough to have an important effect on the makers of the Datsun. In 1933, the DAT Jidosha Seizo Company underwent a reorganization and a year after that was renamed Nissan Motor Company, Ltd. (Japan Industries), with a capital of 10 million yen. Between then and 1938, when passenger car production stopped, Nissan made its first standard-size automobiles, introduced mass-production techniques, and shipped out its first few exports. This advance was achieved with the aid of an agreement with the American Graham-Paige Motor Car Company for machinery and technical assistance. Nissan's relationship with the United States thus began very early in the company's history. It is worth mentioning here that Nissan's principal competitor, Toyota, was also a product of this stimulus to motor vehicle production in the 1930s. Initially a manufacturer of automatic looms, Toyota expanded into automobile manufacturing in 1933 but did not put its first car on the market until 1935.

War and Recovery

As could be expected, the Second World War saw Nissan's energies concentrated on military production. Among other things, the company went into the manufacture of aircraft engines in 1943, and in 1944 there was a major reorganization in which the firm became Nissan Heavy Industries, with a greatly increased capitalization. Before this (1939), much of the vehicle manufacturing was transferred to Manchuria, through an organization called the Manchurian Motor Company.[3] When the war ended, this operation vanished into the hands of the Russians, along with much of its trained personnel. In Japan, most of Nissan's production facilities were taken over by the Occupation authorities. It was a very difficult period, but with what it had left, the company managed to resume the manufacturing of Datsun trucks in 1946 and passenger cars in 1948. In 1949, it resumed the name Nissan Motor Company, Ltd.

The outbreak of war in Korea gave an unexpected fillip to Nissan's revival—in fact to the whole Japanese motor vehicle industry—in the form of orders for trucks for the United Nations forces in Korea. (The American term for this type of procurement was "offshore purchases.") The Japanese producers had two conspicuous advantages. In retrospect the volume of these purchases seems small; Nissan sold 4325 vehicles to the United States Army over a period of nine months, from September 1950 to June 1951, plus another 510 to the Japanese Police Reserve Division.[4] At the time, these orders came as a welcome stimulus to an industry that had habitually produced for a very limited market and was just beginning to recover from a devastating war.

The Japanese motor vehicle industry had, in fact, to be virtually recreated. A British authority observes that at the end of the war, "There was an abundance of engineering capacity that could be directed to their manufacture, but Japan was deficient in up-to-date equipment and technical knowledge. Remedies were sought in technical assistance contracts with foreign firms, such as Austin, Hillman, Renault, and Willys-Overland, and as a result foreign makes of cars were produced under license."[5] These firms were all manufacturers of small cars.

Nissan's involvement in this practice took the form of an arrangement with the Austin Motor Company of Great Britain in 1952 for the assembly and eventual construction of Austin cars by Nissan. This arrangement had the advantage of providing Nissan with technical assistance that Austin was well qualified to supply. Since Austin was the first motor vehicle manufacturer to adopt automatic transfer machines on its assembly line, this association was undoubtedly at least partially responsible for Nissan introducing the same technique to Japan in 1956. There were still problems to be resolved. The beginning of Austin production was handicapped by a 100-day strike, which essentially the company won. The union that had staged the strike was replaced by a new organization and an agreement for closer labor-management cooperation.

Drive for Exports

By the mid-1950s, the Nissan Motor Company was in a promising position. Its plants had been restored, it had a good, diversified product line (both Austin and Datsun), and up-to-date production equipment. It had able, energetic leadership, personified in Katsuji Kawamata, who became President in December 1957. The company was then in vigorous competition with Toyota for leadership of the Japanese automobile industry. Kawamata had ambitious plans for the company's growth, but even he could hardly have foreseen completely the phenomenal expansion that the Japanese automobile industry would presently undergo. Attaining a national output of four-wheel motor vehicles exceeding 100,000 in 1956 offered a bright prospect for the future, but it could hardly compare with the million and more cars produced by both West Germany and the United Kingdom, let alone the 7 million by the United States. Nor, in spite of encouraging signs of the increasing acceptability of small foreign cars in the United States, could he or anyone else at Nissan have fully anitcipated the directions that the American automobile market was about to take. (These developments are described in detail in Chapter 2, The American Automobile Scene in the 1950s.) What mattered was that Kawamata and his associates were resolved that Nissan should grow and were prepared to take risks for that purpose.

Exports were a necessary part of any program of expansion because the Japanese home market was still limited (see Table 1.2). It was growing, aided by tariff and other restrictions that made the importing of foreign cars prohibitively expensive. Domestic sales, however, could not yet support a really major automobile manufacturer, not necessarily on the scale of the American giants but comparable to larger European companies: Renault, Volkswagen, Fiat, or the British Motor Corporation, recently formed from Austin and Morris Motors. Volume production is contingent on volume sales, and the necessary volume was not going to be reached in Japan itself for some time.

The Japanese automobile industry had yet to break the circle that small-scale production meant high unit costs and therefore high prices, which in turn restricted sales and kept production low. In those days, a large proportion of the Datsun passenger cars sold in Japan went to taxi companies. If export sales could raise production to any significant degree, then there could be a feedback in lower unit costs that would mean lower prices and better sales at home. As a further incentive to look abroad, there was an economic slowdown in Japan in 1957 to 1958 (as there was in the United States also), which resulted in Nissan having to reduce its output sharply.[6]

The situation is well summed up in this excerpt from *The Oriental Economist:*

> The demand for new cars may be still further developed if their prices are sufficiently lowered. To that end, a wide curtailment of production costs is considered necessary. In these circumstances, Japanese motor companies have begun to redouble efforts for the promotion of exports. Some of the principal stimulants to export efforts are: 1) the United States is importing the annual average of 200,000 small cars from Europe; 2) the weight of demand for household cars in the United States has continued rising, and such a demand is being focused on smaller second cars economical in operation and requiring a narrower parking space.[7]

TABLE 1.2   *Japanese Motor Vehicle Production, 1946–1960   (Four-Wheel Vehicles Only)*

Year (Jan.–Dec.)	Cars	Trucks	Buses	Total
1916	—	14,914	7	14,921
1917	110	11,106	104	11,320
1918	381	19,211	775	20,367
1919	1,070	25,560	2,070	28,700
1950	1,591	26,501	3,502	31,597
1951	3,611	30,817	4,062	38,490
1952	4,837	29,960	4,169	38,966
1953	8,789	36,147	4,842	49,778
1954	14,472	49,852	5,749	70,073
1955	20,268	43,857	4,807	68,932
1956	32,056	72,958	6,052	111,066
1957	47,121	126,820	8,036	181,977
1958	50,643	130,066	7,594	188,303
1959	78,598	177,485	6,731	262,814
1960	165,094	308,020	8,437	481,551

SOURCE: *A Guide to the Automobile Industry of Japan,* 1965, p. 19.

Three features of this statement deserve attention. First, it pinpoints the fact that if the Japanese automobile manufacturers were to take advantage of the economies of scale ("wide curtailment of production costs"), they would have to export in quantity. Second, the most likely place to achieve the needed quantity was the United States. Third, it is quite definite about what kind of market the United States was expected to offer: namely, a strong second-car market for the small cars the Japanese companies would be selling.

This appraisal is confirmed by Kawamata himself. In a statement published in 1966, he expressed his ambition to make Nissan Motor Company, Ltd., a factor in the world automotive market and gave as some of the principal reasons for pushing exports to the United States: "1. Increased sales to the U.S.A. would give Nissan more prestige and credit in the domestic market as well as other areas. 2. Further price cut is possible through mass producing of export cars."[8]

Entering the United States Market

By 1958, Datsun cars were being exported in small numbers to Southeast Asian countries and the South Pacific area, and sales opportunities were opening up in Latin America which would eventually yield excellent results. Datsun assembly plants were built in Mexico and Peru in the 1960s. These markets were welcome but, for the time being at any rate, very limited. In 1958, Datsun exports totaled 3232 vehicles, which was 31.4 percent of all Japanese motor vehicle exports—another illuminating index of where the Japanese automobile industry stood at this time. At this level, Nissan could not hope to be anything more than a respectable minor producer in the world automotive picture. The route to expansion was obvious, alluring, and risky—gaining a foothold in the massive market offered by the United States.

This was not a step to be taken lightly, and it is clear that the decision was given long and careful consideration. On the positive side, the success being attained in the United States by small foreign cars such as Volkswagen, Renault, and Fiat gave reason to hope that there could be a place for a car like the Datsun. By the end of 1957, in fact, Nissan had received a number of proposals from would-be Datsun distributors in the United States.[9] On the other side was concern among Nissan executives over the fact that the Datsun of that period appeared to compare unfavorably in design, roominess, and technical quality with both the American and European models it would be competing with. Kawamata later expressed what he and his associates must have felt at the time: "As a matter of fact, export to U.S.A. cost us more expenditure, more complicated paper work, and more ingenious market strategies, as compared with those of domestic sales. Especially we must face tough competition in the United States of America, since the U.S. is a country of the automobile."[10]

The consensus style favored by Japanese management makes it uncertain just when and by whom the key decisions were made; entering the American market was in fact a cautious, gradual process. Some encouragement undoubtedly was given by the good showing that Datsuns made in the 1958 Australian Mobil Gas Trial. This was a 10,000-mile endurance run over a course regarded as one of the most difficult in the world. Any car that even finished was considered to have done remarkably well. Yutaka Katayama, Advertising Manager of the Nissan Motor Company and a lifelong sports car enthusiast, persuaded his company to compete. Two Datsuns participated and both completed the course. One, a truck, was first in a field of eight cars in its class (less than 1000cc), and the other was well up among the leaders.[11] This performance naturally brought the Datsun a good deal of favorable publicity and helped to allay some of the misgivings at Nissan about the ability of its cars to hold their own in competition with American and European motor vehicles.

The effect of this success in terms of the decision to go into the American market is difficult to evaluate. It could have been a contributing factor, but it certainly was not the decisive one, because the first step had already been taken by the time the Australian rally was held. In 1957, Nissan made surveys of American market prospects through two of the major Japanese trading corporations, Marubeni and Mitsubishi; Marubeni concentrating on the Pacific Coast and Mitsubishi on the Atlantic. (As the next chapter will show, these were the areas most receptive to import cars.) In November 1957, Mr. Wakatsuki of the Los Angeles office of the Marubeni Corporation arrived in Tokyo with a proposal that Nissan display its products at the forthcoming Imported Motor Car Show in Los Angeles. He found a responsive atmosphere. What Wakatsuki was asking was a minor commitment. If the vehicles were badly received, then the company could simply stay out of the United States until a more favorable opportunity came along. If the reception was good, the company could readily decide how to proceed from there. Another factor to be weighed was that Toyota was in the process of establishing an American sales organization and would be represented at the Los Angeles show. It would hardly do for Nissan to let its principal competitor steal a march in getting established in the United States. So the Marubeni proposal was accepted. What were Nissan's expectations at this juncture? What kind of niche did it see the Datsun as occupying in the American market? In general, beyond the overall goal of increasing exports, the recession that was hurting the company at home could be seen as presenting an opportunity in the United States. American buyers, as described in the next chapter, were visibly turning toward smaller, more economical cars. A more specific suggestion appears in two appraisals, one American and one Japanese, made shortly after Japanese automobiles began to be sold regularly in the United States. *Business Week** observed:

> Japan is plunging into the foreign car market here with two entries, Nissan's four-door Datsun and Toyota's somewhat larger Toyopet Crown. With over 50 foreign car makes already on sale here, the Japanese auto industry isn't likely to carve out a big slice of the U.S. market

*"Seeking a Place on U.S. Roads," *Business Week*, August 2, 1958, p.67.

for itself. [The editor's crystal ball was evidently malfunctioning at this point, although it was a reasonable enough appraisal at the time.]

The Japanese companies, Nissan Automobile Co. and Toyota Motor Sales Co., feel that they have no other choice than making a stab at the small, second-car market here. Unlike Western European automakers, which in some cases can't keep up with local demand, the Japanese face an almost stagnant car market at home.

The *Japan Economic Yearbook* (International Publications Service) for 1958, reviewing a falling off in motor vehicle production from the 181,977 record of 1957, saw some compensation in prospective export gains and also pinpointed the second-car market as the most likely source of American sales for Japanese cars (p. 132): "In the Los Angeles district each family has two motor cars or at the rate of one car per two persons. Because of the limited space available for garaging and parking, however, as the second car a midget model, priced at $2,000 or so, is preferred to a standard one. Thus there is hope that 500 small cars per month will be exported there."

There is some misconception here about what life in Los Angeles was really like, and the term "midget" would have been "compact" in the United States, but the direction of Japanese thinking about their probable place in the U.S. automobile market is unmistakable. They would provide the second car for the American family. No one could have predicted in 1958 that their place would turn out to be far larger.

The First Sales Organization

Nissan's American venture began modestly. In response to the Marubeni Corporation's recommendation, Koichi Iwata of Nissan's Export Department was sent to the Los Angeles Imported Car Show with two passenger cars and a pickup truck. According to his own account, his budget was so slender that he could not afford to have colored advertising brochures printed and had to settle for black and white.[12] Nevertheless, the display did very well. The exposition hall has three floors (basement, first, and second) and the Datsuns were given space in a good location on the first floor, next to Mercedes-Benz. The company record designates the two passenger cars as Datsun L210s, but advertisements in Los Angeles newspapers term both the cars and trucks Datsun 1000. The difference may represent the fact that these vehicles were modified in the hope of making them more suitable for American conditions by giving them a compression ratio of 7:5 and 37 horsepower, rather higher than used in Japan. The Los Angeles Times (January 12, 1959) reported on them: "The Datsun's 988cc OHV plant can move the somewhat tiny, four-door sedan at a 60 m.p.h. clip."

In view of this description and the previous concern in Nissan management about the Datsun's ability to meet American expectations in a motor vehicle, it is a little puzzling that when Iwata found that his cars could not keep up with traffic speeds on the southern California freeways, Kawamata and other Nissan executives were shocked. Presumably, they had expected more of the stepped-up compression ratio and horsepower.[13] Iawata's report resulted in the formation of a special project team to study changes in design to make Datsuns more suitable for the American and European markets.

This step, as Iwata observes, was the beginning of study and planning to develop Datsun models suitable for Nissan's export markets. It was a very significant beginning. Much of the success of Nissan and other Japanese automobile manufacturers in the United States has been due to their willingness to study and respond to the conditions of the American market. They, far more than others, except Volkswagen, grasped the seemingly elementary principle that if they wanted to sell motor vehicles in the United States, they had better find out what kind of cars Americans wanted to buy, and design and build accordingly. It is a simple principle to state, but implementing it demands a great deal of painstaking effort.

The strong and weak features of these first Datsuns to appear in the United States were carefully analyzed by the magazine Road and Track in December 1958. It found the styling to be based on "functional utility" and the interior to be surprisingly roomy for the size of the car, except that the hand brake was awkwardly placed between the driver's seat and the door, and the steering wheel was uncomfortably low. The operation of the shift lever mounted on the steering post was commended, but not the nonstandard shift pattern. In performance, the report said:

> The performance of the Datsun is best described as melancholy. Even though its gearing is well chosen, the engine is just too small to cope with the car's weight. . . .
>
> The car is really quite good, and with a few relatively simple changes it could go over. It is, even in its present form, better than most of the small British cars currently being sold in this country: not so fast, perhaps, but it should be more reliable and it has a nice solid feeling about it.[14]

Whatever deficiencies the Datsun may have had, they had no perceptible effect on the car's reception. The display at the Imported Car Show in Los Angeles brought Iwata thirty-five requests for distributorships or dealerships. There were other showings in 1958. One Datsun was exhibited at the Texas State Fair Automobile Show in Dallas in October, and others at the Los Angeles International Motor Show in November, one of the biggest automobile shows in the nation.[15] However, the process of actually putting Datsuns on the market began with the January exhibition.

After reviewing the applications with advice from Wakatsuki, Nissan selected Mitsubishi as importer and Chester G. Luby, a Chevrolet dealer in Forest Hills, New York, as sole distributor for a region comprising twenty-two eastern states.[16] This agreement was signed on April 29, 1958. On May 15, a similar agreement made Marubeni the importer and Woolverton Motors of North Hollywood, California, distributor for an area including eleven western and southwestern states.

The middle of the country was then too uninviting a prospect for import cars to justify much effort by an embryonic organization with uncertain prospects. Both distributors were already large organizations dealing in domestic and some foreign makes. They established subsidiaries, Luby Datsun Distributors and Western Datsun Distributors, to handle their new line. In September, the heads of these firms went to Japan to sign five-year contracts as agents for Nissan Motor Company. The party consisted of Mr. and Mrs. Chester J. Luby (President, Luby Datsun), Mr. and Mrs. Sam Luby (President, Luby Chevrolet), Mr. and Mrs. William Singer (their connection is not given), E. G. Woolverton (owner of Woolverton Motors), and Mr. and Mrs. Jack Woolverton (owner of Western Datsun Distributors). Sales were scheduled to begin in August, and at the beginning of that month the distributors had 50 vehicles on hand, with 75 more in transit and 125 awaiting shipment in Yokohama.[17] The announced port-of-entry price was $1799 for the four-door Datsun sedan.[18] In anticipation of the start of Datsun sales, Nissan in March 1958, before a selling agreement had been reached, sent Mr. Uno, General Manager of the North American Department, Mr. Hara, General Manager of the Planning Department, and several engineers to the United States to initiate arrangements for testing Datsun cars and dealing with whatever technical problems might come up. The company hoped to be able to ship at the rate of 500 vehicles a month by the end of 1958, but this goal proved unattainable. Datsun's American sales in 1958 totaled 83 units (Appendix B gives year-by-year sales totals and market shares).

Some delay in getting the operation started was predictable. It took time to recruit dealers for an almost completely unknown foreign car—"almost" because some Americans who had served in Japan or Korea had become favorably acquainted with Datsun trucks. In fact, the first Datsun dealer to be appointed could be said to have been drafted rather than recruited. He was Ray Lemke of San Diego, California, still in business as San Diego Datsun. He continued to make firsts. In 1965, he achieved recognition as the first Datsun dealer to sell 100 cars in a month, and in 1979, when he had completed twenty years with Datsun, he was the first to sign the new Perpetual Sales Agreement with Nissan Motor Corporation in U.S.A.[19]

Lemke had begun as a mechanic. He was interested in small

cars and in the late 1940s began selling Crosleys as an adjunct to his service and repair business in San Diego.[20] He says, "I built my dealership from the back end up. We sell cars, but I feel that we have the best service and parts operation in the country."[21] When Crosley stopped production, he took on two now forgotten German makes, Lloyd and Goggomobil, for which Woolverton Motors was also distributor. One shipment of cars included a Datsun, a 1000cc sedan, which Lemke accepted as part of the consignment. To his skilled mechanic's eye, it was the best vehicle in the assortment, and so he began to sell Datsuns on October 8, 1958. (He now regrets that he did not keep this first car when it was traded in some years later for another Datsun.) The following spring, he also made the first sale of a Datsun truck in the United States. The buyer, Richard E. McCutcheon, a navy veteran who had served in Japan, tells how it happened.

> I had been driving a Crosley station wagon and was planning to sell it and get something else when I saw this truckload of Datsuns with a pickup truck, I followed the hauler to San Diego Datsun, determined to buy it.
> I had been over in Japan and I knew how rough their roads were and it figured, if the trucks could take that kind of a beating, they must be something. Well, Ray didn't want to sell it to me, 'cause he wanted to keep it for the showroom, but I talked him out of it.
> It ran great. I owned it for six or seven years and put 70,000 miles on it and the only things I had to replace were the radiator hoses and heater hoses. It still had the original battery and tires. I got $600 for it and traded it in on another Datsun pickup and I put another 68,000 miles on that.[22]

Mr. Lemke confirms this account of the transaction but says he would have been less accommodating about selling the truck if he had realized it would take him three months to get another one. He took no chances on the second truck; it was put on display on the roof of his showroom. McCutcheon paid $1647 for the first truck.

Lemke's mechanical ability was also important in helping to correct some of the defects that appeared in these first Datsuns to be offered in the United States. Because the car had to be driven full throttle much of the time in order to keep up with California freeway traffic, unexpected wear developed in the babbitted crankshaft bearings. He found that this fault could be corrected by a simple readjustment in the bearing inserts, something the dealer himself could do in about an hour. The car was still hard put to maintain American standards of speed, but at least the bearings did not wear out after 20,000 miles. Subsequently, these modifications and others suggested by Lemke were incorporated into the design of the car.

So the Nissan Motor Company came into the American market cautiously, almost hesitantly. The caution was understandable, because the company had much at stake. it could of course withdraw if the venture appeared to be turning out badly, but only at the cost of a damaging blow to its hopes for worldwide prestige. Consequently, it is worthwhile looking at the state of the American automobile market when the Datsun made its bid for a place in it.

2

THE AMERICAN AUTOMOBILE SCENE IN THE 1950s

The market that Nissan chose to enter in 1958 held both great promise and great risk. The United States was, and still is, the world's biggest and most lucrative market for motor vehicles. It is a highly competitive market in which failure has been frequent and success is likely to be temporary. In the late 1950s, this market was in a condition of uncertain flux, with no clear indication of the direction—or directions—it might eventually take. Import cars of various kinds had obtained a foothold, and it was likely that some would stay, but no one could predict with any certainty which ones they would be or in what quantity, and there was no assurance that there was room for newcomers.

The Era of the Tail Fins

When the Second World War ended, civilian motor vehicle production resumed rapidly. There was an enormous pent-up demand for cars, and the manufacturing plant was completely intact, in fact with capacity expanded to meet the needs of military production. This situation attracted a number of prospective new entrants into the field but only one, Kaiser-Frazer, ever got into substantial production. The industry retained the oligopolistic pattern it had attained in the 1930s, with the "Big Three" (General Motors, Ford, Chrysler) controlling 90 percent of the market for passenger automobiles and the rest divided among a small group of independents. Kaizer-Frazer's inability to survive for more than a few years, even with help from low-interest government funding and a war-built plant (Willow Run, sold for a fraction of its cost), testifies to the extreme difficulty that any new entrant faced, domestic or foreign. In addition, there had been little previous interest in foreign cars in the United States, so that the big American companies had every reason to believe themselves to be in an impregnable position as they went into the 1950s.

The return to full-scale automobile production was delayed by shortages of materials and labor problems in the late 1940s and then by the outbreak of war in Korea. When that ended and peacetime market conditions returned, the Big Three domination was stronger than ever. In the mid-1950s their combined share of the market went up to 95 percent. The remaining independents sought survival by merging. Nash and Hudson became American Motors in 1954, and Studebaker and Packard were combined in the same year. Willys-Overland became part of the Kaiser organization in 1953 and continued in business as the manufacturer of Jeeps when the rest of Kaiser-Frazer automobile production was terminated. It was sold to American Motors in 1969. Under these conditions, it was difficult to believe that any new arrival, domestic or foreign, could have the slightest prospect of challenging the grip of the Big Three on the U.S. automobile market.

When hostilities ended in Korea, the American automobile industry for the first time in twenty years was free to expand without the restraints of depression, war, or shortages of materials. The result, in terms of output, was impressive; in terms of product, still controversial. In the mid-1950s, American auto-mobile designers and much of the American motoring public were carried away by glamor, power, and size. The result was an outpouring of chromium-plated behemoths with exagger-ated tail fins and constantly increasing horsepower, each suc-cessive model trying to outdo its predecessors and its competi-tors in size and ornamentation, and designed with style and sales appeal as the foremost considerations.

These automobiles appeared to be what the public wanted. Production figures mounted to new highs. In 1949, domestic output finally surpassed the 5-million-plus record of the boom year of 1929; a year later it topped 8 million (these totals are for all motor vehicles, passenger and commercial), and peaked for the decade at over 9 million in 1955, of which almost 8 million were passenger cars. Efforts to counter the trend to size and ostentation were discouraging. Several domestic makes of small cars appeared on the American market between 1946 and 1965: Crosley, initially produced in 1939; Kaiser's Henry J and Nash's Rambler were both introduced in 1950; Willys-Overland's Aero appeared in 1953; Hudson's Jet, a year later. Only Rambler, by then an American Motors product, remained on the market after 1955.

The failure of these attempts appeared to demonstrate that to the American public, in general, economy was not the decisive factor in purchasing an automobile, certainly not at that time. Even where there was a preference for a low-priced vehicle, the buyer seemed willing to pay $100 or $200 more for one of the lower-priced standard-sized models, and with these small-car offerings the price differential was seldom that great, if it existed at all.[1]

In the regular makes, deviations from the emphasis on power and display had even less sales appeal. In the early 1950s Plym-outh tried a simply designed car, supposed to appeal to the economy-minded buyer, and lost its third-place position to the medium-range General Motors models, Oldsmobile, Buick, and Pontiac. Ford experimented with an emphasis on safety rather than style; customers were not interested. The automobile was definitely a status symbol, the most conspicuous symbol an individual or family had, and the owner wanted the status to show. The residence was the nearest competitor as a status symbol, but the car had the advantage of mobility. It was visible to more people in more places. If this attention to display meant increasing size and power and therefore cost, this was evidently acceptable to the buying public in a period of prosperity to which the automobile boom was a major contributor, and at a time when petroleum was plentiful and cheap.

The Small-Car Challenge

In the face of this trend, it did not seem to mean much that after five years of disappointment, the Rambler managed to sell 80,-000 cars, or 1 percent of the industry's total in 1955. This achievement was due to the persistence of George Romney, president of American Motors, who was convinced that his company must do something different to survive, and also that there was a place in the American market for a small car. As of 1955, this still looked like wishful thinking. Nor did it seem to matter that the volume of imported cars was steadily growing. The proportion of imports to total sales was very small, always less than 1 percent and usually below one-half of 1 percent. Yet the number of imports sold was some 80 percent greater in 1955 than it had been the year before. Although this was still under 1 percent of the total market, the sharp increase might have been seen as a portent that the day of the gas-guzzling dinosaur might be beginning to wane.

In fact, 1955 was a watershed year, even if it was not generally appreciated at the time. The record output of American cars in that year adversely affected demand in the following year. Domestic passenger car production dropped by 2 million, which in turn precipitated a downswing in the economy. A year later came Ford's ill-fated attempt to introduce another large car, the Edsel. This attempt might have succeeded in 1955; by 1957, it was too late.

Dr. Lawrence J. White, in his perceptive study of the American automobile industry after World War II, describes the change thus: "By the second half of 1957 the American economy had lost its expansionary luster and was beginning to go into a recession. Consumers began to look for smaller, cheaper, more maneuverable cars. At the same time European producers began to enter the American market for the first time. Small inexpensive European cars looked like what the new American market wanted."[2] This statement accurately analyzes the immediate situation that had developed by late 1957, allowing for the fact that a number of small European cars had already been selling effectively in the United States and were not recently appearing on the market.

Whether this shift to smaller cars was a long- or short-term phenomenon puzzled contemporary observers. By themselves, the drop in sales of standard-size cars and the Edsel fiasco need not have been interpreted as indicators of a lasting change in public preference. They could just as well have been a normal temporary response to recession conditions, and we know that the American fondness for big cars continued to be strong.

Nevertheless, there were recognizable signs of a more deep-seated change in public attitude. While sales of standard-size American cars floundered, those of Rambler climbed from 80,000 in 1955 to 400,000 in 1959. This example was emulated by Studebaker in 1958 with its own compacts, not as successfully, and the Big Three came into the compact field a year later, in a state of mind graphically expressed by Dr. White: "After much handwringing and protestations that in building a smaller car you take out value much faster than you take out cost and that anyone who wants cheap transportation can always buy a used car, the Big Three finally brought out their own compacts in the fall of 1959."[3]

It was ironic, and for Americans ought to be a matter of some regret, that the American automotive industry, which has led the world for so many years, had to be shown by others that it is entirely possible to build quality into a small car and still keep the cost down. All that is really needed is the incentive to do it.

The Coming of the Imports

This reluctant decision of the Big Three to produce compacts was only partially a response to domestic competition. It was far more a reaction to a phenomenal increase in sales of small import cars. Between 1955 and 1959 total import sales rose by a factor of more than 10, from 58,000 to 614,000 (see Table 2.1), and market penetration from eight-tenths of 1 percent to a staggering 10 percent. This performance, along with the success of the American compacts, was unmistakable evidence that the growing popularity of smaller cars went beyond purely cost considerations.

This feature of the public reaction was described many years ago by Gilbert and Sullivan in *The Gondoliers:* "When everyone is somebody, then no one's anybody." When all cars were designed as status symbols, then none were. If the Pontiac and the Cadillac looked very much alike and the Mercury could not be distinguished from the Ford (except by automobile buffs and teenage boys), then the concept of the status symbol would

TABLE 2.1   *Import Car Sales in U.S., 1949– 1960*

Year	Units	U.S. total (%)
1949	12,251	0.25
1950	16,336	0.26
1951	20,828	0.41
1952	29,299	0.70
1953	28,961	0.50
1954	32,503	0.59
1955	58,465	0.82
1956	98,187	1.65
1957	206,827	3.46
1958	378,517	8.12
1959	614,131	10.10
1960	498,785	7.58

SOURCE: *Automotive Facts and Figures,* various years. (Motor Vehicle Manufacturers Association.)

become meaningless. Increases in size and power had reached the limit of their attractiveness; when buying a new car became likely to mean building a bigger garage to put it in, then it was clearly time to call a halt. An alternative route to status was to buy an entirely different and distinctive type of automobile and this predominantly meant a foreign car of some kind. Thus, a combination of circumstances in the American automobile market of the late 1950s created a situation in which the imported cars satisfied the demands of both economy and prestige.

Imported cars were by no means a novelty in the United States, although they had for the most part been a minor factor in the motor vehicle market. Indeed, the first gasoline-powered cars marketed in the United States were German and French imports in the 1890s, carrying such subsequently famous names as Daimler, Benz, and Panhard. William Steinway, the piano manufacturer, actually contemplated the manufacture of Daimlers under license in the United States about 1890 but found that making pianos and horseless carriages were quite different operations.[4] Panhard still had an important enough place in the American market to be a partner of Henry Ford in challenging the Selden patent during the first decade of the twentieth century.[5] However, when American automobile manufacturing became a large-scale operation, purchases of foreign cars became pretty well reduced to specialized types such as luxury vehicles and sports cars. There was even an experiment in making Rolls Royces in the United States during the 1920s, but it was not particularly successful.[6] Customers who could afford a Rolls Royce wanted the genuine article, not something they suspected of being synthetic. A somewhat similar effort was made in the early 1930s to build and market an Austin two-seater in the United States, named Baby Austin, but the car never became much more than a curiosity.

The place of imported cars in the American market changed drastically after 1945. The pent-up demand of the war years left a situation in which literally anything with wheels and a motor would sell, regardless of origin. On their side, European manufacturers and their governments were eager for American sales in order to aid in the rehabilitation of their economies. Britain, indeed, specifically earmarked a substantial portion of its automotive output for export. These were strong incentives, but the rising volume of import car sales in the United States cannot be attributed simply to these special postwar conditions. It took time for European industry to recover from the war and achieve any substantial amount of production, and by then American automotive output was back in the market in volume. The flow of imports was insignificant until after 1950. It increased during the Korean war, when domestic production was again curtailed and then maintained a continuing upward trend.

TABLE 2.2   *Top Five in Import Car Sales,*
1955–1957

Car	Units	Total imports (%)
1955		
Volkswagen	28,907	49.4
Metropolitan	6,808	11.7
Jaguar	3,573	6.1
MG	3,001	5.1
Hillman	2,778	4.8
Total		77.1
1956		
Volkswagen	50,011	50.9
Metropolitan	7,145	7.3
MG	6,044	6.2
British Ford	4,230	4.3
Jaguar	3,685	3.7
Total		72.4
1957		
Volkswagen	64,242	31.1
Renault	22,586	10.9
British Ford	17,062	8.3
MG	13,496	6.5
Metropolitan	11,791	5.7
Total		62.6

SOURCE: *Ward's Automotive Yearbook, 1960,* p. 177. Published by permission of Ward's Automotive Reports.

If imported cars had merely been replacements during a period when domestic output fell short of meeting demand, then their sales should have declined when the American automobile industry resumed normal production, but they did not. On the contrary, they kept growing. Obviously, the imports were offering something that the American manufacturers did not provide. To some extent the import market continued to consist of the luxury and sports cars of earlier years; however, an analysis of leading imports shows that while these types maintained a fairly steady level of sales, they were a minor part of the import car market, and by the end of the 1950s their share of that market was declining.

Taking the period from 1955 to 1960, Volkswagen was the leader in import sales by a wide margin, although its share of the total import market declined from a peak of 50 percent in 1956. Three prestige and sports cars appeared among the first five imports from 1955 to 1957 (see Table 2.2): Jaguar, MG, and Metropolitan. The last named was a two-seater built for American Motors by the British Motor Corporation at its Austin plant in Birmingham; so while Nissan was making Austins in Japan, Austin was making American cars in England. By 1958, when import sales were really shooting upward, the sports cars had been replaced at the top of the list by standard family car models (see Table 2.3).

Response of the American Industry to Import Cars

The slow-motion entry of the American Big Three into the small-car field has already been noted. Actually the response of the U.S. automobile industry went through several stages. The first was to dismiss the problem as nonexistent. The desirability of an economy car was played down. A contemporary commentator observed: "If G.M. has said it once, it's said it a thousand times: A good used car is the answer to the American public's need for cheap transportation."[7] Next, the challenge of the

TABLE 2.3   *Import Sales Leaders, 1958–1960*

Car	Units	Total imports (%)
1958		
Volkswagen	78,588	20.8
Renault	48,148	12.7
British Ford	33,472	8.8
Fiat	21,156	5.6
Hillman	18,970	5.1
Vauxhall*	17,365	4.6
Simca	17,216	4.5
MG	16,267	4.3
Triumph	16,245	4.3
Opel*	15,686	4.1
Metropolitan**	12,359	3.3
Others	83,045	21.9
Total	378,517	100.0
1959		
Volkswagen	120,442	19.6
Renault	91,073	14.8
British Ford	42,512	6.9
Opel*	39,802	6.5
Fiat	38,468	6.3
Simca	35,190	5.7
Hillman	28,185	4.6
Vauxhall*	23,476	3.8
Triumph	23,072	3.8
Volvo	18,533	3.0
Others	153,378	25.0
Total	614,131	100.0
1960		
Volkswagen	159,995	32.1
Renault	62,772	12.6
Opel*	25,533	5.1
British Ford	23,602	4.7
Fiat	20,773	4.2
Triumph	17,720	3.5
Simca	17,077	3.4
Austin-Healy	16,322	3.3
Mercedes-Benz	14,435	2.9
Volvo	13,926	2.8
Others	126,630	25.4
Total	498,785	100.0

*General Motors.
**American Motors.
SOURCE: *Ward's Automotive Yearbook, 1960*, p. 177; *1961*, p. 167. Published by permission of Ward's Automotive Reports.

import cars was dismissed as inconsequential. It was confidently asserted that when imports reached half a million units per year or 5 percent of the market, whichever came first (with a complacent assumption that neither was likely to happen), the Big Three would take charge of the small-car market with their own products. The 5 percent market penetration was reached and passed in 1958 and the half-million imported vehicles per year, a year later.

Before that, the American firms had reacted to the obviously growing popularity of small cars by bringing their own imports into the United States, somewhat in the spirit of "If you can't lick 'em, join 'em." To their credit, the American automobile firms made no effort to restrict the influx of foreign cars by seeking higher tariff duties or other governmental action. They wanted a free world market in motor vehicles, and knew from past experience, especially with the Smoot-Hawley tariff of 1930, that restrictions invite retaliation and create a situation in which everyone loses.

As a matter of fact, Ford had been importing its British models since 1948, not so much to take advantage of any substantial market for them as to help alleviate Britain's acute postwar dollar shortage.[8] When the market for small cars expanded, Ford accelerated its British imports and in 1958 added its German Taunus. American Motors began to bring in its Metropolitan in 1954. General Motors yielded to the small-car pressure in 1957 by offering Vauxhalls, from its British subsidiary, and Opels, from its German subsidiary, in the United States. Pontiac dealers sold the Vauxhall and Buick dealers sold the Opel.

Chrysler began by marketing the French Simca and bought the company in 1958. Studebaker was relying heavily on its newly introduced compacts, the Lark and the Scotsman, and had no foreign subsidiaries. It joined the import car boom by becoming the American distributor for two German makes, Mercedes-Benz, a luxury car, and the low-priced DKW-Auto Union.

These cars sold well enough for the most part, but they had no perceptible effect on the rising tide of import cars made by independent foreign firms. When these took 72 percent of the import sales in 1959, there was just one further recourse for the Big Three.[9] With import penetration well beyond the 5 percent level that was to call for action, and Rambler sales up to 6 percent of the market, the Big Three in self-defense had to begin manufacturing compact cars of their own. They had been contemplating this step for some time and had done some designing and planning. New car models are not produced overnight; it takes a minimum of two to three years for the designing and tooling. The decision to proceed kept being postponed until by 1958 it was obviously necessary to act. As stated previously, the first Big Three compacts appeared late in 1959: General Motors' Corvair, Ford's Falcon and Chrysler's Valiant.

This was a historic point in the history of the automobile in the United States. For thirty years these three giant companies had dominated the American market, competing among themselves without having to worry very much about what anyone else was doing. Now they were faced with an external challenge of growing proportions. They had tried to ignore it, but it simply would not go away.

The Import Car Market

This was the situation that the Nissan management had to contemplate as it weighed the feasibility of entering the U.S. market. It was an alluring prospect; it was also a chancy one. Given a rapidly increasing demand for import cars, a fairly minor market penetration could have very satisfying results. A sales level of 500 vehicles a month seemed a reasonable goal, and 1000 could be considered attainable.

The market had its complexities. At the beginning of the influx of imports it was easy to assume that people who bought foreign cars did so out of a desire to be different or just from curiosity. There was also a limited but consistent demand for the small sports cars that had become a European specialty. But neither of these motives could account for the great upsurge of import sales just at the time Nissan was making its decision to try to sell in the United States. The boom in imports was manifestly part of a pronounced growth in the popularity of small cars in general; who was buying them, and why?

The most obvious reason was economy, and it was probably the strongest single motivation. The relationship between the recession of 1957 and the sharp acceleration of small-car sales is unmistakable. We have also seen in Chapter 1 how it was taken for granted on both sides of the Pacific that Japanese cars would find their place primarily as second cars for American families, and this was undoubtedly a widely held belief about all small cars, both imports and domestic compacts.

However, there was more to the picture. Table 2.4 presents the results of a survey made in 1957. *Fortune* conducted a direct telephone survey of 153 owners of small foreign cars in eight states, representing all sections of the United States. Some highlights of the survey are given in Table 2.4. It represented a limited sample, but in the absence of evidence to the contrary it can be taken as reasonably representative of import car owners. In general, it bears out the assumptions about economy and use of the import as a second car, but with qualifications. If it was true that two-fifths of the buyers of import cars owned no other automobile, this was an impressive proportion, which indicated a market potential for imports as first cars considerably higher than most people assumed at the time. Second, it is most interesting that half the purchasers in the survey gave economy of *operation* as the primary motive as against a fifth who gave low initial cost. This seems surprising for a period when gasoline was cheap, but the emphasis on economy of operation reflects the fact that with the behemoths of the 1950s even simple repairs were difficult and expensive to carry out. In addition, if customers really preferred economy of operation to low initial cost, then the argument that a used car was the solution to cheap transportation lost its force. Even a good used car is bound to wear faster than a new one and it offers no savings in gasoline mileage. It is worth noting, as well, that by far the largest proportion of import car buyers fell in what was then the

---

TABLE **2.4** *Who Buys Those Small Foreign Cars?*

Do you own any other cars?
    Yes 58%
    No 42%

What was your primary reason for buying a small car?
    Economy of operation 49%
    Ease of handling 20%
    Low initial cost 19%
    "Different" from U.S. cars 3%
    Other 9%

Would you buy a small car again?
    Yes 94%
    No 1%
    Not stated 5%

What would you like changed?
    Nothing 38%
    Less noise 17%
    Better service facilities 14%
    More power 12%
    More space 9%

What is your age?
    29 and under 27%
    30–39 .... 31%
    40–49 .... 25%
    50–59 .... 11%
    60 and over 3%
    Not stated 3%

What is your family income?
    Under $5,000 .... 25%
    $5,000–$10,000 .... 45%
    Over $10,000 .... 24%
    Not stated 6%

SOURCE: Richard Sheehan, "A Big Year for Small Cars," courtesy of *Fortune Magazine*, vol. 56, no. 2, August, 1957, p. 196.

moderate-income group. In other words, they were people for whom low initial cost was a desirable feature in the purchase of a car, but not an exclusive one.

It was also essential that a newcomer understand the geography of the import car market. Table 2.5 shows it accurately enough. Imports sold best along the Atlantic and Pacific Coasts, and a statistical correlation could be worked out between the decline in market penetration and the distance inland.

Table 2.6 pinpoints the situation still more vividly. In both 1959 and 1960, the states with the highest ratios of import car penetration were seacoast states, except for Nevada and Vermont, and both of these are special cases. Nevada is basically part of the California market area; Vermont falls within both the New England and New York City marketing areas.

Ratio of penetration is not everything, of course. Low penetration of a large market may be better than high penetration of a small one; however, as it happened, the regions most recep-

TABLE 2.5   *Import Car Market Penetration by Regions, 1957–1959*

	Percent of penetration		
Region	1957	1958	1959
Southwest Pacific:* Arizona, California, Nevada	8.6	16.3	18.1
Northwest Pacific: Alaska, Idaho, Oregon, Washington	7.1	14.5	15.5
New England: Connecticut, Maine, Massachusetts, New Hampshire, Rhode Island, Vermont	5.3	11.2	12.9
South Atlantic: Alabama, Florida, Georgia, Kentucky, Mississippi, North Carolina, South Carolina, Tennessee, Virginia, West Virginia	2.8	9.1	12.8
Middle Atlantic: Delaware, District of Columbia, Maryland, New Jersey, New York, Pennsylvania	3.6	8.0	10.4
Mountain: Colorado, Montana, New Mexico, Utah, Wyoming	3.5	8.8	9.7
West South Central: Arkansas, Louisiana, Oklahoma, Texas	1.5	5.7	9.5
East North Central: Illinois, Indiana, Michigan, Ohio, Wisconsin	1.8	4.3	5.8
West North Central: Iowa, Kansas, Minnesota, Missouri, Nebraska, North Dakota, South Dakota	1.3	3.8	5.8

*NOTE: Hawaii is included in this region for the first time in 1959. Import car penetration then was 31.1 percent.

SOURCE: *Ward's Automotive Yearbook, 1960,* p. 180. Published by permission of Ward's Automotive Reports.

tive to imports (in fact to small cars generally) were also regions with high sales volume—California and the Northeast. Nissan was well advised when it chose to begin operations in Los Angeles and New York. But this penetration would have to be made in the face of intense competition within the import car field from some of the world's biggest motor vehicle manufacturers: General Motors, Ford, Fiat, Renault, and above all Volkswagen. In addition, there were other newcomers in the American market such as the Swedish firms, Volvo and Saab, who were not among the giants of the world in the automotive industry but would certainly offer stiff competition in the import car field.

The type of vehicle to be offered was self-evident. Apart from the Datsun pickup truck, which was already favorably known to some American buyers, the Datsun sedan fitted among the small, economical cars designed for general family use that had become the most popular import type. But having such a vehicle to sell was not by itself enough. What was needed to make

TABLE 2.6   *Ten Leading States in Import Car Penetration,* [1]*1959–1960 (Penetration, %)*

State	1959	State	1960
1. Hawaii*	31.1	1. Alaska	18.4
2. Nevada	24.7	2. Hawaii	18.0
3. Alaska*	21.0	3. Florida	14.8
4. Florida	20.8	4. Nevada	14.3
5. California	18.2	5. Vermont	12.8
6. Washington	17.3	6. Washington	12.6
7. Oregon	15.3	7. New Hampshire	12.1
8. Connecticut	15.0	8. District of Columbia*	11.8
9. District of Columbia*	14.9	9. Connecticut	11.7
10. Vermont	14.5	10. California	11.3
11. New Hampshire	14.4	11. Virginia	11.3

*NOTE: The District of Columbia is not a state and Alaska and Hawaii were not in 1959, but they have to be listed to give an accurate picture of the areas of highest import car penetration. If they are omitted for 1959, the next three are Maine—13.9; Arizona—13.2; Virginia—13.1. The next two on the list for 1960 are Maryland and New Jersey, each with 11.1.

SOURCE: *Ward's Automotive Yearbook, 1960,* p. 180; *1961,* p. 170. Published by permission of Ward's Automotive Reports.

the grade in the U.S. automobile market was shown in the Volkswagen achievement. Volkswagen had the primary requisite—a well-engineered and economical product—but so did its principal European competitors.

What made the difference was that after a slow start, Volkswagen reorganized its distribution structure in 1954 and imposed on its dealers strict requirements for standards of service and availability of parts.[10] Thereafter the owner of the VW could be sure of getting competent service and replacement parts promptly anywhere in the United States. The dealers were quite willing to comply because sales started to boom and they were soon selling cars faster than the factory in Wolfsburg could make and ship them.

Kawamata and his associates in Tokyo studied the Volkswagen experience carefully and absorbed its lessons, but they could have no assurance that following the VW example would produce the same happy results. They had no way of knowing just what direction the import car market in the United States was going to take. It was growing fast and the purchase of import cars could no longer be dismissed as a passing fad. But there was obviously going to be increased competition from domestic compacts which could check the growth of import sales. Given the power and productive capacity of the American automobile manufacturers, their compacts could conceivably come to completely dominate the United States market for small cars. This was the challenge facing Nissan's management: how to make a place for the Datsun, an unknown on the American scene, in this fluid, uncertain situation and in the face of vigorous, well-established competitors.

=3=

FOUNDING THE COMPANY

The one thing that Datsun's experience in the United States between 1958 and 1960 demonstrated convincingly was that if the car was ever to be a serious competitor in the import automobile market, the makeshift organization with which Nissan had begun operating simply would not do. This fact quickly became obvious to two Nissan officials who were sent to assist the American distributors and to observe and report on the progress of the venture. They were Soichi Kawazoe and Yutaka Katayama, and their mission turned out to have more far-reaching consequences than either they or their superiors in Tokyo could have anticipated.

They were excellent choices. Kawazoe arrived first, specifically assigned to train the mechanics at Luby Datsun in New York, and Luby's dealers, in how to service Datsun cars and trucks.[1] He was an American-educated engineer with a B.S. in mechanical engineering from the University of Dayton (1930) and an M.S. from the Massachusetts Institute of Technology (1931). He was an engineer with both General Motors and Ford in Japan before going to work for Nissan in 1935 as a design engineer. He became a plant manager for the Manchurian Motor Company in 1940, an appointment which resulted in his spending eight years as a prisoner of war in Communist China, working as chief engineer in an army arsenal. When he was finally repatriated in 1953, he became director and plant manager of the U.S. Ordnance Depot at the Fuji Motor Company's plant in Oppama, supervising the rebuilding of Jeeps, Dodge weapons carriers, and GMC trucks. He rejoined Nissan in 1959 in the North American Division and was almost immediately sent to the United States. He thus brought a varied experience to his American assignment, plus a thorough acquaintance with American life and an excellent command of English.

Katayama, who would be known to NMC-USA simply as "Mr. K," had already appeared as the promoter of Datsun's successful participation in the 1958 Australian road rally. He was an economics graduate of Keio University in Tokyo. A brief visit to the United States while he was a student was his total American experience prior to 1960. He joined Nissan immediately after his graduation in 1935, working in advertising and sales promotion. He was also with the Manchurian Motor Company, but he was luckier than Kawazoe in that he was able to return to Japan before the war ended. His enthusiasm for sports cars gave him some international associations; he was the founder of the Sports Car Club of Japan in 1951. This interest also helped to make him an advocate of vigorous development of export markets by Nissan, especially the United States.

Mr. K was sent to Los Angeles early in 1960 with two assistants, one an engineer, Masahiko Zaitsu, to work with Woolverton as Kawazoe was doing with Luby. Zaitsu actually arrived earlier, in September 1959. They had an additional mission, which was to feed back information on American motor vehicles and production techniques with the object of improving Nissan's total operations. Katayama put it: "If I can feed back to the factory, the factory will improve. So, at the beginning, we were in the business of learning something from the United States, then we can make a good car in Japan."[2]

The Datsun Prospect in 1960

Some of what Kawazoe and Katayama saw was encouraging. Datsun sales grew to a total of 1300 in 1959, still an insignificant part of American automotive sales for the year, but evidence that the Datsun was obtaining a foothold—toehold might be more accurate. Public taste, at least a substantial segment of it, seemed to be turning to smaller cars, reflected in the appearance of the American compacts and the rapidly increasing sales of import cars. The yen, at the time, was officially quoted at 360 to the dollar; there was an unofficial rate ranging between 402 and 390 but this could not be used for motor vehicle exports. There were no restrictions on automotive imports other than a fairly nominal tariff duty. There were some American complaints about Japanese competition in other areas, mainly charges of dumping, which the Japanese Ministry of International Trade and Industry (MITI) attempted to control by an elaborate system of export quotas, but motor vehicles were not affected.[3] The volume of Japanese automotive imports in 1960 was much too small to be a matter for concern, quite apart from the free-trade attitude of the major American automobile manufacturers.

On the negative side was uncertainty about the long-term effect on imports of the competition being offered by the domestically produced compacts, accentuated as it was by the entry of the Big Three into the field. The plainly visible immediate effect was a sharp decline in total import car sales in 1960.

There were also problems with the cars themselves, as was described in Chapter 1, which would have to be resolved to make them fully acceptable in the United States. There was nothing basically wrong with their design or construction; as an American commentator later observed, they were simply "underdesigned."[4] This description applies to all the Japanese makes of that period, not just Datsuns. They were sturdy and durable enough, but they were not meant for the prolonged driving at high speeds that was commonplace in the United States. As a result, they were prone to carburetor troubles, their braking systems were inadequate, and they had other largely

minor but frustrating shortcomings. In addition, Japanese automobiles looked plain in comparison with their elaborately
styled American competitors. True, the Volkswagen offered
proof that styling could be dispensed with, but whereas the VW
was ostentatiously *not* styled, the Japanese cars merely appeared
old-fashioned.

For Datsuns, some of these drawbacks were eliminated in the
new Bluebird four-door sedan introduced in 1960 (PL310). This
time *Road and Track* was considerably more complimentary:

> Whereas the car of several years ago had little to recommend it, the new
> model has very much to offer. The appearance of the Datsun Bluebird,
> as it is now called, is improved immeasurably. It no longer looks like
> an exact copy of some other car and the color schemes were apparently
> planned with the U.S. market in mind.
>
> The Datsun Bluebird station wagon is a very useful all-around vehi-
> cle, designed to do many jobs and do most of them well. The consensus
> of our staff is that it is better suited to around-town business than it is
> to cross-country touring. Maneuverability is excellent and with its sat-
> isfactory performance and economy, it should prove to be a practical
> choice for city service. Our staff preferred the station wagon to the
> sedan, but personal needs can play a big part in their choice.[5]

These were encouraging words, but time was needed for the
Datsun to prove itself to American buyers—time and a well-
organized and energetic sales program. Both Katayama and
Kawazoe realized in short order that no such program was possible with the existing Nissan arrangements in the United
States. Kawazoe worked with Luby Datsun only a short time
before he came to the conclusion that if Nissan seriously
intended to sell automobiles in the United States, it had better
buy out its distributors and take over the job itself.

He found the distributorship located in a small warehouse
behind a gasoline station on Queen's Boulevard, New York, and
it employed fewer than ten people. There was no Service Manager and since service problems were accumulating, Kawazoe's
talents were promptly utilized. He described one early experience when he had to fly to Norfolk, Virginia, because some Datsun 210 sedans had developed leaks and the local dealer could

not make repairs: "The dealer had only one garage big enough to park one Datsun. There was a hydraulic jack but no tools. I brought one sedan into the garage and asked where the mechanic was. The dealer said he had quit the day before and took all his tools with him. I knew our distributor didn't have first class dealers, but I didn't know it was this bad."[6] The job was done with tools borrowed from a gasoline station and a crank handle from a Renault dealer (the Datsun's electric starter wouldn't work). Kawazoe worked until after midnight, when the errant mechanic reappeared and received a crash course in Datsun service.

In this same account, Kawazoe remarks that the dealers who had been recruited were "very interesting." One carried hundred-dollar bills in his pockets and always paid cash, whether for cars or parts. Another kept his books by putting all his debits in one pocket and all his credits in another. A third sold the Datsun as a German car because his customers thought the name sounded German and he decided to cash in on the reputation of the Volkswagen.

Katayama arrived in Los Angeles to find the Marubeni America Corporation already urging that Nissan set up its own sales organization and appealing to him for help because neither the distributor nor the dealers seemed able to sell Datsuns. Woolverton had over 100 Datsuns stored in an open lot and deteriorating; they had been bought back from dealers who could neither sell them nor afford to keep them.

Katayama's own study of the situation quickly convinced him that Woolverton did not have the capital and as a multicar distributor lacked incentive to create the kind of sales and dealer organization that Datsun needed. He had very definite ideas about what this should be, expressing the philosophy that both he and Kawazoe had acquired in their service with the Nissan organization:

> A car sale is not completed by getting the money and handing the car over to the customer. That is the start of the sale. And then we can make money on that too. It is not like a book you can sell and get money and

that's it. A car, as long as it's running, is not sold completely. Sales cannot come by one person bringing a thousand cars over and going back home. As long as we sell a car we can't go back.[7]

Thus Kawazoe, Katayama, and the Marubeni Corporation all joined to uge that Nissan establish its own sales organization in the United States. It probably was an additional incentive that rival Toyota had already done so, having created the Toyota Motor Sales Company in October 1957.[8] The recommendation that Nissan do likewise found receptive ears in Tokyo.

Datsun sales had not been affected by the slump in the American import car market; in fact, they even rose a little, reaching a total for 1960 of 1640 by the end of the year. But this was nowhere near Nissan's hopes and expectations. Early in 1960, the company was reported to be seeking 300 outlets with the object of reaching sales of 1000 cars a month,[9] but this goal was still a long way off. Even the earlier target of 500 units a month seemed remote; with the Europeans cutting their prices to try to hold their place in the American market, it was evident that the Datsun faced severe competition and that its position in the United States was far from secure.

Creation of Nissan Motor Corporation in U.S.A.

The outcome was the founding of Nissan Motor Corporation in U.S.A. (NMC-USA), chartered as a California corporation on September 28, 1960. The articles of incorporation appear as Appendix A. The legal work was done by Reid Briggs, a Los Angeles attorney, who continued to be legal advisor to the corporation. The articles of incorporation were signed by Yutaka Katayama, Masahiko Zaitsu, and Takayoshi Sogo, as the first Directors of the new corporation. Zaitsu, who came from the Engineering Department of Nissan Motor Company, Ltd., as factory service representative, returned to Japan in 1966 and became a Director of the parent company. Sogo was a factory sales representative. He had an excellent command of English and early in 1961 went to Houston, Texas, to take charge of NMC-USA's first regional office.

This office replaced a small independent distributorship that Mitsubishi had established in Houston. Since it was in Kawazoe's territory, he was invited to the opening and found the owner, "a big, strapping Texan," and his Sales Manager having a hot argument. As Kawazoe describes the scene:

> There were two flags hung from the ceiling. One was the Star Spangled Banner and the other was a red diagonal cross against a blue background which I had never seen before. I heard later that this was the flag representing the Confederate States of America. I felt very strange that such arguments should erupt in deciding which flag to display in the showroom. I thought there was only one national flag. So the argument went on and the guests started to arrive. I finally suggested that the two flags be left hanging as is, which was agreed to and everyone was happy.[10]

The flag dispute was of no help in selling cars, and the Houston distributorship sold out without protest when NMC-USA was formed.

The corporation's authorized capitalization was 20,000 shares with a par value of $100 each. Nissan Motor Company, Ltd., was the sole stockholder and provided all the capital. At the outset, NMC-USA's capital was established at $1 million.

In the initial organization, Takashi Ishihara, who had been Export Manager of Nissan Motor Company, Ltd., and would in time succeed Kawamata as its President, was named President of NMC-USA. Katayama and Kawazoe became Vice Presidents, in charge of the Western and Eastern Divisions, respectively. The Western Division included fourteen states[11] and the Eastern Division all the rest, although at the beginning its activities were pretty well limited to the Atlantic seaboard. On the surface this structure looked awkward. The President was in Japan, not in close touch with the details of the operation, and having two Vice Presidents, each in charge of a distinct geographical area, was an arrangement likely to create rivalry within the organization.

The reasons for adopting this structure do not appear in the available records, but they can be surmised readily enough. Nissan Motor Company, Ltd., had a reputation for maintaining firm control over its subsidiaries, and this two-division system was well calculated to achieve that.[12] In this case, there was every reason for the parent organization to keep a tight rein over an operation that was very much in the experimental stage. The two divisions made sense under the existing conditions because the best market areas for import cars were along the Atlantic and Pacific Coasts of the United States, with not much immediate prospect for Datsun sales in the interior of the country. If the Divisional Headquarters were at opposite extremes of the country, that was the proper place for them. It may even have been intended that having two separate divisions like this, widely separated geographically and each independently responsible to the President in Tokyo, would generate a healthy competition between them and increase sales. This is precisely what happened; an astute management might well have planned it that way.

One feature of this corporate structure suggests possible miscalculation of the prospective market areas for Japanese automobiles in the United States. The larger share of territory assigned to the Eastern Division seems to indicate an expectation that most promising markets for Datsuns would be found east of the Mississippi and especially in the industrial northeast. There appears to have been some serious consideration given to putting the National Headquarters of NMC-USA in the New York area. It was an understandable position at the time. New York was the financial center of the United States, and the northeast was the country's most heavily populated area. As of 1960, the seaboard region from New England to Virginia, plus Florida, represented the largest total volume of import car sales, although the highest percentages in terms of market penetration belonged to the Pacific Coast, plus Alaska and Hawaii, as Tables 2.5 and 2.6 demonstrate.

The northeast was buying European import cars at the time. Admittedly in 1960 there was not much choice, but it could be assumed that this practice would continue strong, given the factors of geographical proximity and the close cultural and economic ties between the northeastern United States and Europe. It would take time to develop a substantial market for Japanese automobiles. The Pacific Coast was an equally good buyer of import cars, and in the large California automobile market there was a high proportion of import penetration. This region's ties with Europe were not as close, and it had a large population of Japanese origin to make it potentially more receptive to Japanese imports.

Still, as the situation looked in 1960, it was reasonable enough to assume that the eastern United States would provide the largest volume of Datsun sales and that the natural place for NMC-USA's Headquarters would be the New York metropolitan area. The assumption was an error, but not a very serious one, because it was never acted on. The two divisions were left to develop their own territory without discrimination between them. If anything, the fact that NMC-USA was organized as a California corporation put the company's center of gravity in the west at the outset. It certainly shows that there was no positive commitment to an eastern base for the operation.

In any case, whatever deficiencies this initial corporate structure might have had in theory, it served its purpose and functioned on this basis for the next five years. The distributors were bought out, without noticeably vigorous objection on their part, and Nissan took charge of its own American sales. Marubeni, through the Marubeni America Corporation, remained in the picture as the importer, with the responsibility for shipping the cars and bringing them into the United States. This was a sensible arrangement. The Marubeni staff, after all, had the expertise in these matters, which would have been wasteful for Nissan to try to duplicate.

This new beginning was singularly undramatic. The first office of the Western Division consisted of two rooms on the seventh floor of the old Mobil Oil Company building in downtown Los Angeles; the initial staff was Katayama, an engineer (Zaitsu), and an office boy—not even a secretary. It was the office Katayama and Zaitsu had shared before NMC-USA was organized.

This arrangement was short-lived because Mr. K decided that since motor vehicles run on the ground, they could not be sold from the seventh floor. He went looking for other quarters at ground level and with warehouse space and settled on property at 137 East Alondra Boulevard in Gardena, California. This site later became the Headquarters of NMC-USA until it was replaced by the present building in Carson, California, in 1972.

The Eastern Division started with equally modest facilities. Kawazoe located the Divisional Headquarters in Newark, New Jersey, at 200 Frelinghuysen Avenue, because the cars were landed in Newark and he wanted his office to be close to the port. Robert K. Scott, formerly Vice President, Parts, for NMC-USA and now President, Distribution and Auto Service Company (DAS), saw this office late in 1964 and described it as "an old dealership, and the building really should have been ripped down."[13] By that time, the Eastern Division was preparing to move into more commodious quarters, a former furniture warehouse in Secaucus, New Jersey. This move took place early in 1965, so the fate of the Frelinghuysen Avenue structure ceased to be a matter of concern. The Secaucus location had the additional advantage that it was right at the Lincoln Tunnel interchange on the New Jersey Turnpike, so that motorists exiting from the tunnel had the Datsun sign directly before their eyes.

Market Conditions, 1960 to 1962

The state of the American automobile market when NMC-USA came into existence was hardly such as to inspire optimism about the new organization's future. The economy was still recovering from the recession that struck in 1957, and while passenger car sales improved markedly in 1960, they were still a million below the bonanza year of 1955. The principal gains among the domestic cars were made by the compacts, as might have been expected, with the Big Three offerings now coming out in quantity. There was one exception, Studebaker, whose sales fell away—an indication that buyers were avoiding a make that seemed likely to become an orphan in the near future and did. In 1959, the full-size American passenger automobiles had 79.7 percent of the market and the American compacts 10.1 percent; for 1960 the shares were 67.8 for the big cars and 24.6 for the compacts.[14]

For a time it appeared that the domestic motor vehicle manufacturers had in fact succeeded in checking the rising tide of imports. Aggregate import sales of passenger cars in 1960 were over 100,000 less than in 1959, with their share of the market dropping from 10.1 percent to 7.5 percent. This decline continued for another two years, reaching bottom in 1962 with sales of 339,160 and a 4.8 share of the market (Appendix B). In short, NMC-USA started out at about as unfavorable a time as could be imagined. It was going to have to fight for a place in a shrinking market.

There was a very important qualification. The decline in import cars sales was selective. The worst casualties were among the "captive" makes, that is, the products of overseas subsidiaries of American automobile companies, for the simple reason that the American firms were not interested in having their overseas subsidiaries compete with their own compacts. The small-car market offered enough other competition as it was.

In these three years, Opel, Vauxhall, and British Ford lost their positions among the top ten import leaders. Ford's German Taunus, which had not sold well in the United States, was dropped in 1960 and the British Ford imports were limited to its lowest-priced model. General Motors sold Vauxhalls and Opels on order, but made little effort to push them. The American Motors Metropolitan became an unwelcome competitor for the Rambler, itself hard pressed to maintain its pace against the Big Three compact offerings, and was discontinued in 1962. Chrysler cut back sharply on Simca imports. Studebaker was out of the running. It had no overseas subsidiary. It was a distributor for Mercedes-Benz, which sold quite well but was not a compact, and at this juncture, when Studebaker needed all the sales it could get, the German factory could not keep up with the demand.[15]

The experience of the independent participants in the import car market during this period of decline was mixed. Volkswagen was not affected at all; its sales forged steadily ahead, reaching almost 200,000 units and a dominating 56.8 percent of the import car market in 1962. The Swedish companies held their own. So, for that matter, did the Japanese; although, at one-half of 1 percent of import car sales in 1960, their presence in the import car market was still almost imperceptible.

The losses among the "noncaptive" import makes fell primarily on the conventional-type cars whose manufacturers, to quote one authority, "had relied largely on novelty buying and had not bothered to build up a solid dealer and service/repair system."[16] It appears that Renault and Fiat were major offenders in this respect. In Fiat's case, and this may also apply to Renault, there was an element of deliberate choice in what happened. The Italian giant had profitable markets in many other parts of the world and was not willing at this time to make the large-scale commitment that would be needed for it to compete effectively in the United States.[17] But neither one dropped out. Even without the "captives," which did not entirely leave the scene, there continued to be well over fifty competitors scrambling among themselves in an import car market whose aggregate sales were declining; at the same time a consistently larger share of this aggregate was going to a single company.

Starting Operations

When NMC-USA took on the full responsibility for marketing Datsun cars and trucks in the United States, it found itself with a small group of dealers of widely mixed quality, and sales averaging a little over a hundred vehicles a month for the entire United States, including Hawaii, which was not in NMC-USA's sales territory. For comparison, in 1960 domestic motor vehicle production was on the order of 7.8 million and total import sales were over half a million. Manifestly, NMC-USA had its work cut out for it.

The scale of the operation ruled out any elaborate organizational structure. Both Vice Presidents began to gather small staffs. In the Western Division, Katayama had Tadayuki Ide with him. Ide was Comptroller and Director of NMC-USA until 1970, when he returned to Japan. Among the earliest recruits were two mechanics, Jean LaPlant and Joe Slackey. LaPlant had experience with Austins, which had the same engine as the Datsun at that time;[18] Slackey came from Woolverton Motors. He elected to take charge of parts and so could be considered the Western Division's first Parts Manager. He stayed with NMC-USA until early in 1963. LaPlant became the first Service Manager. He later moved over to building maintenance and security and was replaced as Service Manager by Lee Wylie, who remained with the company for many years (but because of failing eyesight later had to curtail his activities and eventually go on a medical leave of absence).

It was all very informal. The titles meant little. When something needed to be done, whoever was available pitched in and did it. For instance, Mr. K frequently delivered cars to dealers himself, usually because there was no one else to do it, but often just because it was a good way to get to know the dealers. These were not just local trips; he frequently went to San Diego and Tucson, with LaPlant in another Datsun to take him back.

The appointment of Ray M. Hoen as its second Sales Manager in January 1961 added somewhat more structure to the Western Division—not much, perhaps, but a definite portent that if the Datsun had its way and the organization grew, the informality of these early days must unavoidably disappear. The first Sales Manager was Ernest Reed, but his health failed before he could accomplish much. Like many of the people recruited by NMC-USA, Hoen had previous experience with small cars, including imports. He had been zone manager for Willys Motors in northern California, selling Jeeps, and then went to southern California as general manager for the John Green Company, distributors for Renault.[19]

The situation in the Eastern Division was very similar, allowing for differences in personality and managerial style between the Vice Presidents. Kawazoe recruited his first office staff by the simple expedient of taking over most of the staff of the Luby distributorship. He also had Masataka Usami as his assistant for Service and Parts. He was a member of the Board of Directors and later became Vice President, Parts and Service, NMC-USA (1971 to 1974). After that he was Vice President and General Manager, Parts, Service, and Technical Engineering, until he returned to Japan in 1976. Another assistant appointed in 1960 was Shintaro Inada, Sales and Accounting. These were highly regarded men from the parent company, whose appointments to work with Kawazoe offer some evidence that the management of Nissan Motor Company, Ltd., initially, did regard the eastern United States as the more promising prospect for Datsun sales.

The first Sales Manager for the Eastern Division was Robert Bathurst, who remained only two years. Ralph Nuzzi was the first Parts Manager and William Renz, the first Service Manager. By the end of 1960, NMC-USA both divisions, had a total of eighteen employees. When the Western Division held its first Christmas party, those present were Katayama, Ide, Sogo, Zaitsu, Slackey, LaPlant, a mechanic LaPlant had hired named Benny Ackermann, and two secretaries, whose names are not on record.[20]

The vital tasks facing the new company were to increase sales and reorganize and expand the dealer network. The two, of course, were interrelated. Without assurance of additional sales, there was no way to recruit more and better dealers; without more good dealers, it would be impossible to achieve sales volume. Reaching these goals would take time and a lot of hard work, and the beginning had to be made under difficult conditions. The year 1961 was worse for imports than 1960. Automobile sales in general were depressed, dropping by over a million from the previous year's figure, and imports fell by a factor of 24 percent. The one exception, as usual, was Volkswagen. There was no general recession to account for this decline in

automotive sales; it was probably the consequence of heavy purchases of compact cars in 1960. Whatever the reason, it was a
poor year to try to sell a relatively unknown car that still had to
prove itself to American buyers.

The Nissan staff tried hard enough. Katayama with all his
long experience in advertising had never actually sold a car
before. Now he went literally door-to-door through the Japanese-American community in Los Angeles trying to sell Datsuns. He buttonholed Japanese gardeners and tried to persuade
them of the virtues of Datsun pickups and, usually with LaPlant
accompanying him, made a point of appearing at meetings of
Japanese-American groups with a Datsun truck for them to see.
The immediate results were disappointing. As far as can be
determined, Mr. K's record of never having sold a car remained
unsullied. Overall Datsun sales for 1961 were 1436, which was
200 less than they had been in 1960, the first decline since Datsun sales had begun in 1958.[21] Kawazoe had no Japanese-American community to canvass, but he was equally dedicated to
seeing that what was needed got done. There was more than
one occasion when he went to a dealership and personally
worked on a Datsun with the mechanics because they could not
correct the problem and the customer was upset.

More was accomplished during those depressing days than
appeared on the surface. The necessary groundwork for future
growth was being laid. The reconstruction of the dealerships
was taken in hand; Hoen proved to be particularly effective at
this. The sales efforts got the Datsun name better known. Above
all, Katayama and Kawazoe incessantly urged Nissan in Japan
to improve the vehicles to make them fitter for the United States
market. There were all sorts of improvements: mechanical, sty-
listic, recognizing that Americans by and large are bigger than
Japanese and so need more headroom. Mr. K even pointed out
that while model names such as Bluebird and Fair Lady might
be popular in Japan, they would not be as acceptable in the
United States. He thought names such as Lion or Tiger would
appeal more to the American buyer. His ideas on this point
were not followed, but in practice Datsun models in the United

States were usually identified by number rather than name—
210, 510, 810, 280-ZX. This policy changed in 1980 with the
introduction of the 1981 810 Maxima.

In matters of styling and engineering, the response was much
more positive. The systematic evaluation of reports from the
United States regarding the quality of Datsun cars, begun in
1958 when descriptions of deficiences started coming back to
Japan, remained an integral part of the Nissan technique.

Beginning in late 1959, new and improved models became
available. In that year the 220–221–222 series, pickup and station wagon, appeared, and the L211 sedan. The major change in
these was a 1200cc, 48-horsepower engine. They were followed
by the 310 series in 1960, which had a three-speed transmission
in place of the previous four-speed system. A year after that
came the 311, sedan and station wagon, with horsepower
increased to 60, plus the well-received four-wheel drive Datsun
Patrol (L60). A four-seater sports roadster was also introduced
in 1960 and a revised model in 1961 (SPL212-213), vigorously
promoted by Katayama, the sports car enthusiast. These first
Datsun sports cars to be offered in the United States did not sell
especially well, but the other models gave NMC-USA the
opportunity to grow. They provided a line of Datsun passenger
cars and trucks that were competitive in performance and price
with other automobiles of comparable size, both imports and
domestic compacts. If the market for small import cars revived,
Datsun was well placed to take advantage of it.

4

THE FORMATIVE YEARS, 1960 TO 1965

The first stage in the growth of NMC-USA can be definitely identified as the years between the founding of the company in 1960 and its first major reorganization in 1966. It might be termed the period of infancy and early childhood, with the reorganization marking the coming of adolescence. Alternatively, and more accurately, it is the phase described by Robert O. Link, now the company's Senior Vice President, as "Creative Evolution," defined as the period when marketing a new product "requires long hours of hard work that are rewarded by modest salaries. It requires a great deal of physical and mental energy to market a new product. Communication among employees is frequent and informal. Control of activities comes from marketplace feedbacks—management acts as customers (or dealers in our case) react."[1]

This is an excellent description of the way NMC-USA functioned during these formative years. Some of the hard work and the informality has already been described. As with most embryonic organisms, NMC-USA had an initial period of uncertainty as to whether it would grow at all, followed by a slow accretion of strength until survival could be regarded as reasonably assured. None of this process was automatic. It took willingness throughout the organization to pitch in and do what was needed, along with the ability to surmount crises and take advantage of opportunities as they arose. Both the crises and the opportunities were produced by continuing shifts in the U.S. market for motor vehicles.

The Import Car Market, 1960 to 1965

The general condition of the motor vehicle market during these early years of NMC-USA was good. After the decline of 1961, sales picked up again and rose steadily for the next four years. This trend applied to Datsun, although import sales as a whole continued to decline through 1962 and did not begin their upswing until the following year. This discrepancy arose from the special situation of the small-car market, which deserves some attention because it was, after all, the segment which most directly concerned NMC-USA.

As noted in the preceding chapter, the entrance of the big American producers into the market for small cars had two immediate effects: it arrested the flow of imports, with the usual exception of Volkswagen; and it cut into the sales of standard-size passenger automobiles. This adverse impact on the sales of standard-size cars was an unforeseen, certainly unplanned, but hardly astonishing consequence of the introduction of the new domestic compact lines; also, like the effect on imports, it was selective. As Table 4.1 shows, between 1960 and 1962, Ford's Falcon and Chrysler's Valiant definitely cut into the market for conventional Fords and Plymouths. Chevrolet was not affected as much by the G.M. compacts, nor were the middle- and higher-range models to any significant extent, except that their gains between 1959 and 1960 may have been smaller than they would have been otherwise. We can only guess. There is no way of knowing which way the people who bought American compacts in 1960 would have gone if these cars had not been available. They might have turned to standard-size automobiles, but if they were looking for smaller cars, there were plenty of imports to choose from. The 1961 figures have to be evaluated in the light of a general decline in motor vehicle sales.

The heavy initial purchases of this first series of American compact cars were undoubtedly due as much to novelty and curiosity as to any marked upsurge of economy-mindedness

TABLES 4.1   *Sales Comparison, Selected U.S. Standard and Compact Cars, 1959–1963*

Car	1959	1960	1961	1962	1963
General Motors					
Chevrolet*	1,349,552	1,614,342	1,201,914	1,495,476	1,625,931
Chevelle**	—	—	—	—	113,774
Chevy II†	—	—	86,310	369,246	312,097
Corvair†	79,441	259,276	316,600	296,687	251,513
Pontiac*	388,856	418,154	244,391	401,674	481,652
Tempest**	—	32,052	115,945	145,676	143,616
Ford					
Ford*	1,352,112	917,087	710,392	722,642	911,496
Fairlane**	—	—	60,443	386,192	318,018
Falcon†	100,757	507,199	486,079	381,558	341,871
Mercury*	156,765	161,787	109,775	109,347	118,815
Comet**	—	198,031	185,844	144,886	150,694
Chrysler					
Plymouth*	393,213	252,453	188,170	177,651	274,735
Valiant†	19,991	231,516	122,275	153,428	221,677
Dodge	192,798	362,808	166,158	216,518	246,425
Lancer**	—	48,858	54,621	35,564	—
Dart†	—	—	—	—	174,876
American Motors					
Rambler/					
American†	378,064	485,745	134,369	117,003	129,665
Classic†	—	—	214,084	297,885	321,916††
Studebaker	153,823	105,902	78,664	86,974	67,918

*Regular.
**Intermediate.
†Compact.
††Negligible sales other than compacts.
SOURCE: *Automobile Facts and Figures, 1964.*

among the buying public. This element in the situation emerged in a short time in the form of customer demand for the kind of accessories and amenities that Americans had become accustomed to in the big cars of the 1950s. The American manufacturers, who had been pushed reluctantly into building small cars, except for American Motors, happily responded by making their compacts less compact.

This indication of customer preferences also enabled the makers of passenger cars in the medium price range to enter the "economy car" competition with reduced versions of their own models. These were not compacts or small cars by any reasonable definition; they became an intermediate category between the standard-size cars and the genuine compacts. The resulting proliferation of models must have left a good many prospective buyers thoroughly confused about what was a compact and what was not.

One consequence of this propensity of the American-built "small" cars to edge up in size was to reopen the door to the imports by leaving the same kind of gap in the market as had existed in the late 1950s. This result was apparently unpredicted and certainly unintended. The domestic automobile manufacturers seem to have been just as astonished by the resultant increase in import sales as they had been the first time around, and their response was almost exactly the same. First they tried to disregard the problem, then they promoted the products of their own overseas subsidiaries, and finally they returned to the small-car market with a new line of what had to be called "subcompacts." But that did not happen until the closing years of the 1960s; in the meantime, there had been other important developments with imports in general and the Datsun in particular.

The three-year slide of import car sales between 1960 and 1962 produced some interesting reshuffling of positions among the import leaders, as illustrated by Table 4.2. Of the top ten in 1960, only Volkswagen continued to gain in both aggregate sales and share of the market. Volvo climbed from tenth to fourth place just by holding its own in sales figures. Renault

TABLE **4.2** *Import Car Sales Leaders, 1961–1965*

Car	Sales	Imports (%)
1961		
Volkswagen	177,308	46.8
Renault	44,122	11.7
Mercedes-Benz	12,903	3.4
Volvo	12,707	3.4
Fiat	11,839	3.1
Triumph	11,683	3.1
Austin-Healey	8,935	2.4
MG	8,806	2.3
British Ford	8,660	2.3
Metropolitan	8,657	2.3
Others	72,922	19.2
Total	378,542	100.0
1962		
Volkswagen	192,570	56.8
Renault	29,763	8.8
Standard-Triumph	15,967	4.7
Volvo	13,157	3.9
Mercedes-Benz	11,075	3.3
Austin-Healey	10,019	3.0
Fiat	9,762	2.9
MG	9,319	2.7
Peugeot	4,926	1.4
Jaguar	4,442	1.3
Others	38,160	11.2
Total	339,160	100.0
1963		
Volkswagen	240,143	62.3
Renault	22,621	5.9
MG	21,270	5.5
Standard-Triumph	20,117	5.2
Volvo	14,175	3.7
Fiat	10,805	2.8
Mercedes-Benz	10,378	2.7
Austin-Healey	8,348	2.2
Jaguar	4,421	1.1
Saab	4,117	1.0
Others	29,229	7.6
Total	385,624	100.0
1964		
Volkswagen	307,173	63.4
MG	24,128	5.0
Standard-Triumph	21,214	4.4
Renault	18,432	3.8
Volvo	17,326	3.6

TABLE 4.2   *Import Car Sales Leaders, 1961–1965*
            (Continued)

Car	Sales	Imports (%)
Opel	14,077	2.9
Mercedes-Benz	11,234	2.3
Simca	9,606	2.0
Fiat	8,988	1.9
Austin-Healey	8,397	1.7
Others	43,556	9.0
Total	484,131	100.0
1965		
Volkswagen	383,978	67.4
MG	22,322	3.9
Standard-Triumph	20,347	3.6
Volvo	18,115	3.2
Opel	16,216	2.9
Datsun	13,201	2.3
Simca	12,994	2.3
Mercedes-Benz	11,994	2.1
Renault	11,431	2.0
Fiat	8,194	1.4
Others	50,623	8.9
Total	569,415	100.0

SOURCE: *Ward's Automotive Yearbook, 1963,* p. 182; *1964,* p. 202; *1966,* p. 174. Published by permission of Ward's Automotive Reports.

and Fiat both lost ground somewhat, but this was partly because both were engaged in remedying their past oversights and reconstructing their United States sales and service organizations, with results that would show in later years.[2] The three "captive" imports that had been among the leaders in 1960 (British Ford, Opel, and Simca) were no longer in the top ten in 1962. There was a marked revival of British sports car imports (Austin-Healey, Jaguar, MG, Standard-Triumph). These were a form of status symbol, hardly in the "economy" category. Their rise in popularity serves to account for the fact that 90 percent of the sports cars built by British Motor Corporation in 1962 were sold in the United States and Canada.[3]

These three years of decline in import sales produced some weeding out of the import car market. *Ward's Automotive Year-*

book described the process thus:

> Some import makes persevered or prospered simply by retaining a degree of frugal functionality beyond that to which the U.S. industry had scaled down its cars. Other imports stuck to the philosophy that a certain segment of the buying public would always have a fondness for the obviously foreign car, particularly for one that could be serviced as readily as sold.
>
> Thus, as smaller American cars took to changes, grew bigger and became more elaborately equipped—and as some tentative sojourners from overseas lost visas to the U.S. market by defaulting in product, service and merchandising—a relative handful of imports emerged more dominant than ever as their aggregate position in this country restrengthened.[4]

The inference in the last part of this statement is borne out by the category "Others" in Table 4.2. The aggregate sales and share of the import car market in this category shrank markedly from 1961 to 1963. They rose again in the next two years, but much of the increase is accounted for by some 6800 Datsun passenger cars and 3030 Toyotas in 1964, and 6400 Toyotas in 1965.[5] Datsun was now in the top ten, no longer among "Others." Obviously some of the weaker entries were being squeezed out. One of the casualties, in fact, was Toyota's first offering in the U.S. market, the Toyopet. It was a car somewhat similar to the early Datsuns, with both their good and bad qualities, plus a name that lacked sales appeal. It suggested both "toy" and "pet." The car was withdrawn from the U.S. market in 1961, and Toyota survived in this country by selling four-wheel-drive Land Cruisers until a redesigned passenger automobile could be offered to American buyers. This arrived in 1965 as the Toyota Corona, following a stopgap model, the Tiara, in 1964.

This increasing domination of the import car market by the leading makes is also evidence of a continuing trend to concentration of the motor vehicle industry throughout the world in fewer and larger firms. The withdrawal of Studebaker in 1964 left the United States with four passenger automobile manufacturers. The British Motor Corporation merged with Leyland in 1968, giving Britain four major passenger car manufacturers also. The story was similar in France and Germany, and Italy was already dominated by Fiat. Japan was an exception. The MITI tried in the 1960s to concentrate the automobile industry about Nissan and Toyota, but the companies had their own ideas on the matter and the MITI plan did not come off. The one important merger was Nissan's acquisition of the Prince Motor Company in 1966.[6] Otherwise, the smaller Japanese automobile companies seem to have benefited from the rapid expansion of the Japanese automotive industry as a whole. However, in general, the number of competitors on the world motor vehicle market was steadily going down, and this was reflected in the number of import makes offered in the United States.

From 1963 to 1965 import car sales climbed steadily and continued to be dominated by Volkswagen, which in 1965 reached a dizzying 67.4 percent of the entire import car market. Volkswagen sales in that year were greater than the total of all import car sales in either 1961 or 1962. The volume of Volkswagen sales would go higher, but the 67.4 percent was a peak that the company would not attain again. Opel and Simca returned to the top ten in 1964, reflecting a renewed effort by the Big Three to cope with import competition (British Ford made it back two years later). By far the most significant change appeared in 1965. Until then the Japanese automobiles had been among the unidentified "Others" in the listings, but in that year Datsun broke into the top ten, in sixth place with passenger car sales of 13,201 (the figures in the tables are for passenger cars only).[7] To this number should be added 5514 Datsun trucks, for a total of 18,715 vehicles altogether. This represented 2.3 percent of the import passenger cars and 39 percent of the import trucks sold in the United States that year—a truly phenomenal growth record in just five years.

Building the Organization

The Datsun feat becomes all the more remarkable when we look at the sales organization with which NMC-USA started. As was stated earlier, at the end of 1960, the company had eighteen employees and the dealers inherited from the distributors that NMC-USA had replaced. The Western Division had forty-seven dealers; the number for the Eastern Division is unrecorded.

The Datsun dealers of those early days and indeed for some years thereafter were a strangely mixed assortment. "Back in those days," says Leroy Stubberfield, now Sales Agreement Manager, NMC-USA, "we were selling them off used car lots or out of service stations, or in some cases the Datsuns were thrown in with other vehicles at a multiple car agency which we called supermarkets."[8] "Supermarkets" sounds impressive, but in 1960 it meant an operation on the order of Ray Lemke's Economy Car Center in San Diego, California, which Lemke himself characterized as a Mom and Pop operation at that time.

In 1961 the sales area that included Arizona; Las Vegas, Nevada; and southern California south of Bakersfield, east of the center of Los Angeles, and all of Orange County had just three dealers. One was a used car dealer in Tucson, Arizona, and another a Pontiac dealer in Redlands, California, each with one Datsun.[9] Both subsequently gave up. The third was Wally Tucker, a used car dealer in Bakersfield who had two Datsuns and was also ready to quit. However, he changed his mind and is still in business as Wally Tucker Datsun. The dealer list also included an undertaker who sold Datsuns on the side (the location of his business is not given), and an individual in Arkansas who held his franchise by selling one Datsun a year to his wife.[10] What she did with them is not recorded. Subsequently he improved his business by selling Arkansas farmers on the virtues of Datsun pickups. There are authentic cases of private homes being used as dealerships, with a single-car garage as the service department and equipment consisting of a tool box, an air compressor, and a water faucet inside the garage.

On the other hand, there were dealers such as Lemke and Ellard Winters of Sacramento, who were committed to the Datsun and whose support was a vital element in the company's success. They were multiple-car dealers because Datsun sales were still far from the volume that would support exclusive dealerships, but the Datsun was number 1 on their list.

This wide assortment of dealer types grew out of the difficulties in recruiting dealers of any kind at the beginning. The Datsun was still unfamiliar to the American public in 1961, and some of the little that was known about it was unflattering. It was not easy to persuade a prospective dealer that there was really a future in selling Datsuns—passenger cars, that is. The Datsun pickup was a different story. Leroy Stubberfield began with NMC-USA in June 1961 as District Sales Manager for the states of Washington, Montana, and northern Idaho. His experience then was:

> Most dealers were not interested in the passenger cars. It was the truck that attracted their attention and that was the way we got most of the dealers at that time, through the truck. It was different. It was a very rugged small unit and it appealed to a lot of dealers up in the Northwest area, and actually that is what started it—started the whole company. It was the truck business actually that got us where we are today because from there it grew into the passenger car business once the public and the dealers realized the durability of Datsun products.[11]

But the company could not have lived on trucks alone; the passenger car had to be sold too.

The task of building the sales organization in the Western Division was done principally by Ray Hoen, whose appointment was described in Chapter 3. He remained Western Sales Manager until 1965, when he became National Sales Manager. He served in that post until his death three years later. His first sales staff was made up of men who all had previous experience in selling motor vehicles on the U.S. market, sometimes domestic cars, sometimes imports, occasionally both. They came from both wholesale and retail selling. In other words, right from the beginning the selling of Datsuns in the United States was in the hands of men who were fully acquainted with the American automobile market and thoroughly versed in American sales methods. Some were men Hoen had known in his previous business experience; others were recruited through newspaper advertisements.

The Eastern Division seems to have been less fortunate in its Sales Managers. The first one, Robert Bathurst, was appointed early in 1961, but was replaced a year later by Lee Stokes. He lasted until the reorganization of 1965, when he was replaced by Donald Dare. It is impossible to judge now what effect, if any, these frequent changes had on the buildup of the Eastern Division's sales organization, or on sales. It was probably not very much. Shintaro Inada was there as Assistant to the Vice President for Sales and Accounting to provide some continuity of administration, and Kawazoe himself was described as "a very sales oriented person for an engineer."[12] The description comes from Jack Nielsen, who joined the sales staff in 1961 and eventually became Fleet Sales Manager for the Western area. This is a high tribute indeed from a sales expert to an engineer! But no one in the Eastern Division seems to have matched Hoen's talent for recruiting strong field representatives to build the dealer network.

The first job of the sales staff was to find dealers, and for this purpose "sales staff" in 1961 and 1962 encompassed practically everyone on the company payroll. It was a process that required long hours on the road locating prospects who could be persuaded to take at least one Datsun, and then when it was sold, to take another. The direct responsibility lay with the District Sales Managers as they were added to the organization; they went about the task according to their individual bent, and with some variation according to the territory they had.

As a rule, they found that bankers were initially hesitant about financing Datsun dealers; however, when they discovered that with a reliable, low-priced import car the repossession rate was markedly lower than with domestic cars, the bankers lost their reluctance.[13] William Cushing found twelve dealers in the San Francisco Region when he came into it as Sales Manager in 1961 and he regarded only one as a real dealer. That was Winter Motors in Sacramento, which is still selling Datsuns.[14] The others were poor quality and all eventually dropped out. In rebuilding his organization, he made a point of recruiting among Volvo dealers, because the Volvo was a good car that sold in a different price range from Datsun; in addition, Volvo did not have a pickup truck. For a time, he had twelve and fourteen Volvo dealers also selling Datsuns. He avoided dealers in American automobiles because he wanted the little-known Datsun to be clearly recognized as an import car and not confused with the growing variety of domestic models. Jack Nielsen, who started out in the sales area that included Arizona, Las Vegas, and much of southern California, was quite willing to sign up a domestic new car dealer if he could. On the other hand, he says that he never started a dealership with one vehicle, although this was permissible. The least he put in was three: a passenger car, a pickup, and a four-wheel-drive Patrol. Nielsen's description of how he set out to beat the bushes for dealers gives us a good idea of what it was like to be with an organization that was starting from scratch, selling a product that was barely over its teething troubles:

> It was fun working in those days. We worked, all of us, quite hard looking for dealers and knocking on doors, but the big thing to do at that time was to drive up on a used car lot that looked like it might be a prospect and to get somebody there to come out and look at the car then sell them on taking a drive in it or ride in it around the block, like a retail purchaser. Because they would say "Datsun—no," and they were just not interested.
>
> I recall that a lot of time was spent driving because of the large territory, covering the desert and all of the state of Arizona. Back in those years our little car certainly didn't look or ride like the car we have today, or even in later years. It was without radio or air conditioning and I was traveling in Arizona in the summer. I also went in the pickup which rode very hard; and, also, several trips in the four-wheel drive, because the desert was a four-wheel drive market.
>
> We were able to get some dealers to sign up with Datsun because of it. The pickup was the strong vehicle saleswise because there was nothing really competitive with it at that time. A dealer could get into the Datsun business for $102.60 for his parts package. Nissan would furnish him with a sign to put up—a Datsun sign—I think it was maybe a 4×5 foot fluorescent double faced sign, and then they would give a dealer an advertising allowance.[15]

The effort paid off. There were 122 dealers in 1961, 144 in 1962, and 225 in 1963. This was net gain, allowing for the gradual elimination of the unsuccessful, the unfit, and the uncommitted. There were no exclusive Datsun dealerships as yet. It was still not possible to make a living by retail selling of Datsuns alone; however, it is safe to say that by 1963, the people who were selling Datsuns were predominantly dealers who believed in the product and were ready to push it.

Selling the Product

The object of a sales organization is, of course, to sell. Datsun's rise in just five years from obscurity to sixth place among the imports shows convincingly that NMC-USA's sales organization was doing its job effectively. The start was understandably slow. The story of 1961 and 1962 was one of much painstaking effort for seemingly trivial results. A dealer was recruited and might sell one Datsun in a month, and then another the next month or maybe two months later, and so on until eventually sales gradually began to mount. In those years an average Datsun dealer in the Los Angeles area might sell three to eight cars a month, and ten or twelve in a good month. In the middle of 1961, Katayama announced that there would be a party when the Western Division hit 100 vehicles (wholesale) a month. The party was held late in the year, with seven or eight people present.

We have already seen how everyone in the organization from the Vice President down pitched in to support the sales effort. Katayama continued to deliver cars to dealers himself; he was especially fond of taking new Datsuns to San Diego so that he could talk things over with Ray Lemke. Jean LaPlant made tow bars for dealers who drove to the Western Division office so that they could pick up a car and drive it back themselves. At the time, this gave some tax advantage as well as a smaller shipping cost, because such tows were not subject to the taxes imposed on other trailer rigs.[16]

No detail was too trivial to get attention. Nielsen recalls an occasion when he and Katayama were working in the Alondra Boulevard office on a Saturday afternoon. No one else was there and the building was locked. When someone knocked on the front door and rattled it, Mr. K answered. It was the owner of a Datsun pickup who needed some minor part—something like a distributor cap—and could not find a dealer open who had one. Katayama invited him in and then went back and searched in the Parts Department until he found what was wanted. He sold it to the man for a dollar because he didn't know how much it ought to be—and had a satisified Datsun customer. Then and later, the company would go still further; when necessary, newly arrived cars were cannibalized to meet emergencies for dealers and customers.[17]

The dealers, certainly the good ones, were equally involved. Many picked up their own consignments of new Datsuns, and not just with LaPlant's tow bars. Early in 1961, Bob Daily began doing business as Balboa Motors, briefly in Chula Vista and then in National City, California. His account of what it was like to be selling Datsuns then is very enlightening:

> We couldn't even get truckers to haul our cars from the Los Angeles Harbor, so my wife would take drivers to the docks, about 110 miles north, and they would drive them back. It was rough going for awhile, but by 1963 we knew we had a winner. National City is basically a Navy town and Datsuns were not strange to Navy men, as many had seen and driven them while on duty in Japan. Their previous exposure was helpful to us, as they knew the quality and engineering that went into our cars. Hard work and total faith in our product has been rewarding.[18]

Daily was basically right about 1963, although it took another year for Datsun annual sales to reach five figures. The trend was clear in March 1963, when Datsun took eighteenth place in import sales, compared to thirty-eighth in 1961. By the end of the year retail sales in the Western Division were up 26 percent over 1962 and the division was beginning to show a profit.[19] The year 1964 was a landmark too. In March, the monthly sales figure, including trucks, reached 500—the target Nissan's management had had when it undertook to compete in the United States; in the following July, the 1000-unit mark was reached— a level of sales that in 1958 had represented hope rather than expectations. Katayama had a party to celebrate that event too; rather larger than the celebration for the first 100-car month, but still with only 20 or 30 people present.[20]

In 1962 the company had a survey made to identify the kind of people who were buying Datsuns. The results are shown in Table 4.3. The survey as published seems defective in some respects. The percentages in item 2, "Age," add up to 92; in item 4, "Income groups," to 90.3; and in item 3, "Occupation," to only 68, with no explanation of why the gaps occurred. Nor is the classification system really satisfactory. Why, for instance, should "Salesman" be a category separate from "White collar"? Nevertheless, there is useful information in spite of the deficiencies. Item 1 confirms the importance of the pickup truck in

---

TABLE **4.3**   *Who Buys Datsuns and What Appeals to Buyers?*

According to a recent survey conducted by the Ernest L. Leon Associates, the main Datsun buyer is a blue-collar worker over forty, conservative, and earning between $5000 and $8999 per year. A summary of the breakdown follows.

1. Models (according to sales figures from June 1961 to May 1962):
   Pickup—45.0%   Sedan—34.5%   Wagon—10.0%
   Sport — 5.5%   Patrol— 4.5%
2. Age:
   20–30—17%   31–40—29%   Over 40—46%
3. Occupation:
   Blue collar—28.0%   White collar   —17.0%
   Salesman — 9.0%   Business owner— 7.0%
   Retired   — 6.5%
4. Income groups:
   Under $5000   —17.0% $5000 to $8999—46.0%
   $9000 to $11,999—17.0%   Over $12,000 —10.5%
5. Additional cars of owners:

Type	No additional car	1 Additional car
Pickup	12%	59%
Sedan	30%	63%
Wagon	44%	55%
Sports	40%	40%
Patrol	—	67%

6. Average monthly mileage:
   Under 500— 9.5%   500 to 1499—58.0%
   Over 1500—30.0%
7. Sex:
   Male—87.0%   Female—12.5%

SOURCE: *Datsun Dashes*, vol. 1, no. 1, January 1963.

Datsun sales—45 percent of the total. It is also evident that most Datsun purchasers at that time bought the Datsun as a second car, just as the management of Nissan Motor Company, Ltd., had anticipated. It was undoubtedly too early in the career of NMC-USA for a thorough and conclusive survey of this kind to be done.

There is more accurate and certainly more thought-provoking information on the geographical distribution of Datsun sales (see Table 4.4). At the end of 1961, the first full year of NMC-USA's operations, the Eastern Division led in total sales, even if

TABLE 4.4   *Geographical Distribution of Datsun Sales 1961, 1963, 1965*

Region	1961 Cars	1961 Trucks	1963 Cars	1963 Trucks	1965 Cars	1965 Trucks
EASTERN DIVISION:						
Connecticut	40	2	71	11	85	11
Delaware	5	8	—	—	10	2
District of Columbia	7	—	4	—	—	—
Florida	48	7	60	15	166	28
Georgia	1	—	66	19	162	37
Illinois	2	—	2	—	78	5
Indiana	—	—	—	3	50	21
Iowa	—	—	—	—	4	—
Kentucky	—	—	—	—	127	11
Maine	4	2	1	—	1	—
Maryland	21	3	23	9	87	14
Massachusetts	46	1	67	8	33	2
Michigan	—	—	16	3	590	11
Minnesota	—	—	2	1	44	6
New Hampshire	2	—	—	3	19	4
New Jersey	113	6	136	8	245	9
New York	93	13	293	23	901	44
North Carolina	44	—	69	14	124	42
Ohio	5	—	3	—	126	30
Pennsylvania	37	1	130	18	321	42
Rhode Island	7	1	—	—	2	1
South Carolina	1	—	5	1	89	29
Tennessee	6	—	18	3	418	72
Vermont	13	1	6	—	8	2
Virginia	33	7	26	4	88	11
West Virginia	—	1	6	2	159	56
Wisconsin	—	—	1	1	42	6
Totals	528	53	1,005	146	3,979	496
	581		1,151		4,475	

	1961		1963		1965	
Region	Cars	Trucks	Cars	Trucks	Cars	Trucks
Houston region						
Alabama	1	—	8	3	283	77
Arkansas	—	—	2	—	55	26
Kansas	1	—	1	1	55	11
Louisiana	—	—	1	1	83	48
Mississippi	—	—	1	1	83	48
Missouri	4	2	4	7	78	10
Nebraska	—	—	—	—	14	14
Oklahoma	—	—	38	19	211	56
Texas	66	24	75	150	335	273
Totals	72	26	142	185	1,268	608
	98		327		1,876	
Totals, Eastern Division	600	79	1,147	331	5,247	1,104
	679		1,478		6,351	
WESTERN DIVISION						
Alaska	—	—	14	12	20	29
Arizona	16	4	162	129	488	247
California	158	102	657	787	3,838	2,054
Colorado	12	5	23	29	158	88
Idaho	—	1	13	64	203	167
Montana	—	—	10	13	159	110
Nevada	—	—	19	38	74	52
New Mexico			5	4	253	103
North Dakota	—	—	—	—	—	3
Oregon	14	15	166	398	939	860
South Dakota	—	1	—	—	7	2
Utah	33	20	36	18	24	13
Washington	39	31	76	103	866	477
Wyoming	—	—	3	2	17	6
Totals, Western Division	272	179	1,184	1,597	7,046	4,211
	451		2,781		11,257	
Totals, NMC-USA	872	258	2,311	1,928	12,293	5,315
	1,130		4,259		17,608	
Hawaii*	285	21	393	55	896	107
	306		448		1,003	
Grand Totals	1,157	279	2,724	1,983	13,189	5,422
	1,436		4,707		18,611	

*Not part of NMC-USA
SOURCE: R. L. Polk and Co., provided by Marketing Planning Division, NMC-USA.

its Houston Region is not included. This was what had been originally anticipated when Nissan decided to enter the U.S. market. Two years later the pattern had changed drastically. The Western Division had a commanding lead, with three times the sales volume of the Eastern Division, Houston Region included; this situation was the same in 1965. Much of the credit for the rapid growth of Datsun sales in the west has to go to the personality and leadership of Mr. K, who had a unique faculty for inspiring enthusiasm and dedication in the people who worked for him—plus the ability to get able people to begin with. In this, he had valuable assistance from Reid Briggs. Briggs did not have much legal work to do for NMC-USA at that time, but he had an extensive acquaintance with both the American and Japanese business communities and so was in a position to open doors for Katayama,[21] as well as to steer him away from the errors that could be expected of a novice on the American business scene.

There were other factors as well. From the beginning, the Western Division outsold the Eastern in pickup trucks. In 1963, in fact, the Western Division sold more trucks than passenger cars, as did the Houston Region. These figures confirm what has previously been said about the popularity of this durable little vehicle in farming areas.

The difference has some geographical justification. The sales figures show marked areas of concentration. In the Eastern Division, the heaviest sales volume was in the metropolitan area: Connecticut–New York–New Jersey–Pennsylvania. In the New York metropolitan area especially, the pickup truck had less universal appeal than it did elsewhere, partly because it could not be used on the New York Metropolitan Parkways, or on Connecticut's Merritt and New Jersey's Garden State Parkways. (This point was brought out in an interview on March 3, 1980, by Masataka Usami, who was Assistant to the Vice President, Eastern Division, through most of the 1960s.) There was another consistently good market in Florida, with Georgia added in 1963, and a surprisingly good showing in North Carolina. Texas and Oklahoma were the mainstays of the Houston Region until 1965, also strong in truck sales. The Western Division had a firm sales base on the Pacific Coast—California, Oregon, Washington—and by 1965 was making respectable penetration eastward. Essentially, until the great upsurge of the middle 1960s, Datsun sales were concentrated along the Atlantic, Gulf, and Pacific Coasts, with very little in the interior between the Appalachians and the Rockies. This meant that the Eastern Division was operating in more distinctively urban territory than either the Western Division or the Houston Region.

Perhaps the most definite sign that the Datsun had arrived on the American automobile market was the appearance in 1965 of Michigan, Tennessee, West Virginia, Alabama, Louisiana, Montana, and New Mexico as important sales areas; all except Michigan, it may be noted, were substantial purchasers of trucks. The Eastern Division had another handicap because of its higher ocean freight costs; the price of its cars was $50 more than on the West Coast.[22] Later, after the two divisions were abolished, this differential was absorbed and the price structure made uniform.

There were supplements to the sales effort that should be mentioned. Advertising for the Western Division was handled from its beginning by Parker Advertising of Los Angeles, which continued as NMC-USA's advertising agency nationally after the reorganization of 1965 and remained so for another twelve years. The Eastern Division had its own advertising agency until 1966. Within the company itself, the Service and Parts Departments operated with the same enthusiasm and informality as the sales staff. There were not many Service Representatives at the beginning. They had to cover wide areas— the first one appointed in the south had territory from Florida to Houston—and they had to function as technical advisors, parts salesmen, and training instructors in addition to their service responsibilities.[23] Frequently they delivered parts to dealerships in person to get cars on the road sooner. Also, when there was an urgent need for parts, office personnel would deliver them to dealers on their way home from work.

In recognition of the sales achievement, and as an incentive to greater effort, fifty-five Datsun dealers with outstanding records were given a trip to Japan in November 1965. There they were able to inspect Nissan Motor Company's production and shipping facilities and get better acquainted with the total operation.

The sales drive was materially helped by the introduction of new and improved models—it would hardly have succeeded without them. The first big step came with the introduction of the SPL310 sports car, which replaced the SPL212 of 1961. It was displayed in shows in the fall of 1962 but was not shipped in marketable quantities until 1963. It was a three-seater convertible with an 80-horsepower, 1488cc engine and clean lines[24] and it sold well for three years. A year later (1964) sedans and station wagons of new design (PL410 and WPL410) were put on the market. The 410 had a 60-horsepower, 1200cc engine, like its immediate predecessors, but its appearance and performance showed the results of the constant feedback of information and suggestions from NMC-USA to its parent company—plus the willingness of the parent to listen and respond. The 410 and its successors also had a run of several years, with engine capacity gradually increased to 1600cc.

The 410 sedan came with a Port of Entry (POE) price of $1696. By comparison, the lowest-priced domestic four-door sedan of 1964, the Rambler American, had an introductory factory retail price of $1793, while the Fiat 1100 D sedan, with a 55-horsepower engine, was listed at $1600 POE.[25] This is not a completely accurate comparison, because the quoted prices excluded delivery and handling charges and federal and state taxes and are, in all cases, suggested prices. However, it is close enough to show that the Datsun was satisfactorily competitive in price with the other small cars. It could also, with the 410 series, hold its own in quality.

Company Growth

As its sales grew, the structure of NMC-USA naturally grew also. The basic organization remained unchanged, but more people and more facilities had to be added to handle the expanding volume of business. The company's payroll rose from the 18 of 1960 to 120 in 1965. Less obvious, but certainly no less important, the capital stock was increased to $1.5 million in April 1962, and to the full authorized $2 million at the end of 1963.[26]

The expansion of facilities at this time was reflected chiefly in the establishment of new regional offices. Houston, the earliest, was opened in 1961 to serve an extensive area more effectively than could be done from either Eastern or Western Division Headquarters. The states included in the Houston Region are listed in Table 4.4. The next regional office was Portland, Oregon (1963), serving Oregon, Washington, Alaska, Idaho, Montana, and Wyoming. Then came San Francisco (1965), covering the northern half of California and all of Nevada except Las Vegas. The creation of the Portland and San Francisco offices at this early date testifies to the very rapid growth of Datsun sales on the West Coast. A regional office was opened in Detroit, Michigan, in 1964. Like other early regional offices, it started in modest quarters, in this case an ordinary dwelling house. There was a one-car garage and the basement became the Regional Parts Depot.[27] This office was closed two years later but reopened in 1968. The Datsun was making its way inland—its progress can be traced in Table 4.4—but it took time to approach the degree of penetration attained in seaboard areas.

The regional offices were conceived of in broader terms than mere branches of the Divisional Headquarters. They were, in fact, a conscious decentralization of the Datsun operation, designed to keep sales, parts, distribution, and service as close as possible to the dealers and their customers. It was spelled out by Katayama a few years later:

> Datsun's basic marketing philosophy is to prosper with the community in which the Datsun dealer does business and tie together two nations—the United States and Japan. Knowing this, it is the basic objective of Nissan U.S.A. to obtain and develop successful dealers and in accomplishing this mission the key element is the Datsun Regional Office. All other activities of the National Headquarters play a supporting role.[28]

Until 1966, this supporting role was the responsibility of the Divisional Headquarters, and those facilities had to be enlarged too. The Western Division kept adding to its space in Gardena to take care of increasing requirements for parts and service. The Eastern Division handled this problem by moving in 1965 from its inadequate quarters in Newark to a more commodious location in Secaucus, New Jersey.

There were personnel changes as well, some of them coming in the normal course of events but others showing the changing needs of a growing organization. Two of these changes deserve attention. In 1963, Joe Slackey, the Western Division's first Parts Manager, left to go to a Volkswagen dealership and was replaced by Tom Yasumi, now Manager of Inventory Control and Systems. Yasumi brought a background of first-class experience to the job. He had organized a parts department for the John Green Company, Renault distributor, and had been general manager of Western Parts Distributor, one of its divisions.[29] When Ray Hoen, who had known Yasumi at the John Green Company, told him of the opportunity at NMC-USA, he was attracted. He turned down the first offer because he and Katayama failed to agree on terms, but a second offer a few months later was acceptable and he joined the company.

Then late in 1965, Robert O. Link became Assistant Sales Manager of the Western Division. He had begun his career working in various capacities for Pontiac and eventually arrived in San Francisco. There he moved to Willys Motors, selling Jeeps in northern California for Ray Hoen. When Hoen became general manager for the John Green Company, he invited Link to join him as sales manager.[30] Later, when Green sold his distributorship to Renault, Link became sales manager in Los Angeles for the British Standard-Triumph. Then Hoen asked him to become his assistant again, and after some consideration Link joined NMC-USA. His appointment was in response to the very rapid growth of Datsun sales in the Western Division; as it happened, it came when the company was on the verge of reorganization, but it had obviously been under discussion for at least a year.

By the end of 1965, some reorganization of the company was imperative. NMC-USA was fast outgrowing its first shell; it had reached the stage that Link designated "crisis of leadership," when sheer increase in the number of employees made it impossible for management to continue to operate largely through informal communication.[31] The number of employees was not all that great as yet, but they were becoming more and more spread out geographically, and the number of dealers had grown from the 47 of 1960 to 423 in 1965.

More important, the rapid expansion in the volume of business brought out the awkward feature in the original structure of NMC-USA. It functioned almost unavoidably as two separate companies, both owned by Nissan Motor Co., Ltd., which operated independently of each other. Simply because of differences in the personalities of the people involved and differences in attitude between the eastern and western United States, the two divisions did not approach problems and policies in quite the same way. In the beginning, when sales were light and markets effectively limited to the East and West Coasts, this arrangement was satisfactory enough. But when sales mounted, problems of supply and distribution arose, not yet of serious proportions, but it was inconvenient to have no one nearer than Tokyo in a position to make final decisions. A four-week longshoremen's strike in January 1965 demonstrated the kind of difficulty that could arise. It affected the Port of New York only, but that meant an interruption in deliveries to the Eastern Division even when they were diverted to other ports, with no one on hand who could balance the needs of the two divisions if it became necessary.

Even without disruptions of this kind, the great increase in sales volume alone brought problems. The United States was not the only market of Nissan Motor Co., Ltd. There were other customers to be satisfied, not the least of which Japan's own fast-growing home market. Between 1961 and 1966, Japanese production of four-wheel motor vehicles—passenger cars, trucks, and buses—rose from less than 1 million to something over 2 million and was continuing upward at an accelerating pace.[32] Nissan's share in this output appears in Table 4.5. It shows among other things that the proportion of the total production going to exports was also increasing, from about one-tenth to one-fifth by 1966, and it can be assumed that these proportions are reasonably representative of the Japanese automotive industry in general. The Nissan figures also have the interesting feature that exports of passenger cars exceeded exports of trucks and buses for the first time in 1964, and then only by a slender margin.

This rapid growth in overall demand was bound to put some strain on both production and distribution facilities, with the possibility that temporary local shortages and delays in delivery might develop. There was no crisis situation as yet in 1965, and measures were taken to enable supply to keep pace with demand. Neverthless, it was clearly desirable that NMC-USA should do some restructuring in order to provide for closer coordination and control of its activities.

The reorganization was effected late in 1965; in fact, it was

TABLE 4.5 *Nissan Motor Co., Ltd., Production and Exports, 1962–1977 (By Calendar Year)*

Year	Total vehicle production	Total exports	Production (%)	Exports to U.S.A.	Production (%)	Exports (%)
1962	253,850	28,007	11.0	2,548	1.0	9.1
1963	322,071	46,654	14.5	4,707	1.5	10.1
1964	433,341	72,042	16.6	10,315	2.4	14.3
1965	436,741	78,800	18.0	18,715	4.3	23.8
1966	517,403	102,563	19.8	30,157	5.8	29.4
1967	726,067	132,507	18.2	46,629	6.4	35.2
1968	979,834	206,657	21.1	57,931	5.9	28.0
1969	1,148,715	300,295	26.1	86,894	7.6	28.9
1970	1,374,022	395,301	28.8	155,019	11.3	39.2
1971	1,591,490	631,205	39.7	245,925	15.5	39.0
1972	1,864,244	715,770	38.4	261,384	14.0	36.5
1973	2,039,341	710,624	34.8	319,007	15.6	44.9
1974	1,809,036	863,986	47.8	245,273	13.6	28.4
1975	2,077,447	884,861	42.6	335,145	16.1	37.9
1976	2,303,703	1,142,967	49.6	350,403	15.2	30.7
1977	2,278,051	1,216,986	53.4	488,676	21.5	40.2

SOURCE: *The Global Datsun Family, 1978.*

announced to the Quality Dealers while they were in Japan. Yutaka Katayama became President of NMC-USA and Soichi Kawazoe became Executive Vice President. These appointments could have been anticipated once the decision was made to transfer the presidency of the company to the United States. Katayama was somewhat senior to Kawazoe in the Nissan organization, and in any event the Datsun sales pattern made it logical that the chief executive and the National Headquarters should be in California. The other principal change was to make Ray Hoen the National Sales Manager. Donald Dare replaced Lee Stokes as Eastern Division Sales Manager at this same time, but that was not part of the reorganization.

On the surface it would appear that the company was little changed except that the chief executive officers were now in the United States; and, in fact, the two divisions continued to go their separate ways for some time. The only immediate structural change was that the Houston Region was tranferred from the Eastern to the Western Division on May 1, 1966. But the reorganization proved to have been judiciously timed. The presence of a National Headquarters in the United States made itself felt in due course, and new developments, combined with continuing rapid growth, came along to accentuate the desirability of having the company's management so structured as to provide effective control over an expanding organization.

=≡5≡=

COPING WITH EXPANSION, 1966 TO 1970

When the restructured management of Nissan Motor Corporation in U.S.A. began to function, Datsun was in a takeoff situation. Sales rose from just below 19,000 in 1965 to over 150,000 five years later—a most impressive performance considering that the Datsun had been an almost complete unknown on the American automobile market as recently as 1960. There was obvious cause for congratulation in this achievement, but success of this kind does not come easily, and the company had to contend with problems as well. Supplies of vehicles and parts became tight periodically. Relations with governmental authorities became a matter of major concern, with agitation for restrictions on imports and legislation on air pollution and safety that affected vehicle design. There were changes in the market for small cars that had to be watched carefully, and there must have been disappointment in the fact that while Datsun was doing very well, Toyota was doing even better. Its sales rose from a little over 6000 in 1965 to almost 190,000 in 1970, putting it in second place among import cars.

The Second Wave of Imports

The surge in Datsun sales was to some extent a reflection of the entire import car market. The preceding chapter has told how the appearance of the American compacts in 1959 to 1960 checked and even reduced the flow of imports, and how the domestic producers then responded to apparent customer preference by adding accessories to their small cars and consequently making them somewhat less small. This latter procedure turned out to be counterproductive if the domestic compacts were really to be the weapon that would meet and hold the import challenge, because it left the market for small, economical cars open to import competition once more; the import firms, conspicuously the Japanese, took full advantage of the opportunity. From their low point in 1962, import sales climbed steadily to higher levels than ever, topping the million-unit mark in 1968.

As described before, the reaction of the American automobile manufacturers was a step-by-step repetition of what it had been in the 1950s: first, to dismiss the competition of the imports as negligible, then to push sales of their own "captive" makes, and finally to put a new line of small cars on the market themselves. But history never repeats itself exactly, and there was one highly significant difference. In the 1950s a 5 percent market penetration by import cars was stated as the point at which the domestic manufacturers would take action and enter the small-car field themselves. Now the alarm was not to go off until the imports reached a 10 percent penetration. In other words, while the American automobile companies might talk about "sweeping the imports into the sea," they had become aware that the import beachhead was much too secure for that to happen and they would have to live with an irreducible level of import car sales. The best they could hope for was to keep that level as low as possible.

The 10 percent penetration was attained by the imports in 1968, and that was the signal for the domestic manufacturers to act. A year later, Ford brought out the Maverick and American Motors, the Hornet; both directly aimed at import competition.

In 1970, still smaller cars—"subcompacts"—appeared: Pinto (Ford), Vega (General Motors), Gremlin (AMC).[1] This time, however, history did not repeat itself at all. These cars did not roll back the tide of imports as their predecessors had done, at least temporarily. Instead, import sales and market penetration moved inexorably upward until in 1970 they totaled almost 1.25 million units and represented almost 15 percent of the entire U.S. market for motor vehicles.

There were familiar names among the import leaders of this period (see Table 5.1). Opel made a striking comback to take second place from 1966 to 1968, and Renault, Fiat, Volvo, and Brit-

TABLE 5.1   *Top Ten Import Sales Leaders 1966–1970*

	1966			1967	
Place	Make	Total	Place	Make	Total
1	Volkswagen	420,018	1	Volkswagen	409,263
2	Opel	31,555	2	Opel	51,693
3	Volvo	25,126	3	Toyota	35,913
4	Datsun	21,726	4	Datsun	33,275
5	MG	21,709	5	Volvo	33,012
6	Standard-Triumph	17,184	6	British Motor Co.	30,929
7	Mercedes-Benz	16,081	7	Renault	20,218
8	Toyota	15,814	8	British Ford	16,636
9	Simca	12,596	9	Fiat	15,933
10	Renault	11,500	10	Mercedes-Benz	14,507
	All others	64,814		All others	57,209
	Grand total	658,123		Grand total	718,588

	1968			1969	
Place	Make	Total	Place	Make	Total
1	Volkswagen	563,522	1	Volkswagen	537,933
2	Opel	80,366	2	Toyota	117,384
3	Toyota	68,779	3	Opel	91,161
4	Datsun	40,219	4	Datsun	58,569
5	Volvo	38,335	5	Fiat	41,519
6	Fiat	28,377	6	Volvo	36,448
7	Mercedes-Benz	23,724	7	Mercedes-Benz	24,693
8	British Ford	22,983	8	MG	21,806
9	Renault	19,359	9	British Ford	20,750
10	Standard-Triumph	18,600	10	Renault	17,735
	All others	81,503		All others	93,619
	Grand total	985,767		Grand total	1,061,617

TABLE 5.1   *Top Ten Import Sales Leaders 1966–1970*   *(Continued)*

	1970	
Place	Make	Total
1	Volkswagen	569,182
2	Toyota	184,898
3	Datsun	100,541
4	Opel	83,189
5	Volvo	44,630
6	Fiat	36,642
7	MG	30,548
8	Mercedes-Benz	28,743
9	Renault	19,589
10	Capri	15,628
	All others	117,371
	Grand total	1,230,961

Figures for truck sales would improve the Datsun showing, since many of its pick-ups were used as passenger vehicles.

NOTE: Data is *Ward's Automotive Yearbook* analysis of new car registrations based on R. L. Polk & Co.'s statistical report.

SOURCE: *Ward's Automotive Yearbook, 1967,* p. 167; *1968,* p. 159; *1972,* p. 119. Published by permission of Ward's Automotive Reports.

ish Ford appeared consistently among the leaders. But there were also important changes. Volkswagen continued to hold its place at the head of the list but at a decelerating pace. In 1969, its U.S. sales failed to increase for the first time in twenty years; in the period from 1966 to 1970, the VW share of the import car market shrank from 62 to 46 percent. Volkswagen was repeating the experience of Ford with the Model T fifty years before—the company was dazzled by its overwhelming success and failed to sense that its single, unchanging model could not maintain its place indefinitely against the pressure of competitors with comparable quality and better style.

There was something still more important behind what was happening to the import car market in the United States. In 1968, Japan went ahead of the German Federal Republic to become the world's second-largest manufacturer of motor vehicles, producing in that year a total of 4,085,826 units, of which 2,055,821 (or 50.3 percent) were passenger cars.[2] It was the first time that the Japanese motor industry's output of passenger cars had exceeded its output of trucks.

The world automotive industry, not just the Japanese, had entered a new era. Ten years before, when Takashi Ishihara, Director of Nissan Motor Company in charge of exports, was participating in the first display of Datsuns in the United States, he heard spectators say, "In what country were these cars made? The Japanese can't make such beautiful cars as these."[3] Now things were different. Americans knew very well where the cars were made and who was making them. Some of this change of attitude was effected by determined, capable salesmanship, including implementation of Nissan's philosophy of "responsible marketing," the belief that responsibility to its customers continued after the sale was made. Much of it, very much of it in fact, is a tribute to the remarkable advances that the Japanese automobile manufacturers had achieved in design, engineering, and production techniques during these ten years. The Datsuns of 1958 were good cars, although with some deficiencies where suitability for the U.S. market was concerned. The Datsuns of 1968 were vastly better and could hold their own against any competitor in the same size and price range.

The effect of this Japanese achievement on the import car market in the United States was emphatic. From 1966 through 1970 sales of import passenger cars rose by almost 600,000; of this increase, a quarter of a million was accounted for by gains in Datsun and Toyota sales alone, with several other Japanese makes beginning to be respectably represented as well. A year later (1971), tenth place among the import sales leaders went to the Dodge Colt, made by Mitsubishi for Chrysler, which had been unable to offer an entry of its own in this new small-car field. The import truck situation saw an even more drastic shift. As late as 1967, Volkswagen had as commanding a lead in the import truck market as it did with passenger cars, with about two-thirds of the import truck sales in the United States. Two years later, VW was virtually out of the running and Datsun was far in the lead.[4] Its truck sales climbed from 8431 in 1966 to 50,954 in 1970; by then Japanese trucks represented an astounding 96 percent of all import truck sales in the United States. (For truck sales see Appendix B.)

Import motor vehicles had moved into an entirely new situation. Instead of being on the fringe of the American car market, they had become an integral part of it, with every indication that they were going to stay that way. Beyond that, the import car market itself had experienced a marked shift. The time when "import car" and "European car" were virtually synonymous had come to an end; now the Europeans were struggling to hold their own against the oncoming Japanese.

The Datsun Growth

It was a novel situation for NMC-USA, also, to move with breathtaking speed from working just to secure a foothold in the U.S. market to being one of the top three contenders in import car sales. Datsun moved up from its sixth place in 1965, to fourth in 1966 to 1969, and third in 1970.[5] As sales mushroomed, the company expanded accordingly. The number of dealerships and employees increased as could be expected (see Table 5.2), and with the dealers there was a qualitative change just as important as the growth in numbers. By 1968, exclusive Datsun dealerships were visibly replacing the used car lots, service stations, and multiple-car "supermarkets" of earlier years.

Along with greater numbers of people, there was phsyical expansion. Handling the mounting volume of business

TABLE 5.2   *Company Expansion (1966–1971)*

Year	Datsun dealers	NMC-USA employees
1966	543	121
1967	544	155
1968	606	221
1969	640	276
1970	899	436
1971	922	950

SOURCE: Data from company records.

demanded additional regional offices: Jacksonville, Florida, and Los Angeles (1968), New York (1969), and Boston (1970). In addition, the Detroit Regional Office was reactivated in 1968 and moved to Chicago two years later—evidence that the Datsun was definitely penetrating inland. The New York Regional Office was located with the Eastern Division in Secaucus. The Los Angeles Office shared space with what was now the National Headquarters on Alondra Boulevard in Gardena, California, until October 1970. At that time a Master Parts Depot was opened in nearby Compton and some of the national offices temporarily moved in there. Plans were already afoot for the present National Headquarters building; the growing organization had to have more space.

There were the visible signs of expansion. The effects of the company reorganization were not equally evident. To all appearances, the Eastern and Western Divisions continued to operate on their own, much as they had before. It took time for changes to make themselves felt, but they were occurring just the same. It made a difference that decisions that had formerly been made in Tokyo were now being made in Los Angeles, and there was a more immediate impact in greater coordination of the national sales effort under Ray Hoen. As part of this effort, the Parker Advertising Agency became the sole advertising agency for NMC-USA, and Datsun had its first national advertising campaign in 1966 with the slogan "Drive a Datsun— Then Decide."

In addition, developments that had nothing to do with the company's reorganization had the unscheduled effect of turning Vice President Kawazoe's attention increasingly to matters of governmental relations. These were questions of trade relations and still more of the growing body of federal legislation affecting the automotive industry. (This topic is dealt with in Chapter 6, Government Relations.)

Kawazoe was certainly the logical person to take charge in this area. He remained in Secaucus after the reorganization, so that he was conveniently located for handling problems in Washington, D.C. With his fluent English, he was better equipped than Katayama to represent NMC-USA at legislative and administrative hearings. It also happened that many of the problems concerned engineering matters such as safety and emission control, for which Kawazoe was, of course, superbly qualified. President Kawamata of Nissan Motor Company, Ltd., quite properly designated him as the official representative of the Nissan organization in negotiating with the National Highway Traffic Safety Administration.[6] He also represented the Automobile Importers of America in these matters, as vice president of that organization. All this was good for Nissan, but it meant that Kawazoe had considerably less time to devote to the day-to-day operations of the Eastern Division.

The sales effort continued to be pressed vigorously, since even Datsuns do not sell themselves, regardless of the state of the market. Early in 1967, a new Dealer Sales Agreement was signed, responding to the requirements of the larger and better dealer network. It was the company's first general dealer agreement. This was followed by a Cooperative Advertising Agreement for joint company-dealer participation in advertising programs. Shortly afterward, Robert O. Link took over Hoen's old post as Sales Manager for the Western Division and Mayfield Marshall came into the organization as Advertising and Sales Promotion Manager. He brought to the position a considerable background in advertising and publishing. He had been advertising and marketing manager of *Motor Trend Magazine* and for several years had been promotion and merchandising manager for the nine magazines published by the Petersen Publishing Company.

The product line kept pace with the sales organization. As these steps were being taken, the first Datsun 510 series came on the market, a series whose qualities appealed strongly enough to American buyers so that its four-door sedans and station wagons jointly sold more than 300,000 units over a five-year span. Robert Link characterizes the 510 as an innovative design in that it had four-wheel independent suspension, along with an overhead cam, 1600cc, 96-horsepower engine. It also had front-wheel disc brakes and optional automatic transmission. The automatic transmission at first came from Borg-Warner's British factory, but deliveries from this source proved uncertain and the source of supply was transferred to the Borg-Warner plant in Muncie, Indiana. Later Nissan joined with Toyo Kogyo (Mazda) and Ford to establish the Japan Automatic Transmission Co., using some Ford patents.[7] The 510 was sufficiently innovative for NMC-USA to organize an intensive training program for its own and its dealers' service personnel. It also proved to be successful as a racing car, an activity on which the worldwide Nissan organization placed a strong emphasis, and in which it enjoyed an excellent record (see Chapter 14, Racing, Rallies, and Sports Cars).

While Datsun sales were forging ahead, the whole company was saddened by the death of Ray Hoen in September 1968, after a period of illness that had compelled him to give up his post as National Sales Manager in the previous July. He had been an important contributor to the rise of Datsun through his success in building the sales staff and extending and improving the dealer organization. For the time being, the company carried on the sales effort through Link in the Western Division and Donald Dare in the Eastern, under the overall direction of Katayama, whose own talents in sales promotion were far from negligible. Then in May 1969, Link was made National Sales Manager.

Some of the salient features of the sales growth appear in Table 5.3. The apparent domination of the Western Division has to be regarded with some reservation, because it now included the Houston Region, containing such high-sales states as Texas, Louisiana, Mississippi, and Missouri. If their sales were credited to the Eastern Division, the count would be more nearly even. Nevertheless, the figures make it unmistakably clear that the Pacific Coast had become the prime market for Datsuns in the United States, understandable in view of the accessibility of this region to Japan and the fact that it had consistently been partial to import cars. Something has to be attributed to salesmanship, although that poses another unanswered, and possibly unanswerable, question: Which took better salesmanship—selling many Datsuns in California or a few in South Dakota?

The most marked feature of this table, as compared with the

TABLE 5.3 *Geographical Distribution of Datsun Sales 1966, 1968, 1970*

Division	1966 Cars	1966 Trucks	1968 Cars	1968 Trucks	1970 Cars	1970 Trucks
Eastern Division						
Connecticut	123	17	290	75	1,820	404
Delaware	36	9	121	25	353	85
District of Columbia	38	—	57	2	165	14
Florida	461	102	1,936	1,337	5,932	3,462
Georgia	308	99	651	434	2,209	1,441
Illinois	342	30	396	90	1,998	277
Indiana	99	38	407	147	1,073	358
Iowa	23	6	132	59	339	120
Kentucky	247	49	289	96	695	223
Maine	64	16	140	80	408	247
Maryland	114	28	365	84	2,163	520
Massachusetts	119	11	313	35	1,487	181
Michigan	513	100	524	177	1,035	364
Minnesota	53	8	86	23	364	123
New Hampshire	119	43	236	85	549	195
New Jersey	360	23	670	96	2,363	297
New York	1,099	97	1,400	247	3,589	679
North Carolina	236	66	439	189	1,553	743
Ohio	199	30	619	262	1,900	634
Pennsylvania	536	79	1,087	226	3,664	859
Rhode Island	15	2	48	16	344	65
South Carolina	137	53	408	246	1,160	479
Tennessee	626	128	1,031	438	1,609	855
Vermont	22	1	39	19	148	55
Virginia	238	63	304	128	1,635	601
West Virginia	282	71	537	264	894	644
Wisconsin	48	12	83	11	355	72
Totals, Eastern Division	6,457	1,181	12,608	4,891	39,804	13,997
	7,638		17,499		53,801	
Western Division						
Alabama	383	87	446	227	1,210	730
Alaska	56	32	78	36	218	144
Arizona	613	298	945	441	1,548	1,211
Arkansas	43	30	180	200	514	477
California	7,215	3,364	12,494	5,820	32,053	19,894
Colorado	401	137	821	233	1,903	643
Idaho	329	229	498	426	700	544
Kansas	67	17	226	87	576	217
Louisiana	271	142	426	319	1,384	960
Mississippi	288	123	373	309	967	823
Missouri	223	21	496	137	1,244	361
Montana	259	169	323	194	485	346

Division	1966 Cars	1966 Trucks	1968 Cars	1968 Trucks	1970 Cars	1970 Trucks
Nebraska	46	20	119	24	293	66
Nevada	45	49	120	75	251	222
New Mexico	366	159	678	350	1,093	530
North Dakota	3	3	6	9	60	50
Oklahoma	363	86	571	246	N.A.	N.A.
Oregon	1,197	1,033	2,013	1,302	4,150	2,747
South Dakota	14	6	37	25	55	41
Texas	613	437	1,699	984	4,166	2,818
Utah	58	20	190	71	538	173
Washington	1,036	607	1,593	912	3,555	2,287
Wyoming	41	11	48	18	120	71
Totals, Western Division	13,930	7,080	24,380	12,445	57,083	35,355
	21,010		36,825		92,438	
Hawaii	1,339	166	3,230	373	3,654	964
	1,505		3,603		4,618	
U.S. government	—	4	1	3	—	—
	4		4		—	
Grand Totals	21,726	8,431	40,219	17,712	100,541	50,316
	30,157		57,931		150,857	

SOURCE: Market Planning Department, NMC-USA.

previous one, is the positive evidence it gives that Datsun sales were becoming genuinely nationwide in scope. While the seaboard states remained the source of the largest volume of sales, the figures for Middle America became more and more impressive. By 1970, only the two Dakotas recorded fewer than a hundred sales of Datsun passenger cars during the year; only eight had fewer than a hundred Datsun truck sales and they were so widely scattered geographically that they show no perceptible pattern. There were now regional variations and fluctuations in Datsun sales, but no longer any segment of the United States where Datsun cars and trucks had not become familiar.

Growing Pains

It might be supposed that a company whose sales had leaped in less than ten years from four-digit figures to six would have reached a position where it would have little to worry about. Actually, this idyllic situation never occurs in the world automobile industry, where miscalculation of the market, unwise expansion, unexpected labor problems, or any of a number of factors can turn yesterday's prosperity into today's adversity. The story of Chrysler, British Leyland, or Volkswagen in the mid-1970s each offers eloquent testimony on this point. Not that NMC-USA was in any such critical position, but it was discovering that while fast growth yields sales totals that are very agreeable to contemplate, it also entails a fair amount of blood and sweat and sometimes even a few tears.

The basic difficulty facing the company immediately after its reorganization in 1966 was very simple: the supply of cars could not keep pace with the demand. This would appear to be a desirable situation for a business to be in, but in reality it is not. No business likes to turn prospective customers away, least of all the automobile business, where variations in consumer preferences are volatile and unpredictable enough. A disappointed customer has other makes to turn to and can very well be a permanently lost customer. The risk in this situation was greater for import cars, since domestic makes were in plentiful supply. For Datsun, specifically, there was a limit to the production capacity of Nissan's plants in Japan, there was a limit to the shipping tonnage available, and neither ships nor ports were yet equipped for handling large numbers of cars efficiently. In addition, seamen's or longshoremen's strikes occurred in the New York port area every year except in 1968, when there were two; also, early in 1969, there was a dock strike covering the entire East and Gulf Coasts.

The effect on NMC-USA shows in the change in the number of dealers between 1966 and 1967—543 to 544. It was necessary to restrict the number of new dealers who could be accepted because it was impossible to supply them with cars; it was difficult enough to fill the requests of the dealers the company already had. Yet the problems were dealt with and sales and the dealerships continued to increase.

The achievement took concerted effort by both parent and subsidiary. Nissan Motor Company, Ltd., opened its great new Oppama assembly plant in 1962 in Yokosuka and the Zama plant for truck assembly three years later. These and the acquisition of the Prince Motor Company properties in 1966 gave it the productive capacity to meet the burgeoning demands of its home and export markets. For the exports, the bottleneck became the problem of getting the vehicles to their destination. Shipping by conventional freighters was unsatisfactory because of the uncertainty of scheduling and still more because too many cars were damaged in transit. To deal with this problem, Nissan first organized the Nissan Motor Car Carrier Co., Ltd., in 1965 for the purpose of operating a fleet of ships specifically designed for the transportation of motor vehicles. The first of these, *Oppama Maru*, went into service late in 1965. It was built and owned by Mitsui O.S.K. Lines, Ltd., and chartered on a long-term contract by Nissan. The subsequent development of this fleet will be described in Chapter 13, Transportation and Distribution. The *Oppama Maru* had a capacity of 1200 cars and had ramps so that the cargo could be driven on and off. Second, in 1967, Nissan opened the Hommoku Wharf in Yokohama, covering 38 acres and built exclusively for loading motor vehicles.

At the receiving end of the line, there was a major improvement in the port facilities at Los Angeles. Until 1970, cars were unloaded at ordinary berths in Los Angeles Harbor and then trucked several miles to Santa Fe Springs, where they were inspected and the necessary cleaning and repairing was done by a concern called Vehicle Maintenance and Painting, which also stored them pending shipment to their ultimate destinations. The process involved a good deal of unnecessary movement with concomitant risk of damage, and there were continual disagreements about responsibility for work done on cars. So, in 1969, NMC-USA, Marubeni America Corporation, and

Mabuchi Kensetzu, a Japanese warehousing firm, established a joint operation under the name of Distribution and Auto Service, Inc. (DAS).[8] This organization built a dock and warehouse complex on 32 acres of land in Wilmington, California, where one advantage was a rail connection that permitted cars to be shipped out directly. The first cars unloaded at the DAS facility arrived in April 1970 on the new Nissan car carrier *Hommoku Maru*. The benefits of this arrangement were not fully effective until the next stage in NMC-USA's history.

The combination of these measures pretty well eliminated shortages of cars as a serious handicap to Datsun growth in the United States for some time to come. There would still be occasional interruptions in the supply line for causes over which the company had no control, such as labor disputes in shipping or at the ports, but these were usually temporary nuisances that could be dealt with rather than crises that threatened to be seriously disruptive. As the decade of the 1960s drew to a close, NMC-USA had arrived at a position where it could really "think big," as befitted a company whose operation had grown in less than ten years from being essentially regional to a fully national scale.

Coming of Age

The company was doing exactly that; not only thinking, but acting big. The year 1969 emerges as important in the history of NMC-USA. Its capitalization was increased twice: to $4 million in September and then to $6 million in October. The first 240-Z sports car was displayed at this time, too, to initiate a distinguished line of Datsun Z-cars. The 240-Z got off to a flying start; *Road Test* magazine chose it as the "Sports Car of the Year" for 1970. Monthly sales in May 1969 reached the 10,000 level[9]— quite a contrast to the situation of ten years earlier, when sales of a thousand Datsuns a month in the United States was a target that seemed highly optimistic but just possibly attainable.

There were significant personnel developments in 1969. The

appointment of Robert O. Link as National Sales Manager has already been noted. He filled a post that had already existed but had been vacant since Ray Hoen's death. Along with this, two additional national offices were created: Robert K. Scott as National Parts Manager and Lee R. Wylie as National Service Manager. This was hardly a startling new departure considering that NMC-USA had been officially operating on a national basis since 1966. It is somewhat surprising that it had not been done before. Evidently the two-division separation had strong survival power. Scott had been Parts Manager for the Eastern Division, coming to NMC-USA, like so many of its staff, from previous experience with import cars. He started working as a grease monkey for a Chrysler dealer in Watertown, Massachusetts, while he was in high school and claims he noticed then that the Parts Manager seemed to have the cleanest job in the place.[10] He got into import car parts when the dealer took on Renault. Scott subsequently operated a distributorship for import car parts and was Parts and Service Manager for Renault when Kawazoe persuaded him to join NMC-USA.

Wylie had been a service manager in various capacities and just before he joined NMC-USA was with the Lincoln-Mercury Division of the Ford Motor Company.[11] His work was mainly in retail service and he wanted to be in wholesale operations, so in 1964 he answered an advertisement in the "Help Wanted" section of the *Los Angeles Times* and found himself Service Manager of the Western Division. What this was like in 1964 can be best told in his own words; it gives some inside view of how far Datsun grew in the next few years:

> I was interviewed and hired without ever having seen the Service Department, its offices, or management personnel. So I went to work on a Monday morning and they said, "We'll take you back to the office," in an apologetic way, "Well, it isn't too much of an office now but things will get better," or words to that effect. So I went back. Here is a cubicle like a foreman's shack built inside the building about 15' × 15' divided in half. The back half of it was the Service Manager's office, which had a large table in it, completely covered with warranty claims.

Wylie says he almost turned around and left, but then he decided there was a challenge here. Five years later, he was National Service Manager, with markedly improved quarters.

These appointments, along with Link's and Yasumi's, confirmed the policy adopted by Katayama and Kawazoe from the beginning when they first started to recruit their sales staffs. This was to seek out people who understood American business practice and were experienced in the methods used in the United States for automobile sales and service. It did not really matter whether the experience was with import or domestic cars. What counted was that the people on the firing line for NMC-USA understood the American market and the American consumer. It was a wise policy. There are subtle differences in business practice between Japan and the United States—the Japanese view of contracts, for example, is more flexible than the American[12]—and it was sound judgment for NMC-USA to build its staff to ensure that its business methods conformed to its market.

These appointments to newly created national positions were hailed within the company as symbols of an "Alliance for Progress" between the Parts and Service Departments,[13] which were undergoing an expansion necessitated by and consistent with the growth of retail sales. Scott was able to mark his promotion by announcing that Nissan Motor Co., Ltd., had upgraded its export parts section into an Export Parts Department, whose function would be "to facilitate the smooth and speedy supply of spare parts for export and to provide relevant technical information."[14] In addition, a new parts storage warehouse was scheduled to open in 1971, with over twice the capacity of the existing building at the Zama plant and a section of it was specially assigned for the use of the Export Parts Department. The further development of Parts and Service is the subject of Chapter 12.

In the light of all these developments, Bob Link could fittingly close the year and the decade by announcing a five-year expansion program aimed at annual sales of 300,000 by 1974 and saying, "If the pattern for Datsun in the 1960s was unspectacular, it was by design. We now have a strong foundation on which to base our plans for launching this program in the future. Our attitude in the 1970s will show a sharp departure from our conservatism in the past ten years. The time has come to flex our muscles."[15] One comment has to be made about this statement: If raising annual vehicle sales from 1300 in 1960 to 82,000 in 1969 was conservatism, it is impossible to imagine what a nonconservative policy might have been like.

The company was perceptibly changing. It had to. The sheer phenomenal growth of its business demanded the expanded physical facilities and the increased staffs, from Vice Presidents to warehouse workers. There were other new developments. The informality of the early days, the close personal relationships in the conduct of the business, were giving way to a more elaborate and structured organization—unavoidably if regrettably. There had to be a greater degree of departmentalization because as the company got bigger, its operation became more complicated.

Two such departments were created in 1970. What is now the Employee Relations Department was first organized in that year as a section of Finance and Administration.[16] Understandably, with a staff of over 400 that was about to double in size, NMC-USA could no longer function in its old way, when almost everyone was hired personally by either Katayama or Kawazoe. At the same time, the Technical Service Department, the precursor of the Engineering Department, was created within the Service Department.[17] It had two sections, which explain its initial responsibilities, Product Support and Emission Control.

Executives and operations alike were thus centered in southern California by 1970. The new departments were located there; the additional administrators had their offices there. The one conspicuous exception was Kawazoe, whose responsibilities required him to stay in the east. His former Eastern Division Service Manager, William Renz, became head of Equipment Approval in the Technical Engineering Department, but he continued to keep his office in Secaucus for some time.

Throughout 1970, NMC-USA was moving steadily toward the

third phase of its organizational development and the direction of the movement was plain. The company was becoming too big to be managed effectively by the somewhat loose administrative system adopted in 1965, which itself had represented a fairly minor modification of the original organization of 1960. Sales for 1969 were close to the 100,000 mark; they would certainly pass it in 1970 (they did—150,000). An efficient, firm administrative structure was needed to ensure that vehicles in this quantity could be shipped across the Pacific in both the required numbers and the desired types, were delivered to their proper destinations, and arrived when they were supposed to. And as the number of Datsuns on American roads proliferated, more elaborate organization was required to see that adequate service facilities existed and that parts were readily available on a nationwide scale.

Achieving these goals meant more centralization of authority and more systematic controls than the existing NMC-USA organization provided. There had been some progress in this direction since 1965, but a considerable residue still survived of the initial arrangement of two separate divisions virtually independent of each other. Between the Eastern and Western Divisions there were variations in managerial and accounting practices and some discrepancies in pricing policies because of the higher cost of transporting cars to the eastern ports. All this had to be changed so that the company could operate as a unified whole.

There was much study and discussion of organizational problems throughout 1970. There could have been a sense of urgency about the process because the company's growth continued to accelerate. Sales went up approximately 80 percent, the number of dealers by 40 percent (from 640 to 899), and employees by 60 percent (from 276 to 436). NMC-USA was far from being a giant corporation, but it was definitely and rapidly outgrowing the organizational shell it had lived in since 1966. Moreover, the area of managerial concern had been substantially and permanently extended by regulatory legislation, both federal and state, that affected the entire U.S. automobile industry, domestic and import alike.

Yet the reorganization process was not rushed; it was too important for that. Mr. K later summed up how it was done: "It was obvious that a change was necessary, but we did not approach this change hastily. We took stock of our organization; we noted our good points and our bad points. We have met, discussed, and evaluated what shape this change should take, and we are now on the threshold of implementing this change."[18]

As part of the taking stock, the management consulting firm of McKinsey and Company was called on for advice. The "threshold" date was April 12, 1971, and it was none too soon. NMC-USA's management was unquestionably wise to go about its reorganizing carefully, but it was also just as well that the task was completed when it was. The next few years were going to see occurrences in the United States and elsewhere that would profoundly affect the world automotive scene. Few if any of these events could have been anticipated and they would present challenges calling for strong, effective management. Under the circumstances, it was fortunate that NMC-USA streamlined its management when it did.

It was fitting that while this major transformation was going on, NMC-USA should be celebrating its tenth anniversary, and "celebrating" is the proper term. The company had come a long way in ten years. The occasion was recognized in two major events. First, there was an anniversary dinner at the Century Plaza Hotel, Los Angeles, on October 1, 1970, at which the principal speaker was Masataka Okuma, then Managing Director and now Executive Vice President, Nissan Motor Company, Ltd. This was followed by the official opening of the new Master Parts Depot, located on West Artesia Boulevard in Compton, California. It was, as the company magazine expressed it, a time when the Datsun family "joined together to bring down the curtain on ten full years of success in the most competitive automobile market in the world, and at the same time they pledged their cooperation in challenging the new decade that promises to be the most exciting in Datsun's history."[19]

=6=

GOVERNMENT RELATIONS

The period of rapid growth for NMC-USA in the second half of the 1960s coincided, as has been pointed out, with a number of new developments on the national political scene that suddenly propelled the company's relationships with government, both federal and state, from being a relatively unimportant consideration into a matter of major concern. This altered situation was, of necessity, a factor in the decision of how to reorganize the company; undoubtedly not the most influential factor, but certainly one that carried far greater weight in 1970 than it had in 1965.

For the first five years of its existence, NMC-USA's involvement with government was essentially routine; meeting customs regulations (this was largely Marubeni's responsibility) and seeing that its cars met the standards for certification by state authority where that was required, as in California. The yen and the dollar were in a stable relationship, and imports of Japanese cars were still not nearly large enough to disturb domestic industry or labor. In selecting the principal causes for

the intensification of NMC-USA's involvement with government, in common with all other import car companies, one of
the correct answers would have been "none of the above." The
dominating element was a sudden upsurge of public concern
about air pollution and traffic safety, which produced a spate of
legislation, several new administrative agencies, and a profu-
sion of regulations, all directly affecting the entire automobile
business.

The "Chicken War"

This new phase in government relations was ushered in for
NMC-USA by a trade dispute in which the Japanese actually
had no part. They were in the position of the innocent
bystander who accidentally gets caught in the line of fire. What
happened was that in 1962, the European Common Market
adopted a Common Agricultural Plan, which had the effect of
drastically curtailing exports of chickens from the United States
to Germany. The U.S. government protested and, when negotiations through GATT (General Agreement on Tariffs and
Trade) failed to provide a remedy, raised tariffs on EEC (European Economic Community goods).[1] Among these was a 25 percent ad valorem duty on trucks valued at $1000 or more, effec-
tive December 4, 1963. The intended target was the Volkswagen
Combi, which then dominated the import market for pickup
trucks in the United States. However, because of "most-favored-
nation" provisions, the tariff had to apply to Japanese-built
trucks as well. Then, as described in the previous chapter, Japanese pickup trucks, especially Datsuns, practically pushed the
VW entry off the market and found themselves in the anomalous position of being the products most affected by a tariff
increase adopted as reprisal against the EEC.

Efforts to have this tariff removed or reduced have been
unavailing. Domestic truck manufacturers have been reasonably satisfied with the situation, even though General Motors
and Ford marketed pickup trucks of Japanese manufacture (Luv

and Courier). The Japanese producers were able to reduce the burden by shipping truck beds and chassis separately and assembling them after arrival in the United States. This operation began for Datsun in Los Angeles, California, at the beginning of 1973[2] and was subsequently extended to Seattle, Washington; San Francisco, California; Jacksonville, Florida; and, Baltimore, Maryland. Obviously, the Chicken War did not materially restrain the sale of Japanese pickup trucks in the United States; the sales figures testify to that. Its major effect has been to introduce an additional cost factor, since except for the tariff consideration it would be just as cheap to ship the trucks as units; so, perhaps the real victim has been the American consumer rather than the Japanese manufacturer.

Emission Control and Highway Safety

By far the most important of the issues that involved Nissan (the whole organization, not just NMC-USA) and all other motor vehicle manufacturers in extensive dealings with government authority were air pollution and traffic safety. Although they had no direct relationship to each other, these two issues arose to prominence at about the same time on the national political scene.

Atmospheric pollution is a problem of long standing, going back as a matter of concern to the smoky industrial cities in the nineteenth century. However, such action as was taken was mainly at the local level and not especially effective. Most of this pollution was produced by factories, railway locomotives, and domestic coal fires. The motor vehicle was not regarded as a culprit until after the middle of the twentieth century, by which time there were heavy enough concentrations of cars in large metropolises for ther exhaust emissions to be identified as a major contributor to air pollution. The phenomenon first surfaced in Los Angeles in the early 1950s when a yellowish-brown haze began to appear in the atmosphere with increasing frequency and intensity. It was termed "smog," a word originally coined to describe the combination of smoke and fog that polluted nineteenth-century London. It was eventually identified by Dr. A. J. Haagen-Smit of the California Institute of Technology as principally a photochemical reaction to motor vehicle emissions, compounded by peculiar atmospheric conditions that periodically prevented the emissions from dissipating. The state of California began to enact legislation in the early 1960s aimed at reducing pollutant emissions, to the concern of the automobile manufacturers. California was too large a market to ignore and yet it would not be economical to build cars to one set of standards for California and another for the rest of the country.

This difficulty was more or less resolved when Congress imposed national pollution control standards by the Motor Vehicle Air Pollution Act of 1965, although California continued to maintain more rigorous standards than the federal laws required. These first laws, both federal and state, have been constantly revised and amplified. They had deficiencies, as was to be expected. Not enough was known about the subject when they were originally enacted. They imposed rigorous restrictions on emissions of unconsumed hydrocarbons and carbon monoxides and overlooked the importance of oxides of nitrogen in creating smog. Criteria were imposed arbitrarily and perhaps somewhat unrealistically. Nevertheless, the requirements were there and the manufacturers of domestic and import cars alike had to comply with them. They came under a considerable amount of criticism for procrastination in doing so, with some justification; in their defense, however, it must be pointed out that many of the clean-air enthusiasts tended to ignore the very complex technical and economic problems that have to be solved to attain their objective.

The safety issue followed a similar pattern except that it had no special point of origin, as the smog problems did in southern California. It erupted as a matter of national concern in the mid-1960s, assisted by the publication of a book, *Unsafe at Any Speed*, by a crusading lawyer named Ralph Nader. Where traffic safety heretofore had focused mainly on such matters as highway improvement and driver training, Nader castigated the automobile manufacturers for failure to design cars for safety. Some of his strictures were justified, others were not, but this intensification of safety agitation was a factor in the passage of the National Traffic and Motor Vehicle Safety Act in 1966.

Like the Air Pollution Act, this law has been constantly elaborated, amplified, and modified. It has the same fundamental problem: Admitting that the objective sought is eminently desirable, what are reasonable standards? Where is the balance struck between optimum safety and economic feasibility, since safety features, such as pollution control devices, add measurably to the cost of the car? How is the choice to be made between alternative methods of achieving the same end, such as seat belts or air bags? The emotional plane on which much of the discussion of traffic safety was conducted tended to impede rational analysis of complex technical problems, and there was too little regard for the plain fact that in terms of the number of vehicle miles traveled, American highways have easily the best safety record in the world.[3] There is certainly room for improvement, but it is most likely to be achieved by careful and dispassionate study of all facets of the problem.

Adapting to these new requirements posed difficulties for all motor vehicle manufacturers but particularly for the makers of small cars. The main reason for this is very simple: a small car has less space to work with. When it comes to modifying design or adding equipment to comply with requirements prescribed by law, a small car is under far more severe constraints of weight and space than a big one; however, if these constraints are removed by the easiest method, enlarging the vehicle, then it ceases to be a small car and loses its primary sales appeal. There are other factors. Small engines are designed to run at higher temperatures because this improves performance in relation to size, but the higher temperature increases output of oxides of nitrogen. In fact, a general response to the first emission control laws was to raise engine temperatures in order to cut down hydrocarbon and carbon monoxide emissions as required by law. This technique, however, had the unexpected effect of calling attention to the equally important role of nitrous oxides as atmospheric pollutants.

The early legislation itself unwittingly discriminated against small cars by prescribing emission standards as a ratio, parts per million (PPM). By this standard a small car could be sending less *total* pollutant into the atmosphere than the large car next to it but still be in violation of the law while the big car was not.

This was the situation that all manufacturers of import cars had to face just when their market in the United States was reaching new heights. The legislation was especially crucial for the Japanese, who were climbing rapidly from the bottom to the top of the import list. To preserve what was being gained would require skillful handling of relations with the U.S. government, both its legislative and executive branches. Fortunately for NMC-USA, Vice President Kawazoe was on the scene and had the qualities that were needed.

His talents in this area were widely recognized. Chapter 5 has told how he was made the official representative of Nissan in negotiations with the U.S. government, and he also acted for the Automobile Importers of America, of which he was vice president. In addition, he was designated as the spokesman for the Japan Automobile Manufacturers Association (JAMA). This combined load eventually proved too heavy and he had to give up the JAMA assignment.

Implementing this legislation demanded an incredible amount of work by both the government and the manufacturers. The government had to organize new administrative agencies which would then formulate the regulations for compliance with the law. The process meant exhaustive hearings and conferences with representatives of the industry—such as Kawazoe—to try to work out techniques and schedules. Then came the problem for the manufacturers of incorporating the techniques and meeting the schedules within some acceptable limit of cost.

The Nissan Response

For Nissan, as for all other automobile manufacturers, the air pollution and safety legislation called for a concerted effort by the entire organization. This included not just NMC-USA but reached back to basic design and engineering for the production line in Japan. President Kawamata has a trenchant description of how the problem looked to the company at the start:

> It is, of course, without question that we automakers should try to make a vehicle as safe as possible for the public good. But again, a key consideration in producing a "safe car" should be given to the cost of the car. I suggest that we refer to the total 26 items of government car procurement safety rules of GSA (General Services Administration) before we make any decision.
>
> For the research and development of the safety car, the cost would be incomparably lower in the U.S. (where annual production by the Big Three exceeds 10 million passenger cars) than those of Japanese made cars of which annual production is not more than several hundred thousand, of which only one tenth are for export.[4] To make matters worse, these safety rules are more strict with the smaller cars than with big ones. Without safety devices, no foreign car is allowed to be sold in the U.S. market.
>
> Another problem is emission control regulations, which go into effect in September, 1967. Our study on emission has just started and therefore we have no relevant data.[5]

The rest of this section of Kawamata's talk deals with the desirability of the entire Japanese automobile industry sharing a patent on emission control held by the Saggino Company, a General Motors subsidiary. His statement emphasizes an important but generally overlooked issue, namely, the regressive effect of the cost of meeting emission and safety requirements. Since the cost of the necessary research and development is about the same whether a large or a small producer is doing it, the burden is heavier for the small company. Kawamata's suggestion of pooling resources made sound sense; however, in the United States, such a step might be considered to be in violation of the antitrust laws. It would be ironic if a long-term consequence of legislation that was largely promoted by forces eager to encourage competition in business were to have just the opposite effect in the automobile industry by making it more difficult for small firms to compete.

The mention of the General Services Administration rules refers to the earliest effort of the federal government to impose safety requirements on cars by establishing regulations that had to be met in vehicles purchased for government use (other than military). Kawazoe attended a hearing in Washington on these GSA standards on May 14, 1965, a year before the passage of the Motor Vehicle Safety Act.[6] The points under discussion were:

1. Padded instrument panel
2. Recessed instrument panel
3. Impact-absorbing steering wheel
4. Four-way flasher
5. Dual braking system
6. Tire specifications

These were all features of subsequent legislation and administrative regulations. Kawazoe notes that the U.S. manufacturers could not guarantee that they could incorporate these features into their 1967 models, and that four import car companies were represented: Nissan, Volvo, Citroen, and Mercedes-Benz.

Further hearings and discussions followed with GSA, and then with the Department of Health, Education, and Welfare (HEW) and the National Highway Traffic Safety Administration. HEW, which at that time was responsible for administration of the Air Pollution Act, agreed to a change in its requirements for the benefit of the makers of small cars: the standard for emissions was made grams per mile instead of PPM.[7]

All this meant intense activity for Kawazoe and his staff, because he had to send detailed and accurate information back to Japan so that Nissan and the rest of the industry could design cars that would comply with the requirements of U.S. law, and do so by January 1, 1968. It must have been an exacting task. The text of the law was not nearly enough for the manufacturers to go on. They also needed to know and understand the myriad of administrative regulations and interpretations by which these laws were being implemented, and what choices of techniques were available to them. Sometimes the process of working these out was even funny, although the hard-pressed designers of Nissan Motor Co., Ltd., were probably not especially amused. Kawazoe recounts how the first hearing on safety standards was held at the General Motors Technical Center in Warren, Michigan, where G.M. engineers had made a mock-up to show what a car complying to the letter with the proposed standards would look like.

> It was interesting to note . . . that if the law was complied with, strictly as written, the knob on the door lock became the size of a golf ball and the front A pillar became so wide that it obstructed the view through the windshield . . . I couldn't help but silently laugh to myself because our engineers had already advised me how our cars looked by following the standard and it was exactly like the GM mock-up.[8]

The elementary difficulty was neatly summed up a number of years ago by a very wise man named William Shakespeare: "If to do were as easy as to know what were good to be done, chapels had been churches and poor men's cottages princes' palaces." (*Merchant of Venice*, Act 1, Scene 2.)

The whole matter was taken seriously enough by Nissan, along with the rest of the Japanese automotive industry. In December 1966 a Safety Mission consisting of the presidents of Nissan, Toyota, and Honda and sponsored by the Japanese government arrived in Washington. Its purpose was to assure the federal authorities of the willingness of the Japanese manufacturers to comply with American safety standards but to request that more time be allowed and that consideration be given to the special problems of small cars, sports cars, and four-wheel-drive vehicles.

This was neither special pleading nor procrastination. While the Japanese were making this request they were also working hard to meet the requirements of the law. The new safety standards were promulgated by the National Highway Traffic Safety Administration on January 31, 1967; in the following April, Kawazoe reported to the NMC-USA staff on what was being done.

At present the new safety standards are being studied by groups of engineers from various manufacturers in Japan under the auspices of the Automotive Industrial Association in Tokyo. New comments and petitions were drawn up and hand carried from Tokyo to my office on January 25. The documents were further studied here and presented to the National Traffic Safety Agency on February 28. As for the exhaust emission control devices, we have had our units tested at the HEW laboratory in Detroit after a 4,000 mile test in our own lab in Japan. I understand that the results were extremely good. However, this is only part of the program. A unit with 50,000 mile test completed will be flown in also for final verification. However, I am quite certain that all of our units will come out with flying colors.

So you can see that Nissan is right on the job to send you Datsuns fully capable of meeting any and all Federal Government regulations for 1968 models whether emission controls or safety. Good selling![9]

All this was just the beginning of an ongoing process in which solutions to the problems that were encountered kept being pushed farther into the future simply because of the difficulty, perhaps impossibility, of defining conclusively the goals to be achieved.

Kawazoe, writing in 1973, pointed out that 70 percent reduction in pollutant emission had been achieved since 1970, but the law required a 90 percent reduction for the 1975 model year. The 70 percent figure represented an average cost per car of $100, while trying to attain 90 percent would run about $500 per car. Yet, he observed: "We still seem to lack sufficient scientific data to precisely pinpoint the necessity for a 90 percent reduction. This is particularly true from the standpoint of cost benefit analysis. How bad is bad? Nobody knows."[10]

Emission and safety matters were definitely going to be a continuing concern for all motor vehicle manufacturers doing business in the United States. Kawazoe's work in Washington grew into the External Relations Department of NMC-USA, formally constituted in 1976. Nissan Motor Company, Ltd., established the Engineering Office of North America in Englewood Cliffs, New Jersey, where Kawazoe also established an office, for the specific purpose of keeping the home company in close touch with the technical requirements of American law. The Engineering Office of North America also maintained an office in Washington.

The Nissan record in meeting the challenge of emission and safety legislation was excellent, evidence of first-class cooperation within the organization. Nissan Motor Co., Ltd., spent over $8 million in the development of Experimental Safety Vehicles and some $60.8 million on safety research and development between 1969 and 1972 and allocated 2000 engineers to this project.[11] Some of this effort was due to the fact that Japan was beginning to impose its own stringent pollution and safety standards, but Nissan still kept the American requirements in mind. Part of the work was done through a research operation called Calspan, formerly Cornell Aeronautical Laboratories, in the form of 50-mile-per-hour front-end crash tests with a modified Datsun 510. The conclusions were:

> The results of the tests come the closest of any work so far to reaching the desired curves for deceleration postulated by the National Highway Traffic Safety Administration.
>
> The front bumper assembly was successful with both flat and pole barriers at speeds up to 10 mph. Except for a slight deformation of right mounting brackets, there was no damage and the passenger compartment decelerations were nominally within the 10 G requirement.[12]

Their efforts brought Nissan a unique distinction for an automobile manufacturer—praise from Ralph Nader.[13]

Other Concerns

Until 1971, the pollution and safety issues dominated NMC-USA's relations with government authorities. There were some others, but they were minor. Except for the Chicken War, tariff rates remained stable. The federal excise tax on motor vehicles was raised from 6 to 7 percent in 1966, but it dropped back again shortly afterward; in any case, it affected domestic and import cars uniformly. Exchange rates were also stable. The official rate remained at 360 yen to the dollar until early in 1971. The unofficial rate fluctuated in the general range of 380 to 400 yen to the dollar from 1962 to mid-1968, when the gap began to close (see Table 6.1).

Then in 1971 came the first of a series of crisis years, in which

TABLE 6.1   *Unofficial Dollar-Yen Exchange Rates, 1962–June,*
            1971*   *(Official Rate 360 Yen = 1 Dollar)*

	1962	1963	1964	1965	1966	1967	1968	1969	1970	1971
January	376.00	396.00	387.00	383.00	389.00	387.00	382.50	373.50	376.00	377.00
February	383.00	400.00	382.00	390.00	388.00	385.00	384.00	376.00	373.00	379.00
March	390.00	389.00	383.00	378.00	389.00	387.00	386.00	378.00	365.00	376.00
April	388.00	399.00	385.00	379.00	387.00	383.00	385.00	375.00	363.00	367.00
May	400.00	399.00	391.00	378.00	389.50	383.00	387.00	374.00	364.00	360.00
June	401.00	398.00	387.50	382.00	389.00	384.00	380.00	376.00	369.00	363.00
July	398.50	398.00	391.00	384.00	393.00	384.00	373.00	375.00	370.00	—
August	400.00	396.00	394.00	393.00	392.00	387.00	370.00	375.00	366.00	—
September	401.00	390.00	380.00	382.00	393.00	380.00	368.00	374.00	370.00	—
October	394.00	382.00	378.00	378.00	385.00	384.00	376.00	372.00	377.00	—
November	394.00	386.00	381.00	388.00	384.00	383.50	374.00	370.00	380.00	—
December	398.50	381.00	380.00	386.00	384.00	386.00	373.00	376.00	380.00	—

SOURCE: Data provided by Market Analysis Department, NMC-USA.
*In Japanese yen per United States dollar at end of month.

the company was confronted by difficult situations that were
not of its making and which no degree of foresight could have
anticipated. All were basically political in nature: devaluation
of the U.S. dollar, tariff surcharges, and the Arab oil embargo of
1973. Under the circumstances, NMC-USA was fortunate in two
respects. One was that it entered this critical period with a
strengthened and greatly improved organization. The other
was that the safety and emissions issues came along when they
did, so that Kawazoe had the opportunity to get acquainted
with the Washington scene and create the organization for handling the company's governmental relations. It was an area that
was going to require increasing highly skilled attention from
this time on.

=7=

REORGANIZATION AND CRISIS

As the decade of the 1970s began, Nissan Motor Corporation in U.S.A. faced it with a thoroughly restructured organization and bright prospects. Sales continued to climb. The years from 1971 to 1973 were good years for all motor vehicle sales (see Table 7.1). Datsun remained firmly ensconced in third place among import cars, with a wide gap separating the top three (Volkswagen, Toyota, Datsun) from the rest of the import field. There were problems to be dealt with, as there always are, but NMC-USA had met and overcome difficulties before, and there was nothing in sight in 1971 that could be considered out of the ordinary.

It could hardly have been foreseen that these years of the early 1970s would be the end of an era—the last time that automotive fuels would be cheap or, as far as the general public was aware, in unlimited supply. The figures were there to show an increasing dependence on imported oil in the United States, but

TABLE 7.1 Motor Vehicle Sales in the U.S., 1971–1974 (In Thousands)

	1971			1972			1973			1974		
	Cars	Trucks	Total	Cars	Trucks	Total	Cars	Trucks	Total	Cars	Trucks	Total
U.S. companies	8,681	2,011	10,692	9,327	2,486	11,813	9,676	2,915	12,591	7,454	2,511	9,965
All imports	1,568	85	1,653	1,623	143	1,766	1,763	233	1,996	1,413	176	1,589
Totals	10,249	2,096	12,345	10,950	2,629	13,579	11,439	3,148	14,587	8,867	2,687	11,554
Imports from Japan	544	82	636	615	141	756	738	232	970	592	175	767
Datsuns	185	60	245	188	74	262	231	88	319	185	60	245
All import market share (%)	15.0	4.0	13.3	14.8	5.4	13.0	15.4	7.4	13.6	15.9	6.5	13.7
Japanese import market share (%)	5.4	3.9	5.1	5.6	5.3	5.5	6.4	7.3	6.6	6.6	6.5	6.6
Datsun market share (%)	1.8	2.8	2.0	1.7	2.8	2.0	2.0	2.7	2.1	2.1	2.2	2.1

SOURCE: MVMA, *Motor Vehicle Facts and Figures, 1979*, p. 22, and Market Research Department, NMC-USA. The totals vary from what appears in other sources, but these appear to be the most reliable.

they were simply ignored. The arrival of this crisis is the subject of the next chapter. When it came, it was not the end of the automotive world, just the end of an era. For NMC-USA it offered the same challenge as the other problems of the period; further progress was contingent on ability to adjust to changing conditions.

The New Organization

The organizational structure adopted by NMC-USA in April 1971 deserves some close attention because it has remained the basic pattern to the present, allowing for adjustments necessitated by continuing growth and by experience with the actual working of the system. The initial outlines of the organization plan had been formulated in close cooperation with Nissan Motor Co., Ltd.; three of the men who became Vice Presidents under it, Kimio Namba, Ryunosuki Miyakoda, and Naofumi Uchiyama came from the parent company in 1969 to join NMC-USA and assist in implementing the plan.[1] The objective was to raise Datsun sales in the United States from the 60,000 level of 1968 to over 300,000—an objective attained in 1973. The major steps in the reorganization were:

1. The two divisions were abolished and replaced by three areas (northern, southern, western), each with an Area Sales Manager in charge (see Figure 7.1). These were Donald Carmack in the northern area (replaced late in 1971 by William B. Akers), Marvin Acklin in the southern, and Gordon Whitby in the western; all men who had come up through the company's Sales Department. They were to operate out of National Headquarters.

   This change was long overdue. Under the market conditions that existed when the company was founded, it was logical to divide it into Eastern and Western Divisions and let them operate as virtually separate entities. But once Datsun was selling in a fully national market, the two-division arrangement made less and less sense, and the rivalry that

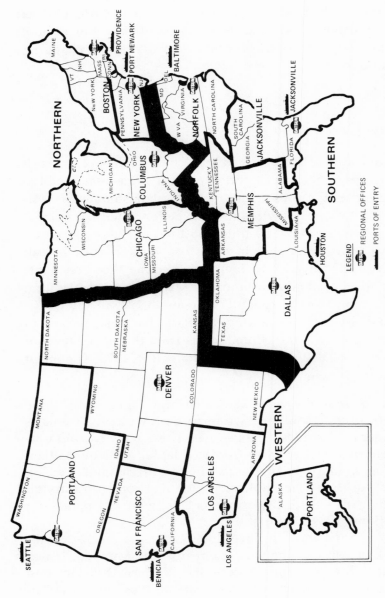

FIG. 7.1 *Nissan Motor Corporation in U.S.A. area and regional boundaries. This map shows the area and regional boundaries as of August 1977. In 1971, the territories now included in the Columbus and Memphis Regions were part of Chicago and Dallas (then Houston) Regions, respectively. Norfolk had previously been in the Jacksonville Region, and the Denver Region was a composite of territories from the Houston, Los Angeles, and Portland Regions.*

inevitably developed between them became a liability rather than an asset.

2. Expansion of the central executive: in the new organization the positions of Katayama, as President, and Kawazoe, as Executive Vice President, remained unchanged. Now, however, there were five new Vice Presidents: Masataka Usami, Parts and Service; Ryunosuki Miyakoda, Marketing; Kimio Namba, Import and Distribution; Naofumi Uchiyama, Finance and Administration; Robert O. Link, Sales. These five, with Katayama and Kawazoe, constituted the company's Executive Committee, which made the basic policy decisions. They supervised seven departments: Finance and Administration, Marketing, Sales, Import and Distribution, Parts, Service, and Technical Engineering.

Figure 7.2 shows the new administrative structure, along with the key management personnel at the time the reorganization went into effect. This structure provided for more effective central control of NMC-USA's operations, which was certainly desirable in view of the company's rapid growth and the national scale of its activities. But it was not intended that there should be a total centralization with everything rigidly concentrated at and directed from National Headquarters.

Two statements by President Katayama explain the objectives of the reorganization so well that they are worth quoting at length, and it is characteristic of Mr. K that the first of them, made on February 11, 1971, was directed to all employees of NMC-USA in order to keep them informed about what was taking place:

> In the past months, I am sure that you have all been reading of the tremendous strides that our Company and its outstanding group of dealers have been making in increased sales. This has not been easy. First, we were faced by the introduction of the domestic subcompacts and then we were threatened by an economic downturn. Through it all, however, our Company has been able to grow stronger. As our sales continued to increase, our dealer organization increased in both number and stature, and our Regional Offices and Parts Warehouse network grew and expanded.
>
> This solid growth in the face of strenuous challenge did not take

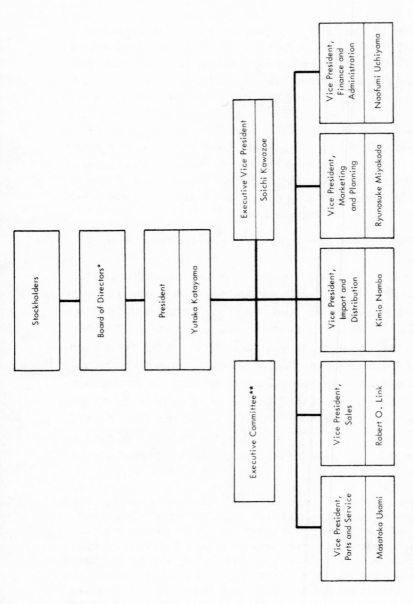

* Board of Directors consists of Messrs. Katayama, Kawazoe, Okuma, Shimamoto and Usami.

** Executive Committee consists of Messrs. Katayama, Kawazoe, Link, Miyakoda, Namba, Uchiyama, and Usami.

FIG. 7.2   *Nissan–U.S.A. organization structure in 1971. (Source: Report of Organization Meeting. April 12, 1971.)*

place by happenstance. It grew from a combination of building a strong foundation, good planning and the efforts of extremely capable people. Part of our strength stems from the fact that we have been ready, willing and able to communicate with all those that had our interests at heart. When we had a problem—we listened. We then determined what we could do to correct that problem and we made the necessary changes.

Now the time has come for us to make another change. This time a major one, and one that will ensure the continued growth of our organization.

Since the inception of the Nissan Motor Corporation in U.S.A. we have operated on a two-division system. An Eastern Division in Secaucus, New Jersey, and a Western Division in Gardena, California, both worked in cooperation with a headquarters staff. In the beginning when our dealers were few and our field force was limited, this system worked admirably. Now things have changed. Our dealers are many and the number of people in the field needed to service this growing dealer body are many. With this unprecedented growth, the two division system has impeded our ability to effect meaningful two-way communications between management and our customers.

Communications are the key to our success and when our ability to "talk" to our customers is hindered due to a ponderous chain of communications, the time has come to adopt a system that once again fosters this communication.

This reorganized system was not approached hastily. We took stock of our organization, noting both the good and bad points. At a meeting held in Gardena last week, top management from both the East and West Coasts were called together and the new organizational system was announced.

The principal change will be the elimination of the two-division system. Now, we are one company. As before the country will be divided into regions. Where there are now eight, there will be nine with the addition of the Norfolk, Virginia Regional Office. And our plans call for three more, making a total of twelve before very much longer. The two divisions were creating difficulties and we have moved to correct that by eliminating them. The Regional Office system has worked well and we are moving to strengthen them.

On a management level, I need help. When the company was young, the decisions came at such a pace that I could cope with them and still keep in touch with all the operations of the different departments. Now there are over 700 people working for the company, and the complexities of a multimillion dollar business need the specialization that only an expanded Executive Committee can handle. To accomplish this, it gives me a tremendous sense of pride to announce that we have reached into our own organization and promoted five very capable gentlemen to the position of Vice President and members of the Executive Committee.

I want each of you to join with me in wishing these men the congratulations that they are so deserving of and to assure them of your continued support.

Joining with these five new Vice Presidents on the Executive Committee will be myself and Mr. Soichi Kawazoe our Executive Vice President. In addition to serving on the Executive Committee, Mr. Kawazoe will redirect his efforts to the multiplicity of areas concerned with safety and emission control and will act as liaison between Nissan, Tokyo, and the federal government. He will continue to operate from the East Coast and will work closely with our liaison office.

Working with Bob Link in the tremendous task of coordinating our sales efforts will be three Area Sales Managers who will supervise geographic divisions of the Country. The Northern Area will consist of the New York, Boston and Chicago Regions. The Southern Area will consist of the new Norfolk Region as well as the Jacksonville and Houston Regions. The Western Area will encompass the Los Angeles, San Francisco and Portland Regions. All three of these Area Managers will be headquartered in Gardena, working closely with Bob Link.

In order to increase uniformity within the Regions and to facilitate improved communications within the various departments, another facet of the reorganization will see the Regional Department Heads reporting directly to the National Department Heads in such areas as sales, service and parts. The aim here is to see that uniform national policies can be established and maintained so that truly we can be one company from coast to coast and border to border.

The second statement was made to an organization meeting on April 12, 1971. It reiterated the description of the reorganization and the reasons for it and added:

I think we should all greet this change with enthusiasm, for it presents us with a tremendous challenge and opportunity for the future. For the first time, we are truly one company, working together to meet opportunities, and working together to reach our common objectives.

The basic objectives of our company are based on a simple marketing philosophy. This philosophy is that we are not doing business simply to make money. We are in business to prosper with the community to which we belong. In our case, our marketing community is the entire United States, and our philosophy of responsible marketing serves not only to allow us to prosper in the United States, but to tie more strongly together the common interest of two nations.

President 1971 Katayama (handwritten annotation)

The expression of our marketing philosophy is found in our company's objectives. If I may, I would like to read to you these objectives which are found in our new Company Organization Manual.

The basic objective of Nissan Motor Corp. in U.S.A., is to develop an expanding and nationwide network of successful dealers. In carrying out its basic objective, the company will strive to make the most effective use of its personnel and facility resources and meet its full responsibilities to customers, dealers, employees, and shareholders. To that end, the following objectives are set forth:

1. To achieve a leadership position in market penetration and sales volume among our primary competitors.
2. To distribute high quality vehicles tailored to the American consumers' needs at a competitive price.
3. To provide the consumer with high quality parts and service through the development and maintenance of superior dealers.
4. To conduct a continuous program of research aimed at improvement of product quality and features, and minimizing of adverse environmental effects.
5. To maintain a strong financial position through effective management of receipts and expenses.
6. To improve and strengthen the corporation's management through acquisition and development of high-caliber personnel and through continuous effort toward simplification of organization structure and procedures.
7. To continuously seek opportunities to strengthen employee morale and productivity.
8. To increase the consumer's awareness of the corporation's responsiveness to customer needs and desires, emphasis on quality and efficiency of operation.

To accomplish these goals and basic objectives efficiently and effectively, we have reorganized Nissan Motor Corp. in U.S.A.

Apart from the basic philosophy they expressed, which had been the Nissan philosophy all along, these statements have some points worth noting. Mr. K made it clear that the new Area Managers would be located at National Headquarters, and that Vice President Kawazoe would continue to have government relations as his special assignment. Most important was the emphasis on the importance of the regional offices. NMC-USA was aiming at a staff-and-line organization in which the regional offices were on the line as the company's direct contact with its dealers and its customers. Headquarters would provide policy direction, advice, and assistance; the regional offices were to be the operational agencies in the all-important function of working with the dealers to sell Datsun cars and take care of them after they were sold. In still another statement, this time to all NMC-USA Managers, delivered on February 17, 1971, Katayama said:

> Let us review the basic structure of our organization. The front line of our organization is the Regional Office. Each Regional Office is in the process of developing into a self-sufficient unit receiving functional guidance from their respective National Department Heads; i.e., policy is formulated at National and implemented in the Region, thus ensuring consistency of operation across the country. Our policies and procedures must be coordinated at the National level and implemented and operated at the Regional level.
>
> We are going through a time of the concurrent development of strong Regional teams and National staff. As individual Regions become more developed, functional dependence on the National staff can slowly be reduced. However, there is always a need for local coordination and teamwork of Regional activities. The Regional Office must grow as a "Team." Acting as Senior Manager in the Region, the Regional Sales Manager is "Captain of the Team."
>
> Even though policy is formulated by National and implemented by the corresponding Department Head in the Region; and even though National will hire and train personnel for assignment in the Region, the Regional Sales Manager must be kept informed of these activities.
>
> The Regional Sales Manager is responsible for the performance of the Region; and all Regional Managers report to him for coordination and implementation of their day-to-day activities.

This arrangement should have provided for adequate intercommunication and apparently did, with the managers of departments such as Service and Parts in the regions reporting both to their National Managers and the Regional Sales Manager. The regions were thus given a partially autonomous status, with ample scope for control of their own local activities but firmly enough linked to National Headquarters to ensure uniformity in the application of company policy. The importance of the regional offices is shown by the fact that at the end of 1971 there were ten, rather than the nine Katayama referred to. One new office was established in Norfolk, Virginia, as he said, and another was added in Denver, Colorado. In the following year, the Houston Regional Office was moved to Dallas, as a more central location for the area it served.

Thus NMC-USA emerged as a thoroughly reconstituted company. The line of authority ran clearly from National Headquarters (temporarily in Compton, about to move to Carson) to the areas and the regions. The total Nissan organization for selling in the United States after completion of the reorganization is shown in Figure 7.3. The thorough planning and equally thorough explanation seem to have been effective in making the reorganization acceptable throughout the company and its dealer organization. There may have been a few disgruntled individuals, but the available evidence is that the change was seen as an improvement that would benefit Datsun's ability to compete in the United States motor vehicle market.

The Crises of 1971

The new organization was almost immediately confronted with a number of serious challenges. Vice President Link compressed them in a single paragraph:

> In 1971 there was, during the months of April and May, a seaman's strike in Japan; July through September, there was a West Coast dock strike during which we had to bring vehicles in through Mexico and Vancouver; October through December, there was an East Coast Dock strike. On August 16th, President Nixon announced his new economic program that repealed the excise tax and added a 10 percent import surcharge.[2]

The economic program also included the cessation of dollar convertibility by the United States, a step which pushed up prices for all imports, and wage and price controls.

None of these, it will be observed, were problems over which NMC-USA had the slightest control. It could only face them and work out ways to deal with them, as in fact, it did. The series of strikes gravely impeded the flow of new cars, so that in May 1971 a moratorium had again to be imposed on the appointment of new dealers. During the West Coast longshoremen's strike, cars were brought in, as Link indicated, through Vancouver, B.C. (actually New Westminster), and Ensenada in Mexico. When the Atlantic and Gulf Coasts were struck, the port of Quebec was used and some cars were shipped by rail all the way from the West Coast. These expedients kept supplies of vehicles from being cut off altogether, but they were limited and costly. Indeed, when the strikes overlapped the import restrictions and the devaluation of the dollar, it worked out that with price fluctuations and variations in freight charges, a dealer could have the same model on his floor at about five different prices.[3]

As if these handicaps were not enough, the EDP (Electronic Data Processing) computer system for warehouse inventory control and billing for vehicles and parts proved inadequate to handle the combining of the records of the Eastern and Western Divisions. Each had its own record-keeping system. They were supposed to be integrated by October 1, 1971, but, they were

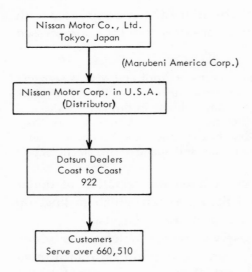

FIG. 7.3   *Selling organization. (Source: Company Outline, 1972.)*

not. It took another year to remove the discrepancies and get a unified system in operation.

Strikes and computer failures could at least be endured as temporary nuisances. It could be reasonably taken for granted that the strikes would be settled sooner or later and that the EDP system would eventually be restored to satisfactory working order (that was achieved in October 1972). The change in U.S. economic policy was another matter altogether, which presented NMC-USA and all other automobile importers with a long-term and tangled problem of fluctuating exchange rates, consistent only in that they kept moving in the least favorable direction for the importers.

President Nixon's announcement suspending convertibility of the dollar on August 16, 1971, threw the world's currency exchanges into confusion. Japan tried briefly to support the existing 360:1 rate and then on August 28 allowed the yen to float. It promptly moved to about 308 to the dollar.[4] This level was accepted on December 18, 1971, in the Smithsonian Agreement, which was an effort by ten countries to fix limits for the movement of their currencies in relation to both gold and the dollar. For Japan, this agreement gave the yen a middle rate in relation to the dollar of 308:1, which represented an appreciation of about 17 percent for the yen, and limits of 314.93 to 301.07.[5] It all added up to a de facto devaluation of the dollar and therefore higher prices for imports in the United States. The devaluation was made official in May 1972, when President Nixon signed the Par Value Modification Act, but this did not produce stabilization because the dollar continued to decline and the yen was revalued. The import surtax exerted additional upward pressure on the prices of imported goods, but it was removed at the end of 1971 when it appeared that the desired result was being attained by current revaluation.

This was a welcome step for importers but it still meant further price adjustment. There is a certain amount of understandable frustration in a bulletin on price revision issued to Datsun dealers on January 14, 1972: "These (suggested prices) reflect the revaluation of the Yen, removal of the Surcharge and the Excise Tax. We trust this will be the final bulletin on 1972 prices."

For Nissan and the other Japanese automobile firms the consequence of all this was to lose much of price advantage they had formerly held over their American-built competitors. Link recalls three price adjustments, all upward, in the last few months of 1971. Yet Datsun sales in the United States grew by a factor of 67 percent over 1970, from 150,000 to 250,000— strikes, transportation difficulties, currency fluctuations, and higher tariff duties notwithstanding. The dollar devaluation and the surtax were too late to affect import car sales appreciably in 1971; in fact, they showed a slight overall gain. The impact was felt in 1972, when the import share of the market fell below 15 percent, but even that was attributable to an upswing in sales of domestic cars rather than to any marked decline in import sales, and this situation lasted only a year. The imports went back over 15 percent in 1973, even with another 10 percent devaluation of the dollar.

In the light of all the unexpected obstacles that were put in its path, it was a remarkable feat for NMC-USA to sell 100,000 more vehicles in 1971 than it had the year before and then continue upward. Some of the achievement has to be credited to the quality of Datsun cars, especially the new 510 series and the 1200 line. They represented the attainment by Nissan designers of parity with anything in the same class that the United States or Europe had to offer. At the same time, it took a highly skilled and well-organized effort to sell even high-quality import cars in the succession of handicaps that cropped up in 1971.

Figure 7.4 shows how sales were distributed among Datsun models in 1971 and what their recommended POE prices were when the year ended. The figures in the table have several interesting features. As recently as 1971, Datsun purchasers opted by more than two to one for standard rather than automatic transmissions, although availability of cars could have had something to do with this in the disrupted shipping conditions of that year. Customers could very well have settled for

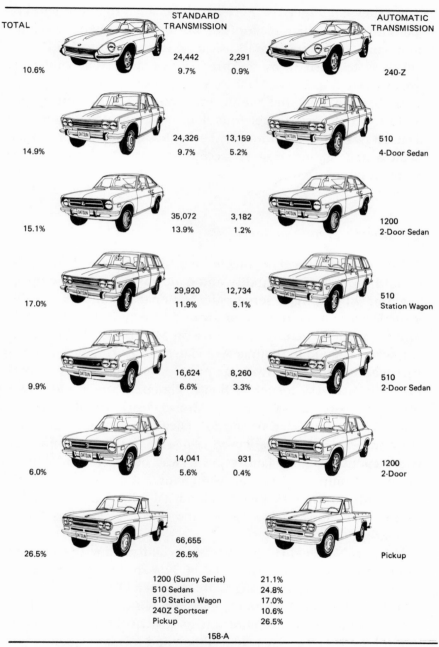

TOTAL		STANDARD TRANSMISSION		AUTOMATIC TRANSMISSION	
10.6%		24,442 9.7%	2,291 0.9%	240-Z	
14.9%		24,326 9.7%	13,159 5.2%	510 4-Door Sedan	
15.1%		35,072 13.9%	3,182 1.2%	1200 2-Door Sedan	
17.0%		29,920 11.9%	12,734 5.1%	510 Station Wagon	
9.9%		16,624 6.6%	8,260 3.3%	510 2-Door Sedan	
6.0%		14,041 5.6%	931 0.4%	1200 2-Door	
26.5%		66,655 26.5%		Pickup	

1200 (Sunny Series)	21.1%
510 Sedans	24.8%
510 Station Wagon	17.0%
240Z Sportscar	10.6%
Pickup	26.5%

158-A

FIG. 7.4   *Retail sales figures and percentages by model for 1971.*

what they could get, not necessarily for what they wanted. The perennially popular pickup did not offer automatic transmission, and the sports car enthusiasts who bought the 240-Z were unlikely to want it, as the proportions show. The buyers of sedans, whether 510 or 1200, may have been reluctant to pay an extra $180 to $190, but the majority were quite willing to pay $140 to $150 more to get four doors instead of two. And the Datsun was overwhelmingly being bought as a family car; sedans and station wagons accounted for 63 percent of the year's total.

Corporate Headquarters

It was appropriate that during this time of crisis NMC-USA should symbolize its stability and continuing growth by opening a new building to serve as its National Headquarters. Construction was announced and ground broken in October 1970, and the formal opening took place on May 10, 1972. The building was designed by Kajima Associates of Los Angeles in a distinctive form to take advantage of the triangular lot it occupies on the southwest corner of South Figueroa Street and 190th Street in Carson, California, close to and clearly visible from the intersection of the Harbor and San Diego Freeways. It is a nine-story trapezoid, glass-walled on two sides, so that it stands out conspicuously in the landscape. It was built by the William Simpson Company, General Contractors, at a cost of approximately $4.5 million, exclusive of land. The site is about 18 miles south of downtown Los Angeles, and 10 miles from Los Angeles Harbor.

The new National Headquarters was dedicated with elaborate ceremony. President Kawamata of Nissan Motor Company, Ltd., came from Japan, along with Masataka Okuma, Managing Director, and Yuji Shimamoto, Director, Nissan Motor Co., Ltd. Both the latter were also Directors of NMC-USA. On the morning of May 10, Kawamata cut a ribbon and formally opened the building. Then he presented Katayama with two pictures to be hung in the lobby, a painting of Mount Fuji by Yusada Yuki-hiko and a spring scene by Kawai Gyokudo. Mr. K accepted them with the observation: "Mount Fuji represents two important aspects of our company. Its natural beauty represents the purity we strive for and its height represents our success. The spring scene represents our growth."[6]

On the afternoon of May 10, Datsun dealers from all over the country toured the building and were given recognition for the contribution made by the dealer organization, which donated the landscaping. That evening there was a cocktail party and buffet for company personnel and their spouses. On May 11, there was a cocktail party and dinner for a thousand business associates and friends of NMC-USA at the Century Plaza Hotel in Century City, Los Angeles. Entertainment was provided by singer Jack Jones and The Establishment, who gave a version of *Jesus Christ, Superstar*. Kawamata was the main speaker.

The best account of this affair comes from *Kashu Mainichi (California Daily News)*, of Los Angeles. It reported that Kawamata "in a low posture speech, spoke with quiet pride of the fact that there will soon be over one million Datsuns on U.S. roads and expressed appreciation to his staff for surmounting the initial hardships to bring that miracle about." Then the editor added: "We have attended non-business dinners where orators spun out fancy words about international amity, understanding, brotherly love, etc. Sometimes, at a business dinner in which ties of international friendship and understanding are forged by the good old-fashioned enlightened pursuit of the buck, one gets the feeling that the ties are more solid."[7]

He also emphasized that NMC-USA is an American company. Of its 1100 employees in May 1972, twenty were Japanese citizens. The annual company payroll in the United States was $11 million; in addition, there were close to 1000 Datsun dealers with their sales, service, and office staffs.

The National Headquarters building has now become the center of a complex. Adjoining structures now house the Service and Engineering Departments, Information Systems (Data Processing), and some of Corporate Administration. Mr. K said "we now have our people gathered under one roof again";[8] even his contagious enthusiasm could not anticipate that in a few years the growth of the company would outrun the imposing structure he was dedicating.

Further Growth

The confidence manifested in the future of NMC-USA at the dedication of the National Headquarters building found justification in continued higher sales even in the difficult conditions that had come into existence. The Nixon program was only partially effective in restraining the flow of import cars. It reduced the rate of increase in 1972, so that the import share of the passenger car market fell from 15.3 to 14.8 percent, but the total of import sales increased slightly. Truck imports actually increased by 68 percent and their share of the United States truck market from 4.0 to 5.4 percent; of the imported trucks some 99 percent were Japanese and over half of these were Datsuns. Datsun passenger car sales went up by 2500 in 1972, keeping pace with the import market in general, while truck sales rose by some 7000. It was a respectable record under the circumstances, enabling Datsun to remain firmly in third place among the imports.

The year 1973 opened in a mood of uncertainty concerning import cars. This uncertainty was accentuated by a second devaluation of the dollar, this time by 10 percent, in February of that year. Foreign currencies again appreciated in relation to the dollar and import prices rose correspondingly. The Volkswagen went up to $2199 from its 1971 price of $1845; the Toyota two-door Corolla to $1998 from $1798; the Datsun 1200 Sedan to $1976 from $1786.[9] By the end of 1973, the yen stood at 280 to the dollar, up about 40 percent over its pre-August 1971 rate. By any ordinary calculation, 1973 should have been an unfavorable year for import cars. It was for some. Volkswagen and Toyota both lost a little ground, VW's share of the import passenger car market dropping to 27.5 percent. But the other import leaders gained, so that the total import share of the passenger car market climbed back to 15.4 percent, and the import truck share reached a new high of 7.4 percent.

These gains for the imports were made in the face of record sales of domestic cars. The year 1973 was a banner one for the U.S. automotive industry. The 9,657,647 factory retail sales total of passenger cars from U.S. plants in that year was not only the highest reached to that time, it was also the high point in passenger automobiles for the entire decade of the 1970s.[10] There is no obvious reason for this boom. The removal of price and wage controls undoubtedly helped, and probably the ending of the war in Vietnam was having some effect on consumer buying habits. It would be dramatic to claim that the motoring public was enjoying a last fling before the era of easy oil came to an end; the reality is that the public, in the United States and elsewhere, did not know that an oil crisis was impending and pointedly ignored warnings about it.

Among the imports Datsun remained firmly in third place in passenger cars. Its sales, however, were up to 231,000, over twice those of fourth-place Capri (from British Ford, sold by the Lincoln-Mercury Division). Datsun truck sales rose to 87,000, markedly stimulated by the introduction of the PL620, named the Li'l Hustler. It was a vehicle with a four-cyclinder, 92-horsepower engine, and a weight of 2286 pounds. Its suggested list price, FOB West Coast Port, was $2236.[11]

NMC-USA was easily the leading importer of trucks into the United States, although it was getting more competition from other Japanese firms. Datsun trucks represented over one-third of the Japanese total, and Japanese trucks accounted for 99.6 percent of U.S. truck imports in 1973.

The combined passenger car and truck sales pushed NMC-USA comfortably over the 300,000-unit mark for the year, a new record, and one of those units was the millionth Datsun sold in the United States. This event, which probably occurred in April 1973, passed unnoticed at the time. The rate of progress for Datsun can be judged by the fact that it took thirteen years to reach the first million and only three more to reach the second.

The achievement of such a record under adverse conditions was the product of an all-Nissan effort on both sides of the Pacific. In the spring of 1973, *Business Week* published an analysis of why Japanese automobile firms, Nissan in particular, enjoyed continued success in the United States in spite of the handicaps they were facing.[12] (Honda, Mazda, and Subaru were now in the top ten imports along with Datsun and Toyota.) Specific items from this article have been cited previously. The general conclusions it reached can be summarized thus:

1. Some of the increased costs caused by dollar devaluation were offset by expansion of the home market in Japan and increasing export sales elsewhere. Greater volume of production reduced manufacturing costs, although some of these gains were absorbed by climbing wage rates.

2. Nissan was installing more highly automated production methods and was investing in closer control of its parts and components suppliers. This was the time when it began to get all its automatic transmissions from the Japan Automatic Transmission Company.

3. Constant effort had overcome the early deficiencies in Japanese cars, and Datsuns were now described as "small, low-priced cars that show a scrupulous attention to detail in design, engineering, and assembly." Along with that went expansion and improvement of service facilities in the United States.

4. Selling costs for Datsun trucks were reduced by expanding assembly operations. In early 1973, a total of 150 trucks a day were being assembled in Los Angeles and another plant was about to open in Seattle. The goal was to assemble half the trucks imported. The assembly consisted of joining the truck bed and chassis, both made in Japan, and by doing so Nissan avoided a 25 percent import duty—a heritage of the Chicken War.

At this same time, NMC-USA reorganized its Technical Engineering Department so as to tighten quality control and product support and improve technical communications with the parent company in Tokyo.[13] These changes were designed to enable the company to cope with new federal and state air pollution and safety standards and to provide adequate surveillance for the almost 1 million Datsuns now registered in the United States. These were certainly minimum requirements if the company was to hold its market position.

The success of Japanese automobiles in the United States drew more than analysis; understandably it drew criticism as well. Since one of the objectives of the Nixon economic program was to correct an adverse balance of payments (this objective was not attained), there was diplomatic pressure on the Japanese to curtail their automotive exports to the United States. Nissan's response was for NMC-USA to slow down expansion of its dealer network. The moratorium imposed in new dealer appointments in 1971 was rescinded in May 1972, but the company simply delayed planned increases. It was not going to penalize its existing dealers in order to retard the growth of sales. In addition, Nissan Motor Co., Ltd., stepped up purchases of components in the United States—$20 million worth of air conditioners, floor mats, and fender mirrors.[14] The truck assembly was also seen as a partial answer to criticism of the imports, since it increased the number of jobs being provided by NMC-USA. Judging by results, the Nissan policies were successful. Through a period of a generally unfavorable economic climate and considerable drawbacks to the orderly conduct of business—there was another West Coast dock strike early in 1972, and a Penn Central Railroad strike in April 1973—Datsun kept strengthening its position in the U.S. market.

Legal Complications

As if currency instability, other people's labor disputes, and continuing undersupply of cars were not trouble enough, NMC-USA also found itself at this time involved with the U.S. antitrust laws. In 1969, the United States Attorney's office in San Francisco began an investigation of NMC-USA's relations with its dealers, following complaints of obscure origin. It was alleged that the company was pressuring and restricting its dealers in various ways: requiring them to sell at list prices, limiting their ability to discount, enforcing territorial limitations.[15] The company denied the allegations but the government felt it had enough of a case to take its evidence to a grand jury. The case was never actually tried. After a period of negotiation, NMC-USA, without admitting liability, entered into a consent decree with the Department of Justice, and this decree became effective on February 26, 1973, to run for ten years. (*U.S. vs. Nissan Motor Corporation in U.S.A.*, United States District Court, Northern District of California.) Under it, the company agreed not to engage in a number of specified activities, which it claimed it was not engaging in anyway, and to inform all its officers, directors, and employees of its obligations and theirs under this judgment.[16]

The consent decree is a quite usual procedure in antitrust proceedings, since it avoids needless litigation and expenditure of time and money by both parties. One feature of this case worth noting is that it was exclusively a civil action; there was never any question of criminal charges. It would have been gratifying if the consent decree had been the end of the matter, but it was not. As almost invariably happens in such situations, NMC-USA found itself defending a large number of class action suits, filed on behalf of individual purchasers of Datsun cars who agreed to become plaintiffs, alleging that they had suffered financial loss because of the practices complained of. Under federal judicial procedure these cases were consolidated for discovery purposes in Dade County, Florida (Miami), where the first case had been filed. This process continued through a variety of legal maneuverings until 1976, when the court ruled that it would try only the Dade County case and then return the others to their separate districts.

When the Miami case came to trial late in 1976, NMC-USA was fully vindicated.[17] The evidence that was introduced for the company was supported by the testimony of dealers from all over the country, and the six-person jury returned a verdict of not guilty. The verdict was later sustained by the court of appeals, and the United States Supreme Court rejected a further hearing. However, since this decision may not be binding on other United States District Courts, the litigation has not yet ended.

This prolonged legal entanglement did not impede the growth of NMC-USA. It was in the nature of a nagging nuisance that could be borne as long as it did not get any worse, and it would be a relief to have it go away. Adverse decisions could have put the company in a very difficult situation, but as far as it was possible to determine from the progress of the litigation, the outlook permitted a reasonable optimism about the eventual outcome. In the meantime, a more deep-seated problem had arisen to confront NMC-USA, along with the entire world automotive industry.

=8=

THE ENERGY CRISIS AND THE WORLD AUTOMOTIVE INDUSTRY

The euphoria of booming motor vehicle sales in 1973 was abruptly interrupted on October 6, when the world was startled by the news that Egyptian and Syrian forces had attacked Israel. It was Yom Kippur, the most sacred of Jewish observances and, therefore, the day when Israeli forces were most likely to be caught off guard. The war itself is not part of this narrative. What mattered most to the rest of the world was that most of the oil-producing Arab states of the Middle East supported Egypt and Syria by imposing an embargo on exports of petroleum to all countries whose foreign policies were presumed to be pro-Israeli. These Arab states were a majority of the members of OPEC (Organization of Petroleum Exporting Countries). They also raised the price of crude oil by a substantial factor.

The immediate impact was a crisis too recent to have been forgotten. As the embargo took effect, shortages of gasoline developed, with long lines of cars at service stations, frantic "topping-off" of fuel tanks (which made the situation worse), and emergency conservation measures such as reduced speed limits, none of them very effective.

The Yom Kippur war came to a negotiated end on October 28, and in due course the embargo was lifted (March 1, 1974). Life could return to normal; at least that was what most people wanted to believe and the majority of them chose to believe. But while the immediate crisis was over, the long-term effects were just beginning. The oil embargo did two things. First, it demonstrated to all the OPEC countries the great latent power they possessed in their control of the bulk of the world's readily available oil supply, and they proceeded to take advantage of it by limiting production and repeatedly raising prices. Second, it brought to a head a situation that had been developing for some years: namely, that the world's known and easily accessible oil reserves were being rapidly depleted and while further supplies might be found, they would be in expensive locations such as the Arctic, or under the oceans, or in other places that previously had not been worth exploring because of the prohibitive cost.

In short, petroleum was never again likely to be low in price or plentiful in supply. This was a situation that neither the world in general nor the automotive industry in particular had seriously anticipated, and for most of the world and all of the industry, adjustment was difficult and painful. For the automotive world, the immediate result of the oil embargo was a slump in motor vehicle use, followed by a severe slump in sales, because people were bewildered and uncertain about what they should do.

The American Reaction

The initial reaction in the United States to the coming of the energy crisis was predominantly one of shocked disbelief. Ample and inexpensive supplies of fossil fuels had been a fact of American life from the beginning, and much of the public found it impossible to accept that this happy situation no longer existed. There was a marked tendency to see the crisis as something contrived by the oil companies to raise prices, which it was not, and the easing of the petroleum shortage when the embargo was lifted restored much of the earlier complacency.

There was enough concern for some action to be taken. A national 55-miles-per-hour speed limit was imposed, which was observed somewhat casually but did have some effect in curtailing gasoline consumption. Also, Congress acted to expedite construction of the then controversial Alaska pipeline so as to provide access to the great oil field recently discovered at Prudhoe Bay on the Arctic Ocean. However, the termination of the embargo and the preoccupation of both government and public with a different kind of crisis, Watergate, took the pressure off the energy problem. There was much discussion, but little meaningful action.

Yet there was plenty of evidence that the energy situation was far more than a temporary inconvenience. The year 1974 became one of worldwide depression accompanied by mounting inflation, both traceable principally to higher oil prices. The rise in the cost of oil hit the developing countries hardest, which was probably not what OPEC intended, by cutting deeply into their exiguous reserves of foreign exchange. The industrial nations were severely affected also. For the automotive industry throughout the world, the depression meant declining sales, and the resultant curtailment of production intensified the economic slump.

Figures on U.S. and Japanese motor vehicle producion offer an interesting comparison. United States output in 1974 dropped from what it had been in 1973 by 23 percent for passenger cars and 14 percent for trucks and buses. In Japan, passenger car production fell by 12 percent, from 4,470,550 to 3,931,842, but trucks and busses held their own and even increased slightly.[1] In spite of an overall decline in production, Japanese exports of motor vehicles actually rose in 1974—but not to the United States. In the American market there was a complete, across-the-board slump in all categories of motor vehicle sales in 1974. For the domestic cars there was an easy explanation; the gasoline shortage turned buyers away from the big gas guzzlers. During the period of the embargo, stocks of large cars remained unsold while buyers looked for models with greater fuel economy. These were in short supply, and although the American Big Three converted plants in record time to shift production from big to small cars, the switch was completed only after the oil embargo had been lifted. When that happened there was a resurgence in the market for the conventional American passenger cars, somewhat less enthusiastic than previously, as most Americans took it for granted that oil shortages were now a thing of the past and they could return to their customary motoring patterns. Many of them had never believed that there was an oil shortage anyway.

In addition to the fuel crisis, there were other events in 1974 that led the management of General Motors to describe it as "the most turbulent year in postwar automotive history."[2] There were layoffs and plant shutdowns while the embargo was in force; then came a revival, interrupted by strikes in the middle of the year. The third quarter (July through September) saw a brief upswing as buyers tried to anticipate price increases on the 1975 models, but then sales slumped again. They remained down through most of 1975. Toward the end of that year the economy was visibly recovering. For domestic passenger car production, however, it was overall a poorer year than 1974; actually the worst since 1962. Trucks were another matter. Domestic truck sales fell away by 14 percent in 1974 and 10 percent in 1975, but the long-term trend was definitely upward. Even the drop to 2,248,000 in 1975 was an increase of 70 percent in ten years.

One other item in the automotive situation of this period should be noted. Under the pressure of the energy crisis, Congress had enacted legislation mandating the achievement of specified standards of mileage-per-gallon performance in future new cars, and the Environmental Protection Agency (EPA) was making tests and publishing results for all new models, both domestic and import. These EPA ratings became an important sales factor because customers had become far more performance conscious than they had been before. This arose not so much from concern about saving gasoline—there was little firm conviction that this was really necessary—as from the simple and obvious fact that gasoline had doubled in price since the start of the Yom Kippur war.

More serious for the motor vehicle manufacturers, domestic and import alike, was the long-range necessity of having to try to comply with conflicting governmental policies—admittedly not an especially unusual or even surprising position to be in. One body of legislation required the industry to install emission control equipment that of necessity lowered engine performance and raised fuel consumption. Another body of legislation required the development of power plants that would get more miles to the gallon. This situation benefited mainly the imports, since small cars have lower emissions and better gasoline mileage to start with.

Import Cars and the Energy Crisis

The energy crisis created a market situation that should have been favorable to import cars and eventually was. At the outset, however, the imports experienced the same adverse effects as the domestic cars. Their sales in 1974 shrank in just about the same proportion, although import passenger cars gained a higher market penetration than ever before, 16 percent. The all-inclusive character of the slump in motor vehicle sales in the United States during 1974 can be seen in Table 7.1. No one escaped it. It struck domestic cars, imports in general, Japanese imports, and Datsuns. If the oil shortage reduced the attractiveness of the big American cars, it created other problems for the manufacturers of import cars. The factories in their home countries were frequently slowed down by lack of fuel. In Japan, steel production was cut back sharply which, of course, imposed a severe handicap on the automobile industry. In addition, shipping was erratic and uncertain because of a scarcity of bunker oil.

Under the circumstances, it was quite an achievement for Japan, the most vulnerable of the industrial nations to a stoppage of its oil supply, to have been able to increase its exports of motor vehicles in 1974, although this was obviously achieved at the expense of the home market. Yet even the Japanese cars shared in the general falling off in sales in the U.S. market in 1974. The bumper sales of 1973 probably had something to do with the falling off in 1974, but most of it has to be attributed to the mood of uncertainty that the energy crisis generated. People simply held back until the situation became clearer.

The year 1975 was a different story altogether. While domestic motor vehicle production remained in the doldrums, the market for imports started up again, with the Japanese by far the principal beneficiaries. After more than twenty years of unchallenged and apparently unchallengeable leadership in the import field, Volkswagen, plagued by financial and organizational problems at home, was finally toppled from its throne. The story is told in Table 8.1. As VW sales continued a decline of several years' duration, Datsun and Toyota swung sharply upward from their dip in 1974. The 1975 figures show

TABLE 8.1   *Import Car Leaders, 1973–1975*

Car	1973	1974	1975
Volkswagen			
Cars	480,602	336,248	268,751
Trucks	247	101	—
Total	480,849	336,349	268,751
Toyota			
Cars	289,378	238,135	283,909
Trucks	37,466	31,243	45,009
Total	326,844	269,378	328,918
Datsun			
Cars	231,191	185,162	263,192
Trucks	87,816	60,111	72,223
Total	319,007	245,273	335,415

SOURCE: Market Research Department, NMC-USA.

Toyota edging out Volkswagen as the leading seller among import passenger cars, but Datsun's combined car and truck sales put it in the proud position of being the number 1 import seller for the year.

Fourth place among imports was taken by another Japanese make, Honda, and fifth by Fiat, both with sales of over 100,000 units. This was a rapid climb for Honda, and for Fiat the result of a long and at times discouraging effort to establish a place in the U.S. market. On the other hand, the "captive" imports lost ground, except for Mitsubishi's Dodge Colt[3]—passenger cars, that is. The Courier and the Luv pickups continued to gain. This development among the "captives" was to be expected. With the domestic models struggling to hold their own, the incentive to push the overseas varieties diminished.

In terms of market penetration, import passenger cars went up to 18.3 percent in 1975 and trucks to 9.1 percent. Over half the passenger cars and practically all the trucks were of Japanese manufacture. These were impressive advances in a market that was still laboring under recession conditions. One message they conveyed unmistakably was that American buyers were becoming more cost conscious. Most of them still saw their cars as status symbols and were far from ready to give that up, but they were developing limits on what they were prepared to pay for status.

An analysis of the consequences of the energy crisis for the import car market in the United States comes out with both pluses and minuses, none of them applying with equal force to all imports. The oil shortage and its aftermath of higher prices made the small import cars more attractive to American buyers. The gas guzzlers were definitely on the way out, even though they had a limited revival for about five years after the end of the embargo. It was strictly an Indian summer. As one round of OPEC price increases followed another, the cost of automotive fuels kept edging up. Prices would have risen much more rapidly than they did in the United States if they had not been closely controlled, so that American motorists remained more favorably situated than their counterparts elsewhere in the world. However, the increases were still uncomfortable enough to make the public more receptive to fuel economy in its cars.

On the other hand, the United States was not as completely dependent on imported oil as were its principal competitors in motor vehicle manufacturing, conspicuously Japan, West Germany, and Italy. For them higher prices for oil meant higher costs for production and transportation. These costs, along with continuing depreciation of the dollar and general instability in the world's currency exchanges, meant that the import cars lost the price advantage that had previously helped them to compete in the U.S. market.

Thus the energy crisis cut both ways. It was not the exclusive reason for the surge in import car sales that occurred after 1974, although it was certainly very influential. Nor do oil shortages or higher prices account for the significant shifts among the import producers. Fiat was just as much affected by the oil crisis as Volkswagen—probably more, since Germany has coal and Italy does not—yet Fiat sales in the United States went up while VW's continued down. Japan had neither oil nor coal, but by 1975 Japanese-built motor vehicles clearly dominated the import car market in the United States. Obviously, there had to be other factors present besides the admittedly drastic change in the world oil situation.

The Volkswagen decline has already been noted as beginning in 1971. The cause lay in a combination of managerial, labor, and financial problems that weakened the parent company in Germany. The additional shock of the energy crunch and the ensuing worldwide recession accentuated these difficulties to the point where Volkswagen was teetering on the brink of insolvency. The root of the trouble was a common ailment—the company had been a brilliant success without serious challenge for too long and it had finally reached the stage where it needed new blood and new ideas. It was also hurt by the decline of the dollar relative to the deutschmark, which pushed up Volkswagen prices in the United States. The company was reorganized and recovered, but it had lost its dominating position among import passenger cars in the United States. By contrast, Fiat had almost lost its footing in the American market ten years before but had spent several years studying and correcting its earlier mistakes, so that even in the depressed conditions of 1974, Fiat sales in the United States went up.

During the oil embargo, the Japanese had severe problems of production and transportation and the shifting yen-dollar relationship was usually adverse. However, they were still able to reap the harvest of their years of steady effort and careful study of the needs of the U.S. market. What happened is well described by the associate editor of *Ward's Automotive Yearbook* (italics by author):

> Import carmakers generally rely heavily on exports for sales volume, and some, *most noticeably the Japanese* developed cars for a portion of the U.S. market which, until 1975, was generally ignored by the Big Four. When the big sales crunch came, imports found themselves with their corner of that market nailed down, buyers banging on the door and most of their problems tied to sluggishly-reacting supply lines which showed up as wildly fluctuating inventories later in the year.[4]

The editor credited these inventories with part of the import car boom in 1975, since there was a carry-over of imports from 1974 while domestic compacts and subcompacts were still in short supply. There were big cars available, new and used, but the demand for them was sluggish. Then the editor added a trenchant summation of the meaning of the crisis for the automobile business in the United States: "In the long run, the durability of import sales in times of economic duress was a beacon in the industry gloom in 1975; a beacon noticed by the Big Four for the first time, and one which will undoubtedly have a permanent effect on the course of the U.S. industry." The "Big Four" is simply American Motors added to the Big Three.

Datsun in the Crisis

The experience of NMC-USA in this period has already been outlined. Sales fell off in 1974, along with everyone else's, and then a year later came the spectacular revival that put Datsun in first place among import cars. This accomplishment involved far more than riding with the current. Great successes are seldom achieved that way. NMC-USA was rewarded for foresight and planning on its own and the parent company's part. When the crisis came, the company was able to meet it with an efficient organization, a capable and dedicated managerial and sales force, and a product that met the needs of the occasion by combining economy with quality.

The product line was enriched at a crucial time, late 1973, by three important additions: the B210 Honey Bee, the 710 line, and the 260-Z. The B210 succeeded the 1200 as a light two-seater and immediately established itself at the top of the EPA mileage ratings. The 260-Z was somewhat more powerful than the 240-Z, which it replaced as the Datsun sports car. It continued the popularity of the line. It had a 2600cc engine of 162 horsepower and a twin carburetor. It sold over 58,000 units in two years. The 710 was similar to the 610, very slightly smaller. Both were offered with a choice of engines, 1800cc, 105 horsepower or 2000cc, 110 horsepower. All these models sold well through the oil shortage, as far as they were procurable, with the Honey Bee in the lead (see Table 8.2).

The 1974 models were presented in a preview at the Dunes Hotel in Las Vegas, in October 1973, a new departure for NMC-

TABLE 8.2   *Datsun U.S. Sales by Models, 1973–1975*

Models	1973	1974	1975
B210	15,133	73,317	140,039
1200	57,241	—	—
PL610	75,511	32,916	18,527
PL710	—	33,366	50,914
240-Z	46,282	821	—
260-Z	15,133	44,507	—
280-Z	—	45,328	50,142
Trucks	87,104	60,118	71,361
Others	774	235	220

SOURCE: Adapted from *Ward's Automotive Yearbook, 1975*, p. 28; *1976*, p. 28. Published by permission of Ward's Automotive Reports.

USA. Previously, new models had been introduced in regional showings; this was a national debut. The Las Vegas exhibition was intended to inaugurate a banner year in Datsun sales, and it probably would have done so if the oil embargo had not come when it did. The sales situation in 1974 has already been described. Datsun could have done much better if more cars had been available, but they were not. NMC-USA had to do the best it could with the limited volume that Nissan Motor Company, Ltd., was able to provide. Once again, it was necessary to stop adding dealers; the company believed that its first responsibility was to the dealers it already had. Indeed, between 1973 and 1974, the total number of dealers fell by eight, the result of normal attrition without any new appointments.

Under these conditions, the company could well have seen fit to cut back or suspend some of its operations and its plans for future growth, but it did not. Early in 1974, the New York Region moved into new office facilities in Piscataway, New Jersey. At the same time, the computerized Equitable Distribution System was put into operation, a most timely step for a year in which demand for Datsuns would be strong and supplies limited. This was a system, as mentioned in the Introduction, for allocating vehicles to regions and dealers on the basis of past performance, sales projections, orders, and other relevant information. Shortly afterward, there was a new Dealer Sales and Service Agreement, further described in Chapter 11, The Sales Structure.

Later in the year came the first Service Management Development Seminar, held at Aspen, Colorado. It was planned as an annual event to keep Regional and District Service Managers fully up to date on Datsun service requirements and procedures. These were acts of an organization with confidence in its future and not unduly disturbed by events that had caused a temporary dip in its fortunes. The confidence was justified. The banner year that the Las Vegas showing in the fall of 1973 was supposed to launch was simply deferred until 1975, when all the preparation and planning paid off richly.

There was a change in the management structure in June 1974 (see Figure 8.1). Robert O. Link became Vice President and General Manager, Sales; Masataka Usami, Vice President and General Manager, Service and Technical Engineering; and Kinjiro Tamaki, Vice President and General Manager, Parts. Four new Vice Presidents were added: Blaine Dorsett, Sales; Charles P. "Chuck" King, Import and Distribution; Mayfield Marshall, Jr., Public Relations; Robert Scott, Parts.[5] Dorsett had joined NMC-USA in 1971, bringing a background of twenty-two years in automotive sales experience with General Motors, Mercedes-Benz, Volkswagen, and Porsche. King arrived in 1972 after seventeen years with Chrysler.

This step was a reinforcement rather than a revision of the organization adopted in 1971. The purpose of these new appointments was obviously to strengthen management control in crucial areas. The emphasis on Sales and Sales Promotion is self-evident, but the heightened status of the executives responsible for service, parts, and distribution was proof of the importance of those areas also.

These steps could have been taken in response to the recession. It would have been logical for NMC-USA to try to bolster its sales organization at a time when the market was shrinking, and still more logical for it to seek to put more emphasis on its Service and Parts operations. Likewise, the Distribution system was vital at a time when the supply problem was particularly acute. But the recession was not the reason for what was done. Datsun sales in the United States in 1974 were only a little less than they had been two years before, practically equal to the 1971 total, and well ahead of what they had been in 1970. On any long-range view, NMC-USA was in a growth situation, only temporarily interrupted. By June 1974 the oil embargo had ended, fuel supplies were returning to normal, although considerably more expensive, and there was every reason to expect that the motor vehicle market would presently pick up, as it did toward the end of the year. It was about to be demonstrated that in the United States the demand for gasoline has remained price-inelastic, at least until much higher levels are reached than was true of the 1970s.

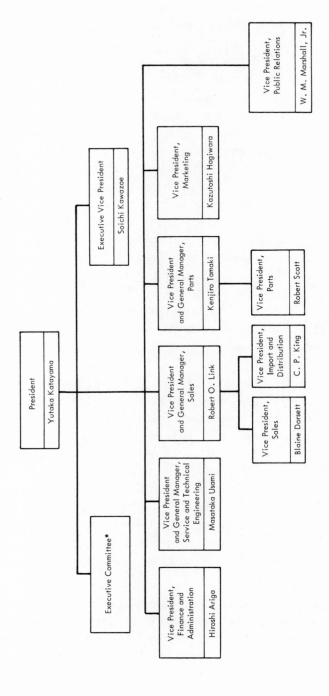

*Executive Committee consists of Messrs. Katayama, Kawazoe, Link, Usami, Tamaki, Hagiwara, and Ariga

FIG. 8.1 *Executive organization, June 1974. (Source: Datsun News, July 1974, p. 6.)*

The administrative changes at NMC-USA in 1974 were prep-arations for future growth, not precautions against decline. The company could hardly have foreseen its rise to the top of the import list in 1975, but it was aiming for a 300,000-vehicle year, with a target of half a million in 1980 (it was reached in 1979). The added executive strength was needed to cope with the demands of an organization that was looking forward to expansion and wanted to be sure that administrative controls remained efficient and effective. The areas that were strengthened were every bit as relevant for expansion as for contraction, more so in fact. With Datsuns coming on the market in greater numbers, there were going to be more and more on the roads of the United States—there were already over a million in 1974.[6] Consequently, the company needed to ensure constant and effective emphasis on the Nissan principle of "responsible marketing," the principle that the responsibility to the customer continues after the car is sold. This meant that the Service and Parts functions must keep pace with Sales and the growing numbers of Datsun vehicles in use nationwide; it meant, also, for the sale of the dealers, that Distribution must be as efficient as it could possibly be made.

The specific objective of this 1974 reorganization was to improve control and coordination in the management structure, based on experience with the functioning of the system adopted in 1971.[7] This was not all. There were broader objectives, which were spelled out at a national sales meeting held in Dallas, in June, at which the principal speaker was Masataka Okuma, Managing Director, Nissan Motor Co., Ltd. (He became Executive Vice President shortly afterward.) Okuma closed the meeting with a definite but realistic tone of optimism, expressing confidence in the Datsun's future without in any way minimizing the difficulties that would have to be encountered. These are some excerpts:[8]

> As your domestic automobile industry prepares to switch its production facilities to at least 50% small cars in 1975, it will become evident to everyone that a dramatic revolution has taken place in the American automotive industry.

You all know that this past year has been one of the most difficult ever faced by our corporation. The worldwide energy crisis has been a traumatic experience. But we have studied the current slowdown and we are convinced that automobile sales around the world will be improving quite soon. In the U.S., your people will adjust to the higher prices of automobiles just as they will adjust to the higher prices of food, clothing, and housing.

Already in Japan our situation is returning to almost normal and we are looking for a sales upturn in both the domestic and the export markets. Our production people are confident that they have the ability to meet the demands for our products both domestically and internationally so I urge you not to hold back on your sales efforts because of any fears you might have that we could not make all the cars and trucks you could sell.

I assure you that the job of meeting your demands for our products here in the U.S. has not been an easy one. The basic logistics of shipping over 300,000 units to the U.S. is truly staggering when it is broken down into items such as port facilities, ships, ports of entry, and so forth.

You have established a very ambitious target of 500,000 sales by 1980 and it is now important for each of you to firmly implant that goal in your thinking and never lose sight of it. The years of huge Datsun sales increases of 40% to 50% per year are over. Now you are faced with the challenge of steady growth. In many ways, such steady growth is much more difficult and demands total concentration toward the problem at hand.

Katayama and Link spoke in the same vein. Mr. K, referring to the half-million sales goal, said:

We realize that it is an extremely ambitious goal, and yet it is one that we can attain if we plot our course properly.

You all see on a day to day basis the nature of our retail competition and you all know how that competition has changed just within the 1974 model year. First, price increases meant that Datsun cars and trucks lost what price advantage they might have had over domestics. Next, Detroit reacted to the energy crisis far faster than anyone could have anticipated.

For years we said that we were filling a need in the U.S. market that was not being filled by Detroit produced products. That is still true for our B210's and Z's and Pickups. That is no longer true for the 710's and 610's. But, we still have a definite edge in one vital area and I am totally confident that advantage is going to be the basis of our strength as we move toward future success.

Quality must be the key to Datsun's success!

Link also dwelt on the price problem and took essentially the same line:

> Compare our price increases with the increase in the cost of living, the increase in the wholesale price index. They are not out of line. Perhaps we are high in relation to domestic cars. We have a history and experience in small car manufacturing that domestic manufacturers cannot compare with. In no way can they compare with us in quality!

The thrust of these messages is very definite. As of mid-1974, with the world in the grip of a recession, NMC-USA was thinking in terms of expansion for the future rather than retrenchment for the present. Its management was well aware that further gains would be harder to come by than they had been in the past, with domestic competition in the small-car market intensifying, but it had confidence in both its product and its organization. This confidence was fully validated in the next year, when the economy began to recover and automotive sales picked up again. So was the expectation that growth would require effort.

The beginning of a fresh stage in the history of NMC-USA was marked by a major managerial change. In January 1975 Hiroshi Majima replaced Katayama as President and Chief Executive Officer; Mr. Katayama became Chairman of the Board. Majima was an engineering graduate of the University of Tokyo, who joined Nissan in 1946 after serving for two years as an engineer officer in the Japanese Navy, where he worked on designing aircraft engines.[9] After a number of years in Production Control, he moved into Marketing and in 1974 became head of the Export Sales Department of Nissan Motor Co., Ltd. With both Katayama and Kawazoe at the age when American business executives would normally retire, this appointment was a logical step. The time had come for the management of the company to be passed on.

So NMC-USA reached an historic landmark. Mr. K was still on hand and Kawazoe carried on for the time being as Executive Vice President, but their era was manifestly approaching its conclusion. It had been a great era. Between them, they had built the company from nothing to the proud position it reached in 1975, when more Datsuns were sold in the United States than any other import vehicles. But like all other things it had to come to an end, and it was undoubtedly wise to bring in the new blood while the momentum of past achievements was still positive. It was also altogether likely that with a large organization requiring more elaborate and formal controls, Katayama's paternal style of management had to be discarded. At any rate, NMC-USA was entering a new stage of its development.

9

DATSUN IN THE SMALL-CAR MARKET, 1975 to 1979

The Majima presidency began auspiciously. As reported, in 1975 Datsun became the top-selling import car in the United States; although it dropped back to second place a year later, its sales progressed steadily forward toward the half-million-a-year goal. The gains were achieved in a very mixed motor vehicle market. In 1975, sales of domestic cars continued to drift downward until the last quarter of the year, while import sales turned upward with the conspicuous exception of Volkswagen. It was a market in which the American consumer was reorienting to the aftermath of the oil embargo. A large segment of the public either remained unconvinced that there had ever been a shortage of oil, or else was satisfied that those days were over for the foreseeable future. So, preembargo ways of life could be safely resumed, subject only to the inconvenience of higher prices for gasoline. This attitude was responsible for the revival in sales of big cars that began in 1975 and continued upward for the next three years.

At the same time, another large part of the buying public had been won over to small cars, partly because of concern about further oil shortages, but probably much more on strictly economic grounds. Gasoline was twice as expensive as it had been in 1973 (although in constant dollars its cost was actually unchanged), and the continuing inflationary rise in the American economy produced continuous increases in automobile prices. The small-car section of the market remained preeminently the domain of the imports, somewhat ineffectively contested by the domestic compacts. The American manufacturers were not indifferent to the small-car market, but the Big Three were giving the greater part of their attention to the reviving market for standard-size and larger cars, which was a more profitable market for them. They were faced with the quandary that a really serious campaign to compete with import cars would inevitably affect sales of their own "captive" imports.

The Automotive Scene in the Late 1970s

This was a period when the worldwide automobile industry was going from year to year without ever being quite certain what the immediate future held for it. Through 1978, conditions were generally good. Production and sales rose to new heights in the United States and Japan, although it was noticeable that the biggest gains for the American manufacturers came from booming truck sales rather than from passenger cars. These were encouraging developments, but in the United States pronouncements from the leaders of the industry during these years have an air of determined optimism, as if they were hoping for the best but really expecting the worst. At the end of 1978, the editor of *Ward's Automotive Yearbook* referred to the U.S. automobile industry as "a bundle of contradictions,"[1] and he had ample justification.

Sales were rising steadily but so were costs, as the United

States, along with the rest of the world, was caught in a seemingly unbreakable spiral of inflation. Thus car prices kept going up, and the only consolation the domestic manufacturers had in this situation was that the declining value of the dollar put the import cars in an even worse price squeeze. In addition, both domestic and import producers had to face increasingly stringent safety requirements and emission controls, although an outburst of public wrath did force the withdrawal of a requirement that cars should be designed so that they couldn't start unless the seatbelts were fastened. Add to these problems a five-week strike against the Ford Motor Company in 1976, a 100-day strike against four major tire producers, and periodic interruptions because of fuel shortages in severe winter weather, and it becomes clear that although these were good years for the automotive industry in terms of sales, they were certainly not easy ones.

In addition to these problems that were common to the industry, two of the American producers had acute difficulties of their own. American Motors, as the smallest of the four-passenger-car manufacturers, had trouble staying in competition with its bigger rivals. The stimulus that the Rambler had given to AMC in the 1950s ended when the Big Three entered the compact field; in the early 1970s it was a serious question whether American Motors could survive. The oil embargo had a shot-in-the-arm effect as buyers went looking for small cars, but sales slumped again in 1975 and 1976. Then, however, a reorganization of management and a change of policy put AMC back on its feet. Production was limited to the profitable lines such as the Jeep, and an agreement with Renault provided for the sale of the Renault LeCar through AMC dealers and financial support for the eventual manufacture of Renault models by AMC.

The Chrysler story was less happy. The company's international expansion in the 1960s (Rootes in Great Britain, Simca in France) turned out to be an unfortunate investment; Chrysler's European holdings were sold to Peugeot in 1978, with Chrysler retaining a financial interest in Peugeot. What was worse was that Chrysler was burdened with obsolescent plants—Chrysler

Main in Hamtranck, Michigan, was the original Dodge Brothers plant of 1914, finally abandoned in 1980—and the management seriously underestimated the demand for small cars. In 1978, Chrysler decided to use VW engines for its new front-wheel-drive small-car offerings, Horizon and Omni, but miscalculated the demand for small cars (it was not alone in this, merely more vulnerable), so that it was caught short when a new oil crisis erupted in 1979. Volkswagen could not supply any more engines than the contract called for because its own sales were climbing and it needed its engine production for its own cars. The result was a Chrysler appeal to the U.S. government for help in the form of a $1.5 billion loan guarantee, which was eventually granted with some qualifications because of the serious unemployment that would result from a Chrysler shutdown.

AMC and Chrysler had company in their troubles. In Britain, the British Leyland merger fell disappointingly short of expectations. It was hoped that the merger would produce a British General Motors but the promoters, including the government, failed to appreciate that just putting companies together was not enough to create a General Motors. An Alfred P. Sloan helps, among other things. In 1977, British Leyland, plagued by labor unrest and delays in production, had to be rescued by the British government, which became its principal stockholder. Fiat was never in the same kind of financial crisis, but in 1975 and 1976 it was also plagued by strikes. Volkswagen was on the mend. A new management and a new model, the Rabbit, rehabilitated the company. In an effort to recoup its position in the U.S. market and protect itself from further appreciation of the mark, VW opened an American assembly plant in New Stanton, Pennsylvania—a former Chrysler installation. The first American-built Rabbit came off the line on April 10, 1978.[2] In the meantime, however, VW had lost its leadership in the American import car market to Nissan and Toyota.

This overall situation in the world automotive industry might well have given General Motors and Ford the opportunity to preempt the small-car market in the United States had they chosen to do so. Table 9.1 shows how, in 1975, at the beginning of a four-year period of rising production, these two firms towered over the rest of the industry; even ailing Chrysler was on the same level as Nissan and Toyota and ahead of Renault, Volkswagen, and Fiat. Clearly the fortunes of all the rest of the automobile industry depended heavily on the way the American giants chose to go. It was not toward the small-car market. Ford and General Motors were doing well with their standard-size and larger models, which offered greater profits than the compacts. While these companies may have talked at times about "pushing the imports right back to the shores,"[3] they were well aware that the time for that was long past. The change of expression is symbolic; now the imports were to be pushed back to the shore, not driven into the sea.

The attitude of the American manufacturers was described thus by *Ward's* associate editor in 1975: "Imported cars have

TABLE 9.1   *Major World Motor Vehicle Producers,*
           1975   (Over 1 Million Units)

Country	General Motors	Ford	Chrysler
United States	6,638,744	2,500,222	1,222,308
Canada	598,876	480,089	285,980
United Kingdom	190,042*	458,759	245,823
Germany	657,539†	640,336	—
France	—	—	473,796**
Brazil	173,948	170,371	—
Totals	8,259,149	4,250,367	2,227,907

	Toyota	Nissan	Fiat
Totals	2,336,053	2,077,447	1,185,964

Country	Volkswagen	Country	Renault
Germany	1,121,937	France	1,391,948
		Spain	205,984
Brazil	502,580		1,607,932
Totals	1,634,517		

*Vauxhall.
**Simca.
†Opel.
SOURCE: Adapted from *Ward's Automotive Yearbook, 1976*, p. 81. Published by permission of Ward's Automotive Reports.

been an irritating but generally ignored part of the U.S. auto market for years, like a boot nail slowly working its way into the heel of the U.S. manufacturers. For a variety of reasons, 1975 became the year for U.S. carmakers to sit and figure out just what was causing the pain."[4] The editor observed that import sales had risen, taking over 18 percent of total U.S. motor vehicle sales in 1975, while "full-sized U.S. built cars staggered through one of the worst sales years in recent times in the North American market place." This situation produced charges of dumping and some agitation from the United Automobile Workers (UAW) to require import cars to have a greater proportion of U.S.-produced components. Yet nothing very much happened. The market for the larger cars turned upward toward the end of 1975 and continued to gain encouragingly over the next three years; this seems to have convinced the domestic industry and the UAW that they could get along with that annoying boot nail a little longer.

It may have been assumed that the impact of the oil embargo had worn off and that American motorists had reverted to their customary preference for big automobiles. It would have been a sound enough assumption if prices for both cars and gasoline had remained reasonably stable, but they did not. The escalating inflation of the late 1970s, along with the rising costs imposed by increasingly stringent standards for safety and emission control, kept pushing car prices upward—there were fifteen separate pricing actions by automobile firms, all increases, in the first six months of 1978 alone.[5] Gasoline and oil, the cost of service and repairs, all followed the same path. Because of price controls and other regulations the price of gasoline and oil in constant dollars actually remained fairly stable, but consumers calculate costs by what comes out of their pockets at the time.

Thus, the big-car revival of these years rested on an unstable foundation, with powerful and seemingly uncontrollable factors in the American economy operating to make consumers more and more cost conscious. This was by no means a com-

Takashi Ishihara; President, Nissan Motor Corporation in U.S.A. (NMC-USA), 1960 to 1965; President, Nissan Motor Company, Ltd., 1977 to present.

Yutaka Katayama; Vice President, Western Division, 1960 to 1965; President, NMC-USA, 1965 to 1975.

Hiroshi Majima; President, NMC-USA, 1975 to 1980.

Tetsuo Arakawa; President, NMC-USA, 1980 to present.

Soichi Kawazoe; Vice President, Eastern Division, 1960 to 1965; Executive Vice President, NMC-USA, 1965 to 1976.

Robert O. Link; Assistant Sales Manager, Western Division, 1965 to 1967; Sales Manager, 1967 to 1969; National Sales Manager, 1969 to 1971; Vice President, Sales, 1971 to 1974; Vice President and General Manager, Sales, 1974 to 1979; Senior Vice President, NMC-USA, 1979 to present.

The Datsun Two-Seater. This was the "Son of Dat," or Datson from which the Datsun name came.

The 1958 Imported Motor Car Show, Los Angeles. The Datsun 1000 that is being inspected was one of the three Datsuns displayed at this first formal showing of Datsuns in the United States.

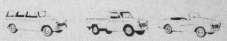

A Datsun advertisement, 1959, by Woolverton Motors, Western Datsun Distributors.

The Western Division Staff, 1961. This picture was taken in front of the Division office on Alondra Boulevard in Gardena, California. The staff, as far as they can now be identified, are as follows. Front row (left to right): Emmett Yeats (Service), unknown, Hershell Broaden (Maintenance), Al Cole (Service). Back row (left to right): Joe Slackey (Parts Mgr.), Jean LaPlant (Service Mgr.), Pauline ? (Accounting), Nancy Goodwin (Parts), Jane Simpkin (Sales), Yutaka Katayama (Vice President), Masahiko Zaitsu (Factory Engineer), Tadayuki Ide (Chief Accountant), Benny Ackerman (Service), Odell Broaden (General Maintenance).

Dedication of Eastern Division Headquarters, Secaucus, New Jersey, July 21, 1965. Front row (left to right): Mrs. Kawazoe; Mr. Kawazoe; Mayor Amico of Secaucus; Mr. Ishihara, then President of NMC-USA; Robert Scott, later Vice President, Parts, and President of Distribution and Auto Service, can be seen standing in the doorway with his arms folded. (Courtesy of S. Kawazoe.)

The Datsun 310 station wagon. Offered in 1960 and 1961, the 310 series foreshadowed the styling changes that came to fruition in the 410 and 510.

The Nissan L60 Patrol. A four-wheel-drive model that was popular in the 1960s.

The Li'l Hustler. The 1971 version of the Datsun pickup that has been an important part of the company's success.

National Headquarters. The building is located on 6.5 acres of land near the intersection of the Harbor and San Diego Freeways in Carson, California, about 15 miles south of downtown Los Angeles and 10 miles from Los Angeles Harbor.

The Datsun 420s on display at the New York Automobile Show in 1964. (Courtesy of S. Kawazoe.)

The 1972 Datsun 510s. Introduced in the 1968 model year, the 510 represented a marked advance in Datsun design and styling and was a very successful model.

The 1972 Datsun 1200 Coupe and Sedan.

The 1975 Datsun B-210 Hatchback.

Mr. Kawazoe, Sparky Lyle, and Little Spark. NMC-USA's Executive Vice President presenting a Dalmatian puppy to the noted New York Yankee relief pitcher Sparky Lyle (1972). Besides being an outstanding pitcher, Lyle raised Dalmatians. (Courtesy of S. Kawazoe.)

Datsun Master Parts Depot, Compton, California. The picture shows the Depot when it was opened in 1971. It has since been expanded.

Port operations, Distribution and Auto Service, Inc. (DAS). In Los Angeles the DAS operation begins (upper left) as any one of the fleet of Datsun super carriers unloads at one of the two berths reserved for DAS at the Los Angeles Harbor. The next step in the process (upper right) is a thorough inspection to determine if there is any damage. Damaged cars are taken to the DAS body shop for repair (lower left) and further inspection before they are put back into the marshalling area. The last step before the cars are loaded for shipment to any one of the Datsun dealers in the Los Angeles region is a complete cleaning (lower right).

The DAS dock and storage yard; Port of Los Angeles.

The Nissan car carrier Violet *entering the Golden Gate.*

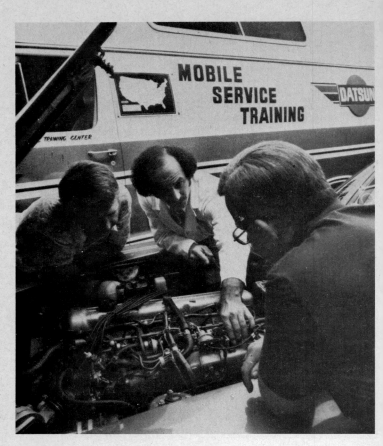

A Datsun Mobile Service
Training Unit at work.

The 1975 Datsun 710
station wagon.

Looking over a racing engine. **Left to right:** *Laurie Leva, Technician; Lee Wylie, National Service Manager; Dick Roberts, National Competition Manager; Tom O'Connor, Competition Parts Manager (1969).*

Road Atlanta winners, 1970. Datsun 240-Zs swept to a 1-2-3 finish in the American Road Race of Champions. **Left to right:** *John Morton, National Champion; Bob Sharp (Wilton, Conn.), runner-up; and John McComb (Hutchivson, Kansas), third.*

A Datsun 240-Z. Driven by John Morton of Van Nuys, California, crossing the finish line at the Phoenix, Arizona International Raceway, September 27, 1970, to win the Class C Production race.

This car is a special Datsun Z with a turbo engine. The driver is Paul Newman.

The 1970 Datsun 240-Z and the Import Car of the Year Award it received from Motor Trend Magazine.

The 1975 Datsun 260-Z and 260-Z 2+2.

The 1980 Datsun 200-SX 2-door Hatchback.

The 1980 Datsun 810 4-door Sedan, the top of the Datsun line.

The 1980 Datsun 280-ZX. Celebrating the 10th anniversary of the Z-cars.

pletely novel situation. The Motor Vehicle Manufacturers Association made a study which showed that the trend to smaller cars dated back at least to 1968 (see Figure 9.1). It was not a phenomenon created by the oil embargo, although the chart shows a marked effect on sales of regular and intermediate models during the period of the embargo. In short, a careful analysis of the indicators could and probably should have suggested that the resurgence of big-car sales was likely to be temporary.

The peak was reached in 1978, with an all-time high of 13 million motor vehicle factory sales from U.S. plants. A considerable proportion of these were lighter-weight vehicles, not necessarily smaller, as manufacturers worked to meet federal requirements for fuel economy as established by the Energy Policy and Conservation Act of 1975.[6] The manufacturers wanted this changeover to come gradually, not from lack of willingness to improve their products but from a concern that, "If the shift to smaller vehicles is forced too rapidly, consumer backlash could result. This could cripple manufacturers at a time when they need all the financial resources they can muster for their costly product redesign programs. In addition, if consumers should decide to keep their older, less fuel efficient vehicles instead of buying new ones which provide higher

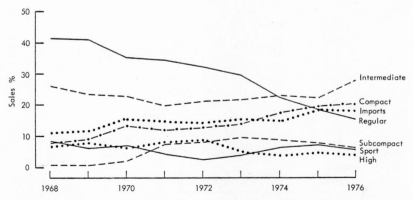

FIG. 9.1   *Percent of U.S. new car retail sales by class. (Source: Motor Vehicle Manufacturers Association of the U.S., Inc.)*

economy, the purpose of the entire exercise would be defeated."[7]

The validity of this assumption was never tested because in the spring of 1979 the revolution in Iran precipitated another upheaval in the world oil market and another gasoline crisis in the United States. Long lines and short tempers appeared at the service stations again, and all the allegations against the oil companies were repeated verbatim from five years before. The emergency period was brief, but it was enough to cause an upheaval in the American motor vehicle market. Consumer preference swung sharply and decisively to small cars. The extent of the reversal appears in Tables 9.2 and 9.3. In 1979, sales

TABLE 9.2   *U.S. Motor Vehicle Sales, 1975–1979   (In Thousands)*

Year	Domestic	All imports	Total	Import (%)	Japanese imports	Total (%)	Imports (%)
Passenger cars							
1975	7,053	1,587	8,640	18.3	817	9.4	51.4
1976	8,611	1,498	10,109	14.8	941	9.3	62.8
1977	9,109	2,076	11,185	18.5	1,387	12.4	66.8
1978	9,312	2,000	11,312	17.7	1,356	12.0	67.8
1979	8,162	2,497	10,659	23.4	1,770	16.6	70.9
Trucks							
1975	2,248	229	2,477	9.2	229	9.2	100.0
1976	2,944	237	3,181	7.4	236	7.4	99.6
1977	3,352	323	3,675	8.7	321	8.7	99.4
1978	3,773	337	4,110	8.2	334	8.1	99.1
1979	3,011	469	3,470	13.5	466	13.4	99.4
All vehicles							
1975	9,301	1,816	11,117	16.3	1,046	9.4	57.6
1976	11,555	1,735	13,290	13.0	1,177	8.8	67.8
1977	12,461	2,399	14,860	16.1	1,708	11.4	71.2
1978	13,085	2,337	15,422	15.1	1,690	10.9	72.3
1979	11,173	2,966	14,139	21.0	2,235	15.8	75.3

SOURCE: *Motor Vehicle Facts and Figures, 1979,* p. 22; Market Analysis Department, NMC-USA.

TABLE 9.3   *U.S. Automobile Market Shares by Size,*
             Class, and Imports in Percent

Year	Small cars		Mid-size cars	Full-size cars
	Import	Domestic		
1970	15.1	23.1	21.8	40.0
1971	15.3	23.6	19.9	41.2
1972	14.8	24.1	21.7	39.4
1973	15.4	27.2	22.5	34.9
1974	15.9	32.4	24.6	27.1
1975	18.2	35.3	23.5	23.0
1976	14.8	33.2	27.0	25.0
1977	18.4	28.8	27.7	25.1
1978	17.7	30.8	27.9	23.6
1979	21.9	34.8	23.3	20.0
1980*	26.9	38.0	19.8	15.3

*Through May.
SOURCE: Unpublished data from U.S. Department of Commerce,
Bureau of Economic Analysis.

of domestic passenger cars were over a million less than in 1978, and, surprisingly, the booming market in trucks went down by three-quarters of a million. However, the market share of domestic small cars rose appreciably, as did import sales of both passenger cars and trucks.

The backlash that the American manufacturers worried about never had a chance to materialize. Whether it would have materialized if there had been no oil crisis in 1979 is another question. There can be no conclusive answer, but two conspicuous features of the years from 1976 to 1979 suggest that the possibility of a backlash in favor of larger automobiles was less than the American manufacturers seem to have believed. One is that American-made subcompact cars were noticeably enlarging their share of the U.S. market even before the 1979 oil crisis—from 9.5 percent at the beginning of 1977 steadily upward to 15 percent at the end of 1978, followed by a steep rise to 24 percent in March 1979.[8] The other is that while sales of domestic cars were very good in the 1976 to 1979 period, sales of import cars did just as well and sales of Japanese cars did even better.

The Import Car Boom

This section could also be entitled "The Japanese Car Boom," because the bulk of the import gains went to Japanese producers. The figures tell the story. Imports dropped off somewhat in 1976 but then rebounded. Imports from Japan gained steadily except for a minor decline (18,000 units in all) in 1978, a year that saw import sales in general fall away by some 60,000 units. Then came the bonanza year of 1979.

The most interesting and important feature of this analysis is the third part of Table 9.2, "All vehicles." Discussions of import car penetration of the U.S. market usually focus on sales of passenger automobiles, but it seems far more meaningful to consider total sales, even if this shows a lower percentage of penetration. Certainly for Datsun and more recently for Toyota, truck sales have been a vital element in establishing their position in the American market. For the 1975 to 1978 period, the "All vehicles" figures yield the interesting information that total import sales went down in 1976 and again in 1978, although the 1978 total was the second highest ever reached by import cars up to that time. However, sales of Japanese cars went up consistently until 1978, and even in that year the Japanese share of import car sales increased. This was true of passenger cars, and the fluctuations in the import truck percentages are hardly significant; the Japanese had almost complete control in this field. In mid-1977, the leading import cars were (in order) Toyota, Datsun, Honda, VW, Colt, Fiat, Subaru; five of the first seven are Japanese[9].

Some of the reasons for this situation have already been discussed. The principal European competitors had internal troubles in the mid-1970s, and by the time they had resolved their problems, the Japanese companies were too firmly established in positions of leadership in the American market to be dislodged. Volkswagen recovered from a six-year decline in 1977 but it lost third place among the imports to Honda.

Fiat came back strongly in 1975 with sales of over 100,000 vehicles to take fifth place in the import car market, just behind

Honda. A year later, British Leyland overtook Fiat but could not hold the pace thereafter. Meanwhile, the Japanese penetration of the import car market continued to grow. In 1976, Subaru moved into sixth place among the imports. In addition, manufacture of the Buick Opel was moved briefly from Germany to Isuzu in Japan, and Mitsubishi made the Plymouth Arrow as well as the Dodge Colt. In 1977, the top year for import sales prior to 1979, three companies—Toyota, Datsun, and Honda— accounted for almost 80 percent of the Japanese passenger car sales in the United States, or about 10 percent of all United States passenger car sales.[10] The rest came from Subaru and Toyo Kogyo (Mazda) and the companies that made automobiles for American firms—Isuzu and Mitsubishi. Toyo Kogyo also made Ford Courier pickup trucks.

Obviously, an import car market that was approaching a fifth of all passenger automobile sales in the United States had moved a long way from the time when import sales had been concentrated in a U-shaped area representing the seaboard states of the United States. There were still variations in import car penetration, which was to be expected. The U-shape was still discernible in 1977, but its edges were fuzzy and its interior could hardly be described as hollow. Only four states—Illinois, Iowa, Indiana, and Michigan—had an import car penetration of 10 percent of less. At the other extreme, five states—Alaska, California, Hawaii, Oregon, and Washington—had over 35 percent import penetration. The Pacific Coast was a particularly strong area for Japanese cars. In 1978, California alone accounted for 21.6 percent of all Datsun passenger car sales, 25.2 percent of the truck sales, and 22.4 percent of the total.

In price, the import cars contrived to hold their own in spite of their severe problems of currency exchange. *Money* magazine compared the smallest of the most popular imports in 1977 with their nearest American counterparts, Chevrolet's Chevette and the Olds Cutlass. All the cars were two-door hatchbacks except the Colt and the Cutlass, which were two-door sedans. The prices were: Datsun B210, $3888; Toyota Corolla SR5, $4188; Honda Civic OVCC, $3637; VW Rabbit, $4524; Dodge Colt,

$3408; Chevette, $3391; Cutlass, $4774.[11] These were suggested list prices. The Ford Pinto and the Chevrolet Vega were in the same price range, but they were excluded from the list because they were heavier vehicles and harder to handle. The high price of the Volkswagen as compared to the other imports was a matter of currency exchange, and it was an important factor in Volkswagen's decision to assemble in the United States. The models listed were selected as samples; the article credited Datsun and Toyota with a sales advantage in offering styles "from sedate sedans and station wagons to flashy coupes."

When the gasoline crunch of 1979 arrived, import cars were suddenly at a premium. Buyers swung sharply to the small automobiles that offered economical gasoline mileage, and the domestic manufacturers were simply unable to meet the demand. Imports went up over 20 percent of passenger car sales. This was very nice for the time being. The catch was that it caused a reaction in the United States. Chrysler was threatened with bankruptcy, Ford lost money on its domestic operations, and they and General Motors were shutting down plants. The result inevitably was agitation for restrictions on imports. Nothing was done at the time and there was no definite agreement on what sort of restrictions might or should be imposed, but there was a warning that the market boom for the imports was not likely to last indefinitely.

The Datsun Record

For any business organization, it is imperative that no matter how well it is doing or has done, it should constantly be looking for improvement and under no circumstances be content to rest on its laurels. This was the Datsun situation when Hiroshi Majima became President of NMC-USA at the beginning of 1975. The company's record was impressive. In fifteen years, it had grown from nowhere to be the second-largest seller of import cars in the United States, from sales of barely 1000 vehicles in a year to more than 300,000. Also, with the active cooperation of its parent company, it had grown from a product that American buyers viewed with some misgiving to a line of cars with an excellent reputation for quality of construction and efficiency in operation.

This was a highly creditable performance; however in the automobile business, gains can turn very readily into losses. The Majima regime began while Volkswagen was losing its former dominant and seemingly unassailable position in the import car market. Competition in this market was intensifying, with more Japanese makes rising to prominence in the United States— Honda, Subaru, Mazda, plus the "captives." Fiat was selling more aggressively, and the prospect of a VW comeback had to be faced. Then there was the uncomfortable fact that since 1968 Toyota sales had outrun those of Datsun. NMC-USA's past accomplishments were a source of justifiable pride and they provided a solid foundation for future growth, but it was clear that continuing effort was needed to keep the company moving ahead, or even just to hold its own.

The Nissan management, whether in Tokyo or Los Angeles, had not been accustomed to thinking in terms of just holding its own, and it had no intention of starting to do so at this point. Majima launched two programs when he took office, both designed to keep NMC-USA moving ahead. One was to develop long-range planning more intensively to give the company and its dealers clear objectives to work for.[12] First of all, there was strengthening of the plan aimed at reaching sales of half a million in 1980; the goal was reached in 1979, with sales of 550,000 units, assisted by the special circumstances created by the oil crisis of that year. This planning program involved intensification of the market analysis and research activities that had begun effectively in 1970 when John Gladen was brought into the company. Gladen had long experience in sales and market research with American Motors and Chrysler, plus two years with Ford.[13] After the 1971 reorganization, which put his work in the Marketing Department; Katayama asked him to start the planning function, so that it was organized and operational when Majima took over; however, there was still no adequate research on advertising effectiveness, that is, which themes and which media produced the best responses in terms of increased sales.

The kind of information that was secured is shown in Tables 9.4 and 9.5, which show the sources of sales of 1978 Datsun buyers. These are samples of much more elaborate data compiled by the Marketing Department of NMC-USA. They demonstrate the kind of detailed data that the company needed in order to implement its planning program, and they provide an interesting perspective on the buying patterns of Datsun purchasers. New Datsun buyers, for instance, were considerably more likely to come from owners of domestic makes than from owners of other imports. There has been much more information accumulated on Datsun buyers and owners, so that the sales force

TABLE 9.4   *Source of Sales of 1978-Model Datsun Buyers, October 1977– March 1978 By Datsun Model Bought   ("Where Datsun Business Came From")*

	Datsun total (%)	Datsun model bought (%)						
		B210	F10	510	810	200-SX	280-Z	620
Previous vehicle owned*:								
Import make	38	29	39	47	55	35	41	47
Domestic make	53	58	53	48	42	53	53	46
Did not own a vehicle	9	13	8	5	3	12	6	7
	100	100	100	100	100	100	100	100
Specific make of previous vehicle owned*:								
Datsun	17	11	15	25	27	15	18	25
VW	7	9	10	7	6	7	5	7
Toyota	4	3	3	4	5	4	5	3
Other imports	10	6	11	11	17	9	13	12
Chevrolet	15	15	16	11	9	14	14	15
Ford	13	14	13	11	9	13	13	14
Other domestics	25	29	24	26	24	26	26	17
Did not own a vehicle	9	13	8	5	3	12	6	7
	100	100	100	100	100	100	100	100

NOTE: 1978 510, 810 and 620 models had a higher proportion of previous Datsun owners.
SOURCE: 1978-Model Datsun new buyer study, May 1978.
*Previous vehicle owned is defined as the vehicle disposed of or the respondent's inventory vehicle if no vehicle was disposed of.

TABLE 9.5   *Reasons for Buying Datsun Over Other Makes
Considered by Datsun Model Purchased*

	Total Datsun (%)	Datsun model purchased (%)						
		B210	F10	510	810	200-SX	280-Z	620
Cost/value	46	50	51	39	40	51	47	26
Good gas mileage/ economy	25	30	20	24	18	21	19	20
Exterior styling	21	20	14	15	10	30	35	17
Recommendation	15	16	13	17	17	11	10	20
Good workmanship/ dependability	13	12	7	17	18	10	18	10
Handling/ performance	8	5	17	7	11	6	18	4
Interior roominess	7	3	6	12	10	3	6	28
Good engine	5	3	1	6	20	3	20	4

NOTE: Cost/value was the major reason for buying Datsun over other makes considered, except for the 620, where it was interior roominess.
SOURCE: 1978 new Datsun buyer study, May 1978 (October 1977–March 1978 buyers).

and the dealers can have the basis for judging accurately where the most promising prospects are to be found. How this information can be used is described by Dale R. Finley, Dealer Advertising Manager:

> Our biggest competitor is the other importers as opposed to the other domestics; that is why we are very careful in selecting the media for our advertising. Let's face it, 12 million cars were sold last year and I think Datsun sold about 525,000, so there are millions of people out there who are not really interested in buying a Datsun. They are not import buyers. So what you have to do in your advertising is go after that individual who fits the profile of an import buyer and tell him our story and why he should buy a Datsun.[14]

The other major Majima objective was to improve product planning. This was an area in which Majima had considerable experience, and he saw a need for better communications between NMC-USA and Nissan Motor Co., Ltd., with regard to the technical qualities of Datsun cars. Katayama had spent a good deal of effort in telling Tokyo what he felt was needed for the U.S. market and had received willing cooperation, which showed in the constant improvement of Datsun vehicles. But Mr. K was not an engineer or a designer, and his proposals were sometimes misunderstood. Furthermore, he thought that all the product planning would be done in Japan, whereas both Majima and Gladen saw a need for an office in NMC-USA to have product planning studied in the light of the special requirements of the American market.

A Product Planning Department was duly created within the Marketing Department in October 1976 with the specific responsibility of improving NMC-USA's ability to respond to market needs.[15] This responsibility required making sure that the designers of Nissan Motor Co., Ltd., had accurate information, in a form they could understand, regarding what American customers liked. Some of the points that needed to be clarified seem minor, even trivial—for example, the floor covering should be a single, wall-to-wall piece. Minor, perhaps, but items such as this could very well determine whether a customer bought a Datsun or something else.

This amplifying and streamlining of staff functions was part of a general revision of the company organization in a process of building for further growth. Two new regional offices were added in 1978, in Columbus, Ohio, and Memphis, Tennessee, after careful study to determine the optimum location for the new offices. These gave the company its planned total of twelve regional offices. More important was an expansion of the sales organization in 1976, which involved the appointment of three Vice Presidents: Robert Kent, Vice President, Marketing Services; Blaine Dorsett, Vice President, Sales Staff; and Charles P. "Chuck" King, Vice President, Sales Operations.[16] All were responsible to Robert O. Link. At the same time, Yasuhiko Suzuki was made Vice President, External Relations, charged with "implementing an organized and systematic liaison program with a variety of organizations in both the public and private sector."

Early in the following year, there was another personnel change at NMC-USA, a truly historic one. In March 1977 the two K's, Katayama and Kawazoe, retired. President Majima

hailed their achievement in these words: 'These two men succeeded beyond anyone's dream. Our stature in the United States
today is due in great measure to their contributions. We will
miss their counsel and leadership, but will continue to think of
them as part of our Datsun family.'[17]

Katayama's farewell was in part:

> Our dream of 16 years ago is now a reality. Everybody knows about us.
> We have more than two million Datsuns on American roads, have made
> great strides to let our customers know how service-minded we are
> toward our product, and we have even reached a point where others in
> the industry have come to us to learn about how we go about doing
> things.

Kawazoe's parting began:

> When the Company was established, having taken over the distribu-
> torship of Datsun products from the American distributors, I became
> Vice President in charge of Eastern Operations, comprising 35 states.
> There certainly have been many trials and tribulations during the past
> years. But fortunately, largely due to the fine cooperation and encour-
> agement I received from Nissan, USA employees, the dealers, and my
> many good friends, I am now retiring with a very satisfying sense of
> accomplishment and fulfillment.

They were certainly entitled to the tribute and to pride in
looking back at a difficult task well done. NMC-USA was now
building on the secure foundation that they had established.

Two years later, in 1979, Robert O. Link became Senior Vice
President, after almost a decade as head of the company's sales
organization. The responsibilities in this newly created post
were to represent NMC-USA in its relationships with the dealer
body, trade organizations, and high-level public affairs, and to
advise the President on policy affecting internal operations.[18]
He also became Chairman of the Policy Review Board, further
described in Chapter 11, The Sales Structure.

Along with these changes in the internal organization, the
company's advertising arrangements were completely trans-
formed in 1977. Until then Parker Advertising of Los Angeles
had been the agency for NMC-USA, for the Western Division
until 1966 and then for the national advertising program. In all

this time, there had been no formal contract. The agency handled NMC-USA's work, which was its largest and almost its only account on a straight commission basis. By 1977, this account had grown to a very substantial annual expenditure, and the new management of NMC-USA concluded that a change was needed in order to meet more effectively the challenges that could be seen ahead. The company conducted an intensive nationwide search, from which the William Esty Company of New York emerged with the NMC-USA account. The new agency produced the "We Are Driven" slogan, followed by the campaigns emphasizing Datsun economy. The advertising policy is discussed further in Chapter 11.

If action is to be judged by results, the sales figures were recording a success story: 350,403 in 1976; 488,217 (just shy of the half-million mark) in 1977; 432,700 in 1978 (slightly down but still well ahead of anything up to 1977); and then a new high point in 1979—574,166. The slight falling away in 1978 must have been a disappointment because the company was aiming for sales of 490,000 vehicles in that year. It had just introduced a new 510 series for the 1978 model year to replace the 710 as the middle-size Datsun entry, and the dealer previews had been favorable. The 510 models had suggested list prices from $4093 to $4683. The company was also about to introduce a cab-and-chassis version of its pickup that could be adapted for recreational or utility vehicles.

In addition, 1978 would be the first full year for the Datsun 810, which was designed as a family car that would let consumers avoid having to choose between vehicles that were "big and gas-guzzling or small and lacking in performance."[19] It was the top of the Datsun line, with a six-cylinder, 240-Z engine of 120 horsepower, electronic fuel injection, power steering and power-assisted brakes. The styling, particularly the interior fittings, was on the order of the higher-priced American automobiles. The suggested retail price when the 810 was first put on the market was $5099 for the sedan and $5499 for the station wagon.

The Datsun models came up to expectations in performance. They had consistently high ratings in emission control and fuel economy. A test in 1978 by the California Air Resources Board put the Datsun in the "very clean" category (see Table 9.6); only the two Swedish cars, Volvo and Saab, gained a higher-ranking category: "outstanding." EPA mileage figures for Datsuns in 1978 are given in Table 9.7. These were performance levels well ahead of the requirements of the law. In fact, the *Los Angeles Times* had pointed out a year earlier that 98 percent of the import cars expected to be sold in California in 1977 would meet the 18-miles-per-gallon standard that the Energy Act was seeking to achieve, while 83 percent of the domestic models would not.[20]

Nevertheless, Datsun sales fell off in 1978, not very much but still off, and short of the hopes for the year. Since most imports

TABLE 9.6 *The California ARB's Cleanest Cars*

Below smog standards (%)	Make-model	Engine size (cubic inches)/ cylinders
72	Volvo 242 Sedan	130/4
72	Volvo 245	130/4
63	Saab 99	121/4
59	Ford Fiesta	98/4
58	Toyota Celica	134/4
58	Toyota Corona	134/4
58	Toyota Corona Wagon	134/4
53	Dodge Omni	105/4
53	Plymouth Horizon	105/4
52	Volkswagen Dasher	97/4
52	Volkswagen Dasher Wagon	97/4
51	Datsun 200-SX	119/4
51	Datsun 510	119/4
51	Datsun 510 Wagon	119/4
51	Volkswagen Rabbit	89/4
51	Volkswagen Scirocco	89/4
50	Audi Fox	97/4
50	Audi Fox Wagon	97/4
50	Toyota Corolla	97/4

SOURCE: *Los Angeles Times*, April 16, 1978, part 1, p. 50.

were similarly affected, the decline has to be attributed to causes outside the Nissan organization and largely beyond its control. Part of the reason certainly was stiffer competition from the lighter-weight domestic cars such as the Chevette and the Chrysler Horizon and Omni.[21] Another factor was the competition of newer Japanese makes—Honda, Subaru, Mazda—in the U.S. market. Their sales went up in 1978 while both Datsun and Toyota were going down, possibly because these newer arrivals had an aura of novelty. However, the most important cause was the continuing fluctuation of the currency exchanges. Further decline of the dollar relative to the yen and the deutschmark kept pushing up prices of import cars during 1978, offset to some extent, it is true, by the fact that the same inflation raised the prices of domestic cars.

This situation generated some cautious speculation that the rapid climb of import sales might be over and that import car penetration of the United States market would drop back to the 15 to 16 percent level of the early1970.[22] These forecasts were

TABLE 9.7   *EPA Mileage Figures Datsun, 1978*

Model	49 States			California		
	City	Hwy	Combined	City	Hwy	Combined
B210 GX* M/T	36	48	40	30	42	35
B210 M/T	28	41	33	29	41	33
B210 A/T	24	28	26	24	30	26
F10 M/T	28	40	33	29	40	33
510 M/T	24	32	27	24	32	27
510 A/T	24	28	26	24	29	26
200-SX M/T	24	33	28	24	32	27
200-SX A/T	23	28	25	23	28	25
810 M/T	16	23	18	18	24	20
810 A/T	17	21	19	17	21	19
280-Z M/T	18	27	21	18	25	21
280-Z A/T	17	23	19	18	22	19
620 M/T	23	30	26	23	29	25
620 A/T	23	26	24	22	25	23

*With optional five-speed transmission.
SOURCE: NMC-USA Records.

made by well-informed observers of the automotive field. The usually reliable *The Economist* predicted in the fall of 1978 that cheap imported Japanese cars were on the way out because of the changing value of the yen, so that the Japanese would have to compete in the higher price ranges.[23] These predictions could have proved more accurate if it had not been for the unforeseeable oil crisis in 1979. As it was, Datsun's unrealized hopes for 1978 were attained and liberally surpassed a year later.

═10═

DATSUN IN 1980

When Nissan Motor Corporation in U.S.A. reached its twentieth year, it was a vigorous, successful organization. It was securely established as the second-largest seller of import cars in the United States—close enough to the leader, Toyota, so that reaching first place could be seen as a reasonably attainable goal. Sales continued to be strong. In fact, the impetus given to purchases of small cars in 1979 carried on as fuel prices kept escalating, so that each successive month saw new records in Datsun sales. The half-million target set for 1980 five years before had already been reached and passed; the 1980 sales figures would top 600,000. Behind NMC-USA stood Nissan Motor Co., Ltd., now the world's fourth-largest manufacturer of motor vehicles, following General Motors, Ford, and Toyota in that order.

As the year began, NMC-USA was an organization with a capitalization of $6 million, and 1582 employees. The largest number, 680, were at the National Headquarters complex in Carson, California; the others were in the regional offices: Boston, 77; Chicago, 83; Columbus, 43; New York, 86; Jacksonville, 88; Dallas, 78; Memphis, 42; Norfolk, 84; Denver, 68; Los Angeles, 109; Portland, 47; San Francisco, 41; Sacramento (Parts Warehouse opened in 1978, replacing San Francisco and Portland depots), 56.[1] There were 1083 dealers, with a total of 30,215 employees.[2]

What this meant to the American economy can be judged by a study made by Harbridge House, Inc., in 1978, dealing with the possible effects of curtailing automobile imports on employment. It concluded that Datsun imports in 1977 represented a total direct employment in the United States of 26,670, composed of NMC-USA staff, Datsun dealerships, and port operations, plus another 9565 jobs supplying goods and services to Datsun operations.[3] The total payroll, corporate and dealership, was estimated at close to $272 million and total net assets at $813.8 million. About $13 million worth of United States–manufactured goods were expected to be purchased in 1978 for use in the assembly and manufacture of Datsuns, including catalytic converters, carpeting, upholstery, spark delay valves, and circular sealed beam headlights. Datsun dealers spent $216,430,000 for goods and services from 54,080 local businesses.

As is appropriate for an important anniversary occasion, 1980 was a year for looking and moving forward as well as for looking back at what had been accomplished. A fresh stage in the development of NMC-USA began in January, when President Majima returned to Japan and was replaced by Tetsuo Arakawa. Like his predecessor, Arakawa is an engineer, a graduate of Keio University in Tokyo, and served as head of the North American Export Division of Nissan, Ltd. Prior to that he spent nine years in Mexico establishing Nissan Mexicana. This change was recognized in a reception at the Century Plaza Hotel in Los Angeles' Century City on January 31, in honor of both Mr. Majima and Mr. Arakawa. Some 700 members and friends of NMC-USA attended.

Then there was the introduction of the NAPS-Z engine (Nissan Anti-Pollution System). This was a design produced by the engineers of Nissan, Ltd., to meet rigorous Japanese emission requirements. It is a 2-liter, four-cylinder motor with hemi-spherical combustion chambers in the cylinder heads. Like most technical innovations, the NAPS-Z engine is based on devel-opment from known principles—over 250 patent applications have come from the development work on it.[4] The advantages of the hemispherical combustion chamber in providing more efficient burning and better engine performance have been known for half a century, but these advantages were offset by higher cost of manufacture plus the handicap that the more complete combustion reduced hydrocarbon emissions but increased nitrous oxides (NOx). This problem was overcome by finding ways to increase the amount of exhaust gas recirculated into the incoming fuel (the most common method of reducing NOx emissions) without impairing engine performance.

This achievement required fine-tuning the engine in every possible way. "This was accomplished," states a graphic descrip-tion, "by using the most up-to-date computer and electronic technology. . . . To achieve their goal Nissan's engineers had to blend induction, ignition, valve timing, and exhaust in such a way that the desirable result occurred. It's one of those pro-cesses where if you change one thing, it produces change in all the others, and the number of possible combinations is infinite."[5]

During the development of the engine, the Engineering Department of NMC-USA worked closely with the Nissan engineers in Japan, providing supporting technical information to finalize the engine and specifications so as to meet U.S. mar-ket requirements. The NAPS-Z engine, adapted for American standards, became standard equipment on the 1980 Datsun 510 and a new 200-SX. For the special requirements of California, each combustion chamber had two spark plugs. Cars with this addition were expected to be one-fifth the number of those models sold in the 1980 model year,[6] a commentary on the importance of the California market.

The EPA ratings for these models put the 510 and the 200-SX at the level that the Energy Act had stipulated was to be attained by all cars in 1985—27.5 miles per gallon. (These mileages are not required for every individual vehicle; the manufacturer's performance is measured on the basis of CAFE, or Company Average Fuel Economy.) At any rate, with this engine, Datsun was in good shape to meet increasingly stringent standards of fuel efficiency and pollutant emission, a notable achievement since the two objectives are likely to conflict with each other.

There is an impressive supporting cast to go with the NAPS-Z–equipped Datsun models: the 210 and 310 are basically economy models; the 310 has front-wheel drive. They are rated at 28 to 31 miles per gallon for city driving and 40-plus on the highway, depending on the type of transmission installed. The 810 remains the deluxe entry in the Datsun line, with some improvements on its 1979 version, and the 280-ZX continues at the top of the sports car list.

The Automobile Market in 1980

If reconciling fuel economy with emission control had been Datsun's only problem in 1980, the management of Nissan, both in Japan and the United States, could have looked forward to an easy and very profitable year. That was a problem which, however difficult, was at least susceptible to a straightforward technological solution. Market conditions in the United States were as favorable as could be desired. The switch to smaller cars that had been precipitated by the 1979 oil crisis was turning into a virtual stampede; with domestic manufacturers unable to meet the demand, the imports were reaping a harvest. In two years, from January 1978 to January 1980, the annual rate of import car sales rose by a million, while domestic car sales went up only half a million and began to decline in 1980; imports took 27 percent of the passenger car market in February 1980 and appeared certain to reach 30 percent for the year.[7]

The Japanese share of the import market in 1979 was 71 percent for passenger cars and over 99 percent for trucks and growing, helped not only by the change in American consumer preferences but by some recovery of the dollar in relation to the yen in 1979. From this situation it followed that Datsun and Toyota sales led the surge in import car sales in the United States in 1979 and 1980. In January 1980, in fact, Toyota went ahead of ailing Chrysler to become the third-largest seller of motor vehicles in the United States,[8] and Datsun was close behind. Actually some of the smaller Japanese companies had been gaining somewhat faster than the Datsun and Toyota, not only in the United States but in Japan as well, possibly because of the attraction of Mazda's rotary piston engine and Subaru's four-wheel drive.[9] Nevertheless, Datsun and Toyota easily maintained their dominating position. Table 10.1 shows the relative positions of the Japanese automobile manufacturers in production for the five years prior to the market change in 1979.

From one point of view, the prospect for import cars in 1980 seemed glowing. The domestic manufacturers could not begin to meet the demand for small cars and would not be ready to do so until late 1981 or 1982 at the earliest. The imports could sell as much as their factories could produce and ship. This was an important limiting factor for an organization such as Nissan, which was striving to outdo Toyota in their home market and

TABLE 10.1   *Japanese Automobile Production, 1974–1978*

By makers	Production (in 1000 cars)					Production share (%)				
	1974	1975	1976	1977	1978	1974	1975	1976	1977	1978
Toyota Motor	2115	2336	2488	2721	2929	32.3	33.7	31.7	32.0	31.6
Nissan Motor	1809	2077	2304	2278	2393	27.6	29.9	29.4	26.8	25.8
Toyo Kogyo	739	643	717	800	850	11.3	9.3	9.1	9.4	9.2
Mitsubishi Motors	496	520	648	776	973	7.6	7.5	8.3	9.1	10.5
Honda Motor	429	414	560	665	743	6.5	6.0	7.1	7.8	8.0
Daihatsu Motor	245	257	261	319	328	3.7	3.7	3.3	3.7	3.5
Fuji Heavy Industries	164	176	241	287	305	2.5	2.5	3.1	3.4	3.2
Suzuki Motor	204	184	202	240	248	3.1	2.6	2.6	2.8	2.7
Isuzu Motors	248	245	336	341	408	3.8	3.5	4.3	4.0	4.4
Hino Motors	74	61	59	58	62	1.1	0.9	0.8	0.7	0.7
Nissan Diesel Motor	29	27	27	31	30	0.5	0.4	0.3	0.4	0.3
Total	6552	6942	7841	8515	9269	100.0	100.0	100.0	100.0	100.0

SOURCE: Japan Automobile Manufacturers' Association.

had other vital export markets besides the United States that had to be supplied with Datsun vehicles.[10] On the surface, a motor vehicle manufacturer could scarcely ask for more—a market that would take everything that could be produced.

However, business has its own form of Newton's Third Law—for every action there is an equal and opposite reaction. What was bonanza for the import firms was near catastrophe for the domestic manufacturers. In just a year from the spring of 1979, the market share of large and intermediate-size cars dropped from 42 to 33 percent.[11] These had been the money makers for the American firms, and while the Big Three were moving to increase their output of small cars, they were quite unprepared for the radical market shift of 1979. Bad judgment on the part of the American automobile industry? To some extent, yes, in that the American producers had persistently underestimated the import competition and their own periodic entrances into the small-car market had been at best half-hearted, yielding to external pressures rather than acting from their own conviction. On the other hand, as one prescient commentator points out, the argument that Detroit

> persisted wilfully in trying to shove gas guzzlers down the public's throat overlooks two things: the public wanted those big cars and the government encouraged it to want them by holding gas prices down. Just before the Iranian crisis, gasoline cost no more in real dollars than it had seven years before. Small cars languished in import and domestic showrooms alike, and Ford was rationing V-8 engines among its customers.[12]

As late as March 1979 there were waiting lists for Ford LTD's and Dodge St. Regises, and General Motors was thinking of converting a compact car plant to make Oldsmobiles. The market for big cars was booming, and the industry, as previously noted, was concerned about rushing the public into buying small cars it didn't want, or, as President Philip Caldwell of Ford put it: "We all faced the specter of forcing the American people to buy something they hadn't indicated they wanted to buy in large quantities."[13] Just a year later an observer of the autombile industry could remark of the oversupply of big cars: "Detroit's dilemma is that it must sell cars that no one wants to get the cash to make the cars that people will buy."[14] These two statements offer an interesting comment on the assertion frequently made that the automobile industry controls its market through high-powered advertising and pressures purchasers into buying cars they don't really want.

As it was, the American automobile industry faced a difficult dilemma in 1980. Its dealers were overstocked with big cars that they could not sell, and yet these were the models that had given the best profit margins in the past. So the Big Three were faced with making heavy investments in plant and tooling to increase their output of small cars, while their revenues were shrinking. As a result, Ford lost money on its North American operations and Chrysler's situation became still more precarious. General Motors, with its more than 60 percent market share of domestic production and 48 percent share of the total U.S. motor vehicle market, fared somewhat better; however, all three experienced plant shutdowns, some complete closings, and extensive layoffs. American Motors was less severely affected; it was not dependent on sales of big passenger automobiles and its arrangement with Renault gave it a stronger position in the small-car market.

The Detroit automakers should be absolved from the charge that they ignored the small-car market. They may have miscalculated it and at times misjudged what kind of vehicle should be designed for it, but they were quite aware of its existence as at least a potential threat. In addition, it was obvious that their own customary offerings were going to have to be reduced in size and weight to comply with the government-mandated standards of fuel economy. Consequently, by 1979 to 1980, there were cars on the drawing boards and to some extent in production that were not, like the earlier compacts, mere cut-down versions of standard-size vehicles but were designed from the start as small cars. The General Motors X-body model, a small car with front-wheel drive, was on the market for the 1980 model year, with other new designs close behind it. Ford had its front-wheel-drive model in the works. If the 1979 oil crisis had been delayed a year or so, the U.S. automobile manufacturers would have been in better shape to meet it.

The Rise of Protectionism

Whatever the prospect for the future, in 1980 the American automobile industry was in marked distress. Sales were down and unemployment was up—over 300,000 layoffs by the middle of the year. At any time this would have been a matter of serious national concern, because for many years the American economy had risen and fallen with the fortunes of the automotive industry. The year 1980 was a special case. The slump was more acute than at any time in the previous thirty years. More important, 1980 was an election year, which put pressure on the government to take some sort of action, not just because of the critical importance of the industry to the whole economy but also because the automobile workers who were being laid off had the powerful international union, United Automobile, Aerospace, and Agricultural Implement Workers of America, better known as the UAW, to plead their case for them.

The most obvious explanation—not necessarily the most accurate one—for the plight of the domestic automobile industry was the competition of import cars and most of all of Japanese cars. It did not escape attention that in 1980 at least one of every four motor vehicles sold in the United States was an import, and that three of every four imports were Japanese. There had been mutterings about import competition in previous years, but nothing on the scale of the crescendo that developed in 1980. Various measures were proposed: restricting imports to the level of some previous year, such as 1977; requiring Japan to relax its restrictions on the import of American cars; requiring companies selling over 200,000 vehicles a year in the United States either to build assembly plants in the

United States or to include some specified proportion of American-built components in their products.

These proposals were aimed primarily at the Japanese imports as the dominant element in the import car market, and specifically at Nissan and Toyota. The issue that was pushed most vigorously was the opening of U.S. assembly plants, which was certainly the most direct way to provide employment for automobile workers. Among European producers, Volkswagen had already taken this step, Renaults were scheduled to be built by American Motors at Kenosha, Wisconsin, and none of the others, even Fiat, was a major competitor in the American market. Japanese imports were dominated by the two big Japanese automobile manufacturers, Toyota and Nissan, which made them conspicuous targets. Third-place Honda had announced plans for an assembly plant next to its motorcycle plant in Marysville, Ohio, to begin turning out 10,000 cars a month in 1982, with an estimated cost of $200 million.[15] Lack of room to expand its Japanese production was partially responsible for this decision. Honda, moreover, is more dependent on its U.S. sales than either Nissan or Toyota. The other Japanese producers were like the Europeans, minor competitors—quite apart from the fact that three of them, Mitsubishi, Isuzu, and Toyo Kogyo, had ties with the American Big Three.

Neither Nissan nor Toyota was enthusiastic about the idea of building assembly plants in the United States. They were under pressure to comply from their own government, which was concerned about possible adverse effects on Japanese-American trade relations if some sort of restrictive action should be taken by the United States. However, they faced a more complicated decision than is generally appreciated. An automobile assembly plant is a heavy investment in buildings and tooling. It would be two or three years from the time of the decision before cars began to come off the line; in the meantime, the new General Motors and Ford small cars would be fully ready for the American market.

Studies of the level of production needed to achieve economies of scale in automobile manufacturing reach varying conclusions, but there is some consensus that ten to twenty years ago the minimum for straight assembly, without fabrication, to be competitive in the U.S. market was 200,000 units per year on a single line operating one shift.[16] For stamping operations the minimum was at least twice as high owing to the need to make maximum use of the dies. Since that time, assembly operations have been elaborately automated and computerized, emphatically so in the Nissan assembly plants; while this increases efficiency and lowers unit costs, it also calls for considerably higher investment and hence requires larger output in order to liquidate the cost. Nissan and Toyota would wish to use these techniques in American assembly plants, and indeed would have to in order to be competitive. An unofficial estimate puts the cost of a passenger car assembly plant in the United States for either company at approximately $1 billion, with a minimum output of a quarter of a million units annually for a single model to make the operation economically feasible.[17] No single Datsun or Toyota model has sold that many in the United States even in the peak years of 1979 and 1980. Honda apparently expects to be able to operate on a more limited scale because it is already making motorcycles on the same site.

This is why Nissan and Toyota were reluctant to commit themselves. By the time they could get such plants into operation—1982 or 1983 at the earliest—they would be facing the competition of the American producers, this time battling in earnest for the small-car market. They were being asked to take a highly speculative gamble; big as they are, General Motors and Ford are still bigger.

The Nissan/Toyota attitude was understood in the rest of the Japanese automobile industry, even though the other firms were not under the same pressure from American sources. A spokesman for Toyo Kogyo observed early in 1980 that his company saw the favorable position of import cars in the United States market as "a temporary situation which will in all probability last only until such time as the U.S. automakers start producing small cars in sufficient quantity."[18] He also made the point that his own company's Mazda sales in the United States were currently too small to make an American assembly plant economically viable.

The protectionist sentiment had plenty of opposition within the United States. The case against restricting automobile imports was forcefully put by Robert M. McElwaine, president of the American International Automobile Dealers Association (formerly Imported Automobile Dealers Association). At an association meeting in February 1980 he said: "At the end of our first ten years as an association and as we enter the decade of the eighties, we find our industry beleaguered as never before. Not because we have failed, but because we have, in the eyes of our competitors, been too successful. We have been too successful in providing a product that answers the demands of our times and meets the needs of our customers."[19] He endorsed the idea of building assembly plants in the United States, pointing out that the association had been instrumental in persuading Volkswagen to do so, but he went on to warn that restraints on imports of Japanese automobiles could produce reprisals against Japanese imports of American products—aircraft, for example, which would hurt a good many members of the UAW.

The *Los Angeles Times* wrote in a similar vein. It urged Toyota and Datsun to assemble in the United States as good business, but went on to say:

> It would not make any sense to try to slap limits on imported cars, for such protectionism would only invite retaliation against U.S. products, and in the end both countries and their workers would be the losers. So would American consumers lose by being restricted in their buying choices. Japanese cars sell well here, not because they are cheaper than comparative American models—they aren't—but because they have a reputation for good fuel economy and sound quality. People buy them in large numbers because they are the kinds of cars that people want to have. It's that simple. Don't blame the Japanese or try to punish them with quotas just because they build cars that Americans like, and because they had the foresight to see what the market would be.[20]

This position was corroborated by a large number of American consumers, voting with their dollars.

The assumption that restrictions on the importation of Japanese-made motor vehicles would cure the troubles of the American automobile industry is difficult to support. Robert T. Samuelson, economics writer for the *National Journal,* summarizes the situation this way: "Imported car sales [excluding those from Canada] will probably total 2.4 to 2.7 million this year (1980), up from 2 million in 1978. Meanwhile, sales of U.S. cars have tumbled from 9.3 million to about 6 million. Even if imports hadn't increased by a single car, the U.S. industry would be in deep trouble."[21] In other words, the import competition was not the basic cause for the drastic decline in domestic automobile sales. Worsening economic conditions and a continuing inflationary spiral were at the heart of the matter. There was a dramatic switch in consumer preference, but it was from large to small automobiles, not from domestic cars to imports.

During this same period the domestic small cars increased their share of the total U.S. motor vehicle market at just about the same rate as the imports (see Table 10.2). The domestics' share of the small-car market declined slightly in 1979 and 1980, but that was because there were simply not enough of them being turned out to meet the sudden increase in the demand for small cars; so, buyers turned to what was available, namely the imports.

The leading position of Japanese automobiles among the imports was a product of the way the import car market had developed over the previous ten years, when the Japanese companies had overtaken and forged ahead of their European competitors. It also happened that in 1978 the dollar rose appreciably in relation to the yen, so that the Japanese cars could keep their prices stable while in Europe the dollar remained low. In 1980, six Japanese automobile makers (Toyota, Datsun, Honda, Mazda, Subaru, Mitsubishi) led the import list in the United States. Volkswagen came next, down because its U.S. production was now providing the larger share of its American sales, and this was ranked as domestic. These were the only imports selling in six-digit figures. Fiat was working hard but was still handicapped by labor troubles, as was another potential competitor, British Leyland.

The import totals suggest that the troubles of the American motor vehicle industry have other causes than import competition. The onset of recession in 1980, tight credit, high interest rates, and a continuing rise in the rate of inflation were more important as contributors, along with an uncertain international situation and concern over the instability of the dollar. These were all in varying degrees factors influencing consumers to defer new car purchases, and there was quite definitely some disposition to wait for the new small-car models that were on the way. The 1980 automotive situation has to be looked on as exceptional and is certain to be temporary. In the last quarter of the year there were some signs that the recession was bottoming out and that domestic motor vehicle sales might begin to improve, stimulated by the new small-car models that the American Big Three were introducing—General Motors X-

TABLE 10.2   *Share of U.S. Compact Car Market Held by Domestic and Foreign Manufacturers 1970–1980* *

Year	Share of compact car market		Total compact cars sold (in thousands of units)
	domestic (%)	imported (%)	
1970	59.5	40.5	3175.6
1971	60.7	39.3	3973.9
1972	61.9	38.1	4278.6
1973	63.8	36.2	4877.1
1974	67.2	32.8	4296.0
1975	65.9	34.1	4641.9
1976	69.1	30.9	4858.8
1977	60.9	39.1	5285.6
1978	63.5	36.5	5474.0
1979	61.4	38.6	6024.0
1980			
January	56.9	43.1	504.8
February	58.0	42.0	523.8
March	61.5	38.5	584.4
April	58.7	41.3	490.2

*Includes subcompacts.

SOURCE: Unpublished data from U.S. Department of Commerce, Bureau of Economic Analysis.

and J-cars (the X-car in 1979); Ford's Escort and Lynx, termed "world cars" to indicate that they utilized the best technology from all over the world, although manufactured in the United States; and Chrysler's K-cars. However, when the year closed the signs of revival had faded and the hoped-for rise in domestic car sales had failed to materialize.

The managements of both Nissan and Toyota were aware that some response to the pressures on them was necessary. Nissan acted on April 17, 1980, when Takashi Ishihara, President of Nissan Motor Co., Ltd., and first President of NMC-USA, announced that Nissan would construct a factory that would eventually manufacture Datsun trucks for the U.S. market. The cost was estimated at $300 million. Production was scheduled to begin in 1983 at a level of 10,000 units a month, and about 2200 people would be employed. The operation was estimated to purchase about $120 million worth of parts and materials annually in the United States, with an eventual target of over 50 percent value added in the American assembly. The decision to begin with trucks was made because truck manufacture is in many ways simpler and less risky than passenger car manufacture. It does not, for instance, demand an annual model change. Mr. Ishihara expressed Nissan's thinking in this way:

> Trucks are subject to less frequent model changeovers, which is important for a new facility. Demand for light trucks is expected to continue firm in the future, and, accordingly, we will be able to compete with the United States manufacturers. Regarding passenger cars, with the United States automakers gearing up for small car production, we are not assured of our capability of competing with the big automakers. Given our limited production scale and the price competitiveness of the large United States manufacturers based on high volume, we would be no match for them.[22]

A company to operate this plant, Nissan Motor Manufacturing, U.S.A., was incorporated in Delaware and subsequently Marvin T. Runyon, former vice president of Ford Body and Assembling Operations, was appointed as its head. The site chosen for the plant was 850 acres in Smyrna, Tennessee, 15 miles south of Nashville. This project is the largest single investment by a Japanese company in the United States to date.

This decision had an additional stimulus in a change of United States tariff policy on truck imports. This was a reclassification, issued on August 20, 1980, that put a chassis with cab on the same basis for tariff purposes as a complete truck, so that it would have to pay the 25 percent Chicken War duty rather than the 4 percent applied under previous rulings.[23] If this ruling stood, then the technique of bringing in truck chassis and beds separately and putting them together after they passed through customs no longer offered any advantage.

Nissan–U.S.A. Turns Twenty

These decisions on the expansion of Nissan operations in the United States were made at Nissan's head office in Tokyo; they were not made by NMC-USA, but they were certainly going to have a profound effect on the future of the American company. It is also quite obvious that they had been under consideration for some length of time, certainly before the agitation of early 1980. Officials for Nissan Motor Co., Ltd., assisted by NMC-USA, were engaged in making studies for possible assembly operations, one of them interestingly being Masahiko Zaitsu, the engineer who had come to Los Angeles late in 1959 to give technical help to the Woolverton Datsun distributorship and had been one of the signers of NMC-USA's articles of incorporation.[24]

What it adds up to is that NMC-USA would celebrate its twentieth birthday in an exciting atmosphere. Its first two decades had certainly not been dull, as new sales records were established year after year, each in turn to be promptly superseded. The 1980 goal of 600,000 was certainly going to be reached and passed. Sales figures for the first quarter of 1980 showed that on a model-year-to-date basis Datsun sales were 35 percent ahead of the 1979 model year and for April and May

1980, Datsun was number 1 among the imports. As a result, Vice President King announced that the sales forecast for the 1980 model year was being revised upward to 650,000 retail sales, compared to 524,000 for the 1979 model year.

The company was ready. The distribution system was geared to handle around 800,000 units if need be, with the aid of a new computer, an IBM 3033.[25] Offsetting this bright prospect were some uncertainties. Datsun import totals might be slowed down by restrictions imposed by the U.S. government, and sales could be adversely affected by the economic recession that was plainly developing by the summer of 1980. As early as May, Datsun dealers were feeling the squeeze of governmental restraints on credit.

President Arakawa sounded an additional note of caution soon after he took office, pointing out that the number of Datsuns that could be imported was limited by the capacity of the Nissan factories and the availability of ships, so that it could not under present conditions go very far beyond the half-million level.[26] He reiterated the case against a Datsun car assembly plant in the United States and emphasized that the immediate problem for NMC-USA was going to be to keep its sales up in the face of the fierce competition that would develop once the U.S. automobile industry concentrated its attention on small cars.

One way and another, 1980 loomed up as an eventful year in the history of NMC-USA. It was the twentieth-anniversary year, certainly an occasion to commemorate in the light of the record of progress since September 28, 1960. It also promised to be an eventful year in itself; record sales were in prospect and they were record sales threatening political repercussions. There was thus an interesting past to look back on and an equally interesting present and future to contemplate. Astute and skillful management was just as necessary as it had been when NMC-USA was struggling just to exist.

At this point it seems desirable to interrupt the chronological narrative in order to look in detail at some of the salient parts of the organization that made the Datsun achievement in the United States possible. The selection is somewhat arbitrary; no segment of the NMC-USA structure is more vital than any other. However, the activities that are described in the following chapters appear to illustrate most effectively what has been responsible for the highly successful growth of Nissan Motor Corporation in the U.S.A. in its first twenty years.

=11=

THE SALES STRUCTURE

Nissan Motor Corporation in U.S.A. is first and foremost a sales organization. The other functions the company performs, such as product planning, technical engineering, truck assembly, promotion of racing and rallies, exist for the sole purpose of contributing to the selling of Datsun cars and trucks. Hence, it is appropriate that the sales operation should be selected for special study. Some of its history has already been told in previous chapters. The early sales efforts have been described, and the formation of the Datsun dealer organization, along with the problems encountered in making a place for the Datsun in the U.S. market.

Within the company, the sales structure began with the Sales Managers of the Eastern and Western Divisions and their District Sales Managers. There was little in the way of a national sales structure until the abolition of the divisions in 1971. It is true that Ray Hoen was made National Sales Manager in 1966, but between his failing health and the built-in handicaps of the two-division system, he did not have the opportunity to create a genuinely nationwide Datsun sales organization. That was achieved by his successor, Robert O. Link, who became National Sales Manager in 1969 and Vice President of Sales in the reorganization of 1971. From there, growth of Datsun sales can be seen reflected in the expansion of the sales structure. Link became Vice President and General Manager, Sales, in 1974, with three Vice Presidents (Marketing Services, Sales Staff, and Sales Operations) reporting to him. Then in 1979, Link was promoted to Senior Vice President and his place as Vice President and General Manager, Sales, was taken by Charles P. King. Marketing Services was separated administratively from Sales.

This is the apex of the sales structure, the high command. It functions, as high commands do, through appropriate staff departments: Sales, Distribution, Import, Dealer Development, Dealer Support. At the next level are the twelve regional offices, each headed by a Regional Sales Manager who is, as stated in Chapter 7, responsible for the performance of the region. As "captain of the team" he provides the necessary local coordination of regional activities. The regions are grouped in three areas, each with its Area Sales Director (see Figure 11.1). In April 1980 these were reorganized as eastern (Boston, New York, Norfolk, Jacksonville); central (Chicago, Columbus, Dallas, Memphis); and western (Denver, Portland, Los Angeles, San Francisco). It is worth noting that over half the regional offices are not actually located in the cities they are named for. The Boston Regional Office is in Mansfield, Massachusetts; New York in Piscataway, New Jersey (moved from Secaucus in 1973); Chicago in Hinsdale, Illinois; Columbus in Worthington, Ohio; Norfolk in Portsmouth, Virginia; Los Angeles in Costa Mesa, California; San Francisco in Walnut Creek, California (moved from South San Francisco in 1980). This represents a conscious policy, partly to locate in lower-cost sites but more to have ready access by road for shipments of cars and parts.

The role of the regional offices can best be described as providing the immediate logistical support for the people who actually sell the cars, the Datsun dealers. They are the members

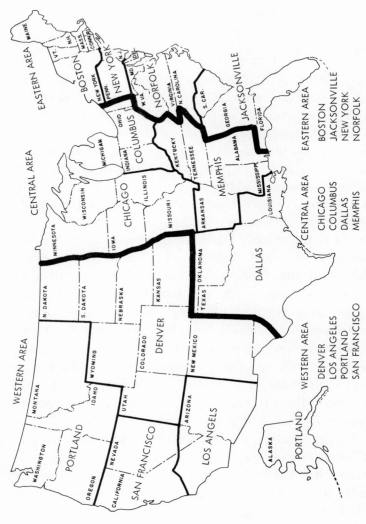

FIG. 11.1 *Nissan Motor Corporation in U.S.A. area and regional boundaries in 1980. This map shows the company's geographic organization as it was reorganized in 1980. Through all the changes, the western area has remained virtually identical with the original Western Division. The one difference is that Kansas and Nebraska were in the old Houston Region and therefore were in the Eastern Division until 1965.*

of the sales structure who are in direct contact with the buying public, and basically they are what the rest of the organization exists for.

The Datsun Dealers

From its beginning, NMC-USA has followed the philosophy enunciated by Mr. Katayama: "Dealers make money, then we make money." The principle seems simple and obvious, but the history of manufacturer-dealer relationship in the U.S. automobile industry offers some evidence that the principle has occasionally been ignored in practice. The record of generally good relations between NMC-USA and its dealers can be explained in terms of a successful mixture of Japanese methods of management and American techniques of organization.

The story of how the early Datsun dealers were recruited has already been told. It had all the earmarks of a hit-or-miss operation at the beginning. Practically anyone who was willing to try to sell Datsuns could become a dealer. The results were surprisingly good under the circumstances. There were the failures and the poor choices that could have been expected, but there were also conspicuous successes, such as those already mentioned: Lemke and Daily in San Diego, California; Tucker in Bakersfield, California; Winters in Sacramento, California; along with Ben Wilson in Norwalk, Connecticut, who became the first eastern Datsun dealer, on November 19, 1958.

At first Datsun dealers' contracts were individual arrangements between the dealer and the company, although in practice they were modeled on the standard dealer contract used by the domestic automobile manufacturers. This situation was changed in 1967, when a general Datsun Dealer Sales Agreement was introduced in the Western Division and adopted throughout the company. It still followed the general pattern of dealer agreements in the American automobile industry, as it should; NMC-USA was selling Datsuns on the American market through sales staff and dealers whose experience and training were in American sales methods and organization.[1] This agreement was written for a specific term, normally one year, with automatic renewal as long as the conditions were met.[2] Then in 1974, a new agreement provided for a five-year basic term and this in turn was superseded in 1979 by a perpetual agreement, with, as we have seen, Ray Lemke as the first signer. This agreement was perpetual for established dealers; for newcomers there was a probationary period, and specific grounds were stated upon which a dealership might be terminated. There was also provision for a Policy Review Board, for the purpose of reviewing dealer complaints that might arise over the appointment of new dealers or over terminations. It consists of three Vice Presidents of NMC-USA, all from departments other than Sales.

This succession of Dealer Sales Agreements tells part of the story of a relationship between the company and its dealers that kept growing closer, as the progression from short- to long-term contracts demonstrates. But formal documents very seldom tell the whole story; history written from them exclusively is incomplete and very likely to be inaccurate. The evolution of the Datsun dealer organization was far less a matter of the letter of the agreements than of careful cultivation of personal associations, of offering encouragement and incentive in preference to cracking the whip.

One of the earliest indications of this policy was the institution of trips to Japan as a reward for Quality Dealers. These trips became known as the "Factour." In 1978, the term "Quality Dealer" was changed to "Award of Merit," judged on the basis of excellence in new and used car sales, truck sales (new and used), parts, service, customer relations, and business management.[3] There are other bonuses as well, such as trips for selected dealers to Mexico City and Acapulco.[4]

These incentives were certainly helpful to dealer morale; other actions by the company were probably even more helpful. As a notable example, when the east and gulf ports were closed by a three-month dockworkers strike in 1971, the Datsun dealers in the affected regions (New York, Boston, Norfolk, Jacksonville, Dallas) were given the following statement of company policy:

> To provide dealers in the eastern and gulf portions of the U.S. with sufficient vehicles to do business, we have the following avenues open to us:
>
> A. Unload ships at the U.S. west coast ports, which are presently operating, rail car them cross-country to points within the Region(s) and motor-carrier ship them to the individual dealership(s).
> B. Unload ships at Ensenada, Mexico, and motor-carrier ship them direct to dealership(s).
> C. Unload ships at New Westminster, Canada; rail car them cross-country through Canada and/or the U.S. to points within the Region(s) and motor-carrier ship them to the individual dealership(s).
> D. Unload ships at Quebec City, Canada; rail car them to Sharon, Vermont; and motor-carrier ship them to the individual dealership(s).
>
> NMC, as stated in the Dealer Sales & Service Agreement (Para 2), reserves the right to ship by whatever mode of transportation, by whatever route and from whatever point we may select. Please be assured that NMC will employ every means at our disposal to select and employ the fastest and least costly routing and methods of transportation from all of these points, and any others that may become available.
>
> Under the price freeze program, phase 1, we are allowed to pass along the actual transportation costs, dollar for dollar, in the full amount. *However,* NMC recognizes the importance of keeping its DATSUN dealers competitive in the marketplace and is therefore, because of the extreme distances and costs involved in transporting vehicles from one coast to the other, adopting a policy of asking DATSUN dealers to absorb 50% of the excess transportation cost up to a maximum of $100 *over and above* the dealer's usual transportation cost from his normal port of supply. NMC will absorb the other 50% *and* 100% of anything over the $100 maximum. For example, a dealer with a normal transportation rate from port to dealership of $60 would not pay over $160 per vehicle under this strike condition situation. Unbelievably, but nevertheless true, cross-country rail transportation will run as high as $212 per vehicle just to get it from the west coast to a dealer's normal port of entry. In this example NMC will absorb all in excess of $100, or $112.
>
> In cases where the inland freight is less than $200, dealers would absorb 50% of the actual freight. For example, if the freight is $114 the dealer would absorb $57 and NMC $57. Add this $57 to $60 regular for a total to dealer of $117.

To prevent delays in shipments of vehicles, we are also adopting the following temporarily expedient, policies on damaged vehicles:

Ships unloaded in U.S. west coast ports; Ensenada, Mexico; New Westminster and Quebec City, Canada—damaged units of $100 or less will be released directly to dealers. A repair order will be placed in each damaged vehicle's glove compartment showing the dollar amount of the damage.[5]

In short, NMC-USA would share the financial burden of the strike with its dealers. As it turned out, it did not become necessary to resort to transcontinental hauls.

As the dealer network developed, it changed in character as

TABLE 11.1   *Datsun Dealers, Totals*

Year	East	West	Total
1960		47	
1961	66	56	122*
1962	90	54	144*
1963	98	127	225*
1964	190	177	367*
1965	228	195	423*
1966	250	293	543
1967	240	304	544
1968	275	331	606
1969	302	345	647
1970	502	397	899
1971			922
1972			937
1973			948
1974			940
1975			948
1976			989
1977			1028
1978			1061
1979			1081
1980**			1087

*These are estimates only—as we have been unable to locate old records. 1965 figure was furnished by *Automotive News*.

**As of May 5, 1980.

SOURCE: Dealer Development Department, NMC-USA.

well as numbers. The numbers are in Table 11.1, showing a persistent increase in spite of an occasional moratorium on adding new dealers when there was a shortage of cars. The qualitative change is recorded in Figure 11.2. When NMC-USA was formed, no Datsun dealer could be rated as exclusive; they all had to be selling something else besides Datsuns. As time passed and sales increased, it became feasible for more dealers to handle Datsuns exclusively and the number of these grew steadily. By 1972 the exclusive Datsun dealers were in the majority—52 percent. The regional distribution offers some interesting variations. The exclusive Datsun dealers were in the majority in just half the regions, scattered across the country. The Los Angeles and San Francisco Regions were highest, as could have been expected, with 80 and 62 percent exclusive dealers, respectively. On the other hand the lowest ratio, 41 percent, was in the Portland Region, which has also been a strong area for Datsun sales.

Since 1972 the proportion of exclusive Datsun dealers has continued to grow steadily. Nationally the proportion of exclusive Datsun dealers reached a high of 60 percent in 1978, then fell off slightly and in 80 stood at 58 percent. By 1980 ten of the twelve regions had a majority of exclusive Datsun dealers. The fluctuations that appear are readily accounted for by normal changes in the composition of the dealer body; a few dropping out, more new ones being added. The most striking changes are the climb of the Portland and New York Regions from 41 and 43 percent exclusive Datsun dealers in 1972 to 56 and 61.5 percent, respectively, in 1980.

The National Dealer Advisory Board

The excellent dealer relationships that NMC-USA enjoys were founded on person-to-person relationships. When the company was small and the number of dealers was on the order of 200 to

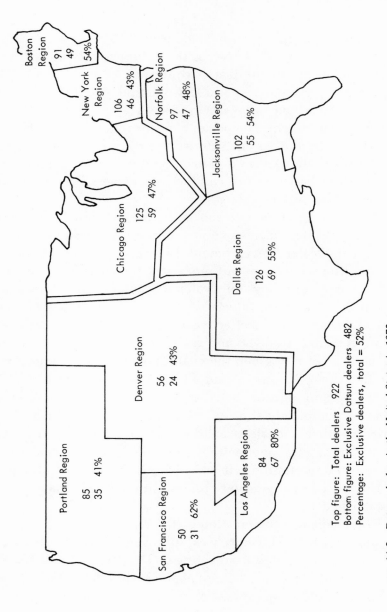

Boston Region
91
49 54%

New York Region
106
46 43%

Norfolk Region
97
47 48%

Jacksonville Region
102
55 54%

Chicago Region
125
59 47%

Dallas Region
126
69 55%

Denver Region
56
24 43%

Portland Region
85
35 41%

San Francisco Region
50
31 62%

Los Angeles Region
84
67 80%

Top figure: Total dealers   922
Bottom figure: Exclusive Datsun dealers   482
Percentage: Exclusive dealers, total = 52%

FIG. 11.2   Datsun dealers in the United States in 1972.

300, there was no need for a formally structured dealer organization; Katayama, Kawazoe, and their Divisional Sales Managers could be in direct touch with all their dealers, and in fact made a point of doing so. We have seen how Mr. K frequently delivered Datsuns to dealers himself as a way of getting to know the dealers. However, as the volume of Datsun sales and the number of Datsun dealers continued to grow, this kind of relationship became less and less practical; eventually the time came when it had to be superseded by a more structured and formal relationship. The personal factor was never totally abandoned; it remained a characteristic of management-dealer relationships in the Datsun organization, but it could no longer be a sufficient basis for the conduct of business between NMC-USA and its dealers.

The coming of change can be definitely identified in 1969, when a business management program was started under the National Dealer Development Manager and a standardized accounting system was put into effect.[6] By that time, also, there were some rumblings of dealer discontent because many of them felt that they interfaced only with their District Sales Managers and had no effective access to the higher echelons of management.[7] It does not really matter whether this was actually so or not; given the characters and management styles of Katayama, Kawazoe, and Link, it is highly unlikely that direct communication between them and the dealers would ever be completely shut off. What did matter was that a sufficient number of dealers saw their relationship to the company in this light. Moreover, with the number of Datsun dealers well over 600 and climbing, it was obvious that a more structured form of company-dealer relationship would have to be established.

The result was the creation of the National Dealer Advisory Board in 1970.[8] The idea was approved by NMC-USA's first Executive Committee at a meeting on December 16 and 17, 1969, in these simple terms: "National and Regional Dealer Advisory Boards should be organized to communicate with dealer councils."[9] The way it was done is lucidly explained by Benjamin A Machinist, National Dealer Organization Manager:

> The National Board consists of 12 dealers. Actually there are 13 because there is the President, also a dealer, who does not have regional responsibility at the time of his office as President. The purpose of the Advisory Board is to have a method of communication, a formal method of communication between the dealer body and ourselves, so that we can resolve any differences of opinion, differences of policy, and so that we can have a method whereby we can receive input/ideas from the dealers. It's a kind of employee suggestion box approach where we open the lines of communication so that they can tell us what is on their mind and we can either answer it and say "we can't change it" or respond to them and get the problem or recommendation off their mind and into our system if we can. That is the essence of it.
>
> As far as the electoral process goes, they are all elected by their fellow dealers. To qualify, they must be a 25% or better owner of a Datsun dealership and active in the Datsun dealership business on a day-to-day operations basis. In other words, if a person is an absentee owner, he cannot be a member of the Advisory Board. If he doesn't have 25% ownership, but is very active in the dealership, maybe even the general manager, we just don't feel he represents the dealer body in that he has no investment of facility and capital. It is a question of being credible among your peers when you are on that Board and if you are not an owner, you lose credibility. Now, we take those dealers that meet those eligibility requirements and they are placed on a ballot by district. If there are 15 or 20 dealers in a district, each dealership is represented unless they don't have anybody qualified; then the dealership is not represented. It is not essential to our system that each individual dealership be represented; other than that, we afford them the opportunity. If they don't meet the criteria, then, of course, they cannot participate. They elect what we call a district Dealer Representative and that District Dealer Representative then automatically becomes a member of the Regional Board.
>
> The Regional Board comes together for a meeting twice a year in preparation for the National Meeting. As I said before, the Regional Board consists of District Dealer Representatives. These gentlemen, and there is basically one from each district, then get together as a Regional Board and elect two officers. They elect a Chairman and a Vice Chairman for the Regional Board. The Chairman automatically becomes a member of the National Board. The Vice Chairman does not; he is an alternate in case the Chairman is sick and cannot attend National Meetings. The Vice Chairman also acts as Secretary of the Regional Board.

When the Regional Chairmen all meet in conclave here at National, that represents our National Board. Now, the National members (The Regional Chairmen) elect one officer each year. They elect a Vice President of the National Board. He, the next year, automatically becomes President.[10]

The first meeting of the National Datsun Dealer Advisory Board was held at the International Hotel in Los Angeles on March 9, 1971. Paul Naylor, of Paul Naylor Motors, Lakeland, Florida, became the first President. The organization has carried out its purpose of giving the Datsun dealers an effective avenue of communication with their company's management, and it has been able to do so because it was set up to be genuinely representative. The National Board meets twice a year. There is an Executive Committee to act at other times and a structure of functional committees for such concerns as product, distribution, parts, service, etc. Other dealer organizations supplement the work of the Advisory Board, such as Parts and Service Clubs for bringing together Parts and Service Managers to compare notes and provide mutual assistance.

Datsun dealers have also been active in the American International Automobile Dealers Association (AIADA) and the National Automobile Dealers Association (NADA). The latter runs study groups and seminars for dealers that Datsun and other import dealers find helpful. NADA also has a program of "20 Groups," which will, for example, take twenty Datsun dealers from across the country for a group session discussing and analyzing each others' operations.

Then the Century Club was established in 1969 to recognize outstanding retail salespersons. The first qualification was to sell at least a hundred units within a year. In 1973, the program was revised to provide for several levels of awards, rising from the basic 100 to 200 and more, with further recognition for maintaining eligibility over specified continuous periods of time, beginning with five years. In that year, 1973, 839 Century Club awards were given. Fifty-two Datsun salespeople sold over 200 cars, 9 over 300, 2 over 400, and 1 reached the astounding figure of over 500 Datsun sales in one year.[11] Altogether, Century Club members sold over 120,000 cars and trucks in 1973, or approximately one-third of Datsun's total sales in the United States.

Marketing and Sales Promotion

While the Sales Department has the primary responsibility for selling Datsuns, it has powerful support in the Marketing and Marketing Services Departments. The former was created in 1971 as part of the reorganization of the company in that year. It now includes Market Planning and Market Research, Product Planning, and Information Systems, all concerned with the compilation and analysis of information and the making of projections based on these compilations and analyses, and all described in earlier chapters. Much of this work is unpublicized, but it is vital to the systematic and orderly planning of the total sales effort of NMC-USA. It should be added that as a byproduct of its activities, the Marketing Department has supplied much of the factual information contained in this book.

Marketing Services was part of Sales until 1979, when it was made a separate department. Its responsibilities are advertising, merchandising, and public relations. Some bits and pieces of NMC-USA's advertising policies have appeared in previous chapters. Good advertising is essential to the success of any business. For Datsun it was especially vital because it was first of all necessary to make the vehicle known to the American public and then to persuade this public to buy it. The record of Datsun sales offers evidence that NMC-USA has done well in its advertising.

When the company started, the Eastern and Western Divisions each had their own advertising agency. For the Eastern Division it was Allen York, whose office was in New York City and who lived part of the time aboard a Chinese junk that he had brought from Hong Kong.[12] The agency for the Western Division was Parker Advertising of Palos Verdes, California. Its position was based on a personal relationship between Katayama and John Parker, the owner of the agency, established when both were just starting out. According to Mr. K, he had approached a large advertising agency and been brushed off as too trivial an account to bother with.[13]

Shortly after that Parker appeared in Katayama's office looking for business and agreed to do some charts that Mr. K wanted for a presentation. That began the business relationship. When Katayama became President of NMC-USA, he dropped York and made Parker the company's advertising agency nationally.

A year later, in 1967, the company instituted a Datsun Dealer Cooperative Advertising Agreement whereby advertising costs were shared between the company and the dealers. With the limited sales volume of that period, an arrangement of this kind was necessary. Datsun dealers needed support if they were to maintain any sort of effective advertising program, and NMC-USA stood to benefit more from good regional and local advertising than from nationwide campaigns. Not that the national scene was ignored. Parker launched the "Drive a Datsun—Then Decide" campaign in 1966, and this theme remained central to Datsun advertising for a number of years. It was appropriate; the most important step in selling Datsuns was to get a prospective customer into one so that he or she could discover the qualities of the car by experience.

The next major program added an incentive: "Drive a Datsun, Plant a Tree." It came in 1972, guaranteeing that for every licensed driver who took a test drive in a Datsun between July 15 and October 15, a tree would be planted in one of seven national forests.[14] The program was developed in cooperation with the United States Forest Service's Cooperative Outdoor Environmental Program. There were eighty-seven commercials on prime-time television, and for the first time national magazine advertisements in *Time, Newsweek,* and *U.S. News & World Report* supported the local retail promotion. There was also national advertising through the *Wall Street Journal,* the *Christian Science Monitor,* and the *National Observer.* The TV commercials featured Ansel Adams, the famous nature photographer, and entertainer Steve Allen. Each individual who took a test drive during the campaign was given an Ansel Adams poster.

"Drive a Datsun, Plant a Tree" was a conspicuous success in attracting nationwide attention, most of it favorable. The program won two awards. It was named "Program of the Year" by the Los Angeles chapter of Marketing Communications Executives International and became one of the eight finalists in the organization's international competition; also, NMC-USA's Advertising Department received the 1973 Arbor Day Award from the National Arbor Day Foundation, an award based on "How effectively the winning nomination has communicated the story of trees to the public."[15]

The adverse reaction came in part from sources that were disturbed because the Forest Service appeared to be encouraging sales of Japanese cars and thereby accentuating the United States' trade deficit with Japan. A congresswoman from Michigan was particularly outspoken about an agency of the government helping to send money out of the country "whatever the benefits to America."[16] Nothing was done because high-level trade negotiations were in progress and it was deemed unwise to risk upsetting them. There were also objections from some environmental groups who disapproved of *any* automobile company, domestic or foreign, being allowed to participate in a conservation program. It seems an odd approach to enlisting support for protection of the environment, but there it was. The "Plant a Tree" campaign did not markedly increase 1972 Datsun sales over 1971, but the publicity it achieved undoubtedly contributed to the great upswing in 1973. Actually, "Plant a Tree" was not really intended to sell cars. It was put on at a time when Datsuns were in short supply and it was meant chiefly to keep the Datsun name favorably before the public—which it did—until the shortage could be remedied.[17]

Two years after "Plant a Tree" came "Drive a Datsun—Help Send a Kid to Y Camp." In this program, which ran from July 1 through August 21, 1974, NMC-USA contributed a dollar to the YMCA campership fund in the name of each person who took a test drive in a Datsun during this period. It was reported to be the most heavily promoted national advertising campaign in Datsun history up to that time, with a $2,400,000 media effort, over $4 million in cooperative dealer advertising, and

$250,000 earmarked for the YMCA in addition to the test-drive dollars.[18] Steve Allen again was the radio and TV spokesperson.

This campaign was not considered as successful as "Plant a Tree." Datsuns were in good supply again, but 1974 was a poor year for motor vehicle sales, so that even imaginative advertising was limited in its effectiveness. There was less reaction of the kind that "Plant a Tree" stimulated. It would have been difficult to object to sending underprivileged children to camp, even if it was being done by a "foreign" company. Probably a more compelling reason was that in the summer of 1974 the American public was in a state of shock over the oil embargo and the continuing reverberations of Watergate.

After 1974, the advertising emphasis shifted for a time to variations on the theme of "Datsun Saves," an obvious and effective response to the rising cost of gasoline. Meanwhile NMC-USA had embarked on a novel promotional scheme aimed specifically at college students. They were a difficult market to reach but an alluring one. As of 1974 the "youth market" (ages twenty to twenty-four), according to the Bureau of the Census, numbered 16.9 million persons, of whom 8 million were students on college campuses.[19] Sixty percent of all college students owned an automobile and 80 percent of them preferred small cars— hence the attraction of this market for Datsun. The approach was made through a company-sponsored magazine, *America. The Datsun Student Travel Guide,* with a million copies to be distributed free over 150 campuses at an estimated annual cost of $600,000.[20] The feature that gave the idea real force was that distribution was to be handled through an organization named Approach 13-30 Corporation, which was managed by young men in their twenties and specialized in service publications for the student market. NMC-USA launched this drive with almost $2 million in national TV and radio advertising, supplemented by about twice that much in the Datsun Dealer Cooperative Advertising Program.

There were other national advertising campaigns on a smaller scale. In 1968, NMC-USA was informed that shipments of cars equipped with automatic transmissions would jump from 250 to

2500 units a month, this because the source of supply had been moved from Borg-Warner's British plant to Muncie, Indiana. Small import cars had seldom had automatic transmission, so Datsun advertising concentrated on the feature that theirs came from Muncie and put on a program based on "The Music Man," with the big scene in the town square of Muncie.[21] Another interesting campaign was Datsun sponsorship of a transcontinental bicycle race in 1976, for which NMC-USA received a Certificate of Appreciation from Bikecentennial for "generous support toward Research, Development, and Promotion of the Trans-American Bicycle Trail." These national campaigns were always coordinated with local dealer-sponsored advertising. Mayfield Marshall defined the relationship in this way when he was National Advertising Manager:

> Our national avertising campaign can go only so far. It can create awareness of Datsun—create interest in our complete product lineup— motivate the customer towards the dealer showroom. But, in the final analysis, it's up to each Datsun dealer to hitchhike on the national advertising with his own individual advertising and promotion so that the potential customer knows just where to go to see the Datsun of his choice. In other words, our national advertising is designed to set the stage for the millions of dollars which will be spent by you individual dealers to bring the customers through your doors.[22]

Revision of Advertising Policy

The advertising arrangement begun by Katayama worked well, judging by the growth in Datsun sales, but that very growth in due time created a need for change. When Mayfield Marshall first took charge of NMC-USA's advertising in 1967 his annual budget was $250,000; his last one was $18 million.[23] A quantitative difference of this order of magnitude becomes a qualitative difference also; in this situation it added up to a sweeping revision of NMC-USA's advertising strategy. Understandably, the reorganization occurred after Mr. Majima replaced Mr. Katayama as President.

The first step was to discontinue the Dealer Cooperative Advertising Program. Vice President Link explained it to the Datsun dealers in these terms:

> This is to advise you of a major change in marketing strategy for Nissan Motor Corp. in U.S.A. Effective October 1, 1975, the Datsun cooperative advertising program will be discontinued and replaced by substantially increased national advertising programs.
>
> We realize that this is a major step for N.M.C. and we want to assure you that this decision was not made lightly. In fact, it follows a substantial period of planning, consideration and discussion. As you know, N.M.C. has been the only major automobile company with a co-op program for the past two years. The co-op program has served N.M.C. and its dealers well for over eight years, and our original objectives have been met.
>
> Co-op was instituted at a time when we had very few dealers and were selling about 30,000 vehicles per year. Sales were limited. Dealers needed the financial assistance to advertise, and, of course, we by no means had the truly "national" success that we now enjoy.
>
> All of this has changed. We just closed July retail with 33,881 units nationally (more in one month than we were selling annually in 1967). You dealers are financially sound. Our sales more closely approximate population concentrations and industry sales.
>
> It is our sincere conviction that national advertising is the most effective and efficient stimulant to our continued mutual growth.
>
> Details of our new plans will be made known to you at the beginning of our new fiscal year (October 1, 1975), and we're sure you will be pleased.
>
> For the time being, I can tell you the following:
>
> - Our policy of dealer involvement and consultation will continue. We will continue with quarterly "dealer group meetings," and will be vitally interested in your local needs and ideas.
> - The Parker Advertising field force will remain to service us locally and to work closely with dealers, Regional Sales Managers and local media.
> - Our National Marketing Services Department will continue to supply you with high quality, retail-oriented advertising and promotional materials. In fact, your Datsun Advertising Planner is being totally redone to make it work even harder for you than ever.[24]

The Cooperative Advertising Program was substantially replaced by Datsun Dealer Advertising Associations. These were voluntary groups of dealers, ranging from two to fifty, who combined to support joint advertising programs in their areas.[25] The associations concentrated mainly on television advertising because of its high cost; radio and newspaper advertising were handled principally by the individual dealers. When the plan started some of the larger dealerships were concerned that as the major contributors they would be helping their smaller associates get a larger share of their local market. However, experience showed that each dealer was getting the same proportional share of a larger pie. Not only was Datsun getting more exposure in the areas where these associations operated, but their advertising had a special local flair and impact.

By the beginning of 1980, there were 66 such associations representing 487 Datsun dealers and about 43 advertising agencies—some agencies handled more than one association.[26] The attitude of the participants was that after their initial hesitation when NMC-USA proposed it, they came to ask, "Why haven't we been doing this all along?" The company's relationship to the Dealer Advertising Associations is advisory only. It does not attempt to tell them how to advertise in their own local markets, because the dealers are in a better position to judge. It sends them information—the Datsun media schedules, prepared materials that can be adapted for local use, radio scripts, research materials from marketing surveys. For instance, the Dealer Advertising Associations are told whether people in their areas are more likely to watch the early or the late news and what the characteristics of Datsun buyers are so that they can select the most suitable media and times for their presentations.

A more far-reaching change followed. NMC-USA's relationship with Parker Advertising had continued through all these years to rest solely on a personal arrangement between Katayama and Parker. There had never been any formal contract, just a verbal agreement that Parker would handle Datsun advertising for a straight 15 percent commission. When Datsun's advertising budget shot up to be many millions of dollars, this was a profitable relationship for Parker Advertising but it was not acceptable to the NMC-USA management that succeeded Katay-ama. The new administration felt that there was too much money involved to continue to go along on this casual basis; it wanted a contract, with payment by fee rather than commis-sion. Negotiations to this end were started, but without satisfac-tory results. Then the company began to consider the advan-tages of switching to one of the big national advertising agencies, which could provide more services, had more media-buying power because it controlled several large accounts rather than just one (NMC-USA was virtually Parker's entire business), and had its own research operations.

The upshot was that in 1977, NMC-USA invoked the advice of a firm of marketing consultants (Canter, Achenbaum and Heekin) and went looking for a new advertising agency. After a ten-week search, the choice fell on the William Esty Company of New York City. Esty proposed the advertising theme, "Nobody Demands More from a Datsun than Datsun. We Are Driven," and was judged to have offered the most promising program for advertising that would be both quality-oriented and would differentiate Datsun more sharply from Toyota.[27].

The "We Are Driven" theme became the thrust of Datsun advertising for 1978, superseding "Datsun Saves." As Vice Pres-ident Kent explained: "We feel Datsun's image of economy is well established. Now it's time to move on and point out the significant quality and engineering features of our lines."[28] "We Are Driven" remained the dominant theme in Datsun advertis-ing until the oil crisis of 1979 swung all automobile advertising to an emphasis on economy and efficiency. Then Datsun came up with "Put Your Money in the Bank, not in the Tank," and "It's a Long Way to Empty," but still echoing "We Are Driven."

Datsun advertising took other forms, some before the agency change. In 1976, NMC-USA was sponsoring broadcasts of National Basketball Association games on CBS-TV and of the home games of the Kansas City Royals baseball team.[29] The lat-ter was part of a plan to develop the middle western market area where Datsun had been weakest,[30] but it could have been an expression of the Japanese enthusiam for baseball as well.

Some time earlier, Kawazoe had given the New York Yankees a Datsun car to bring pitchers from the bullpen and presented a Dalmatian puppy to relief pitcher Sparky Lyle.[31]

After the agency change, Datsun advertising on sports programs expanded greatly. The biggest prize was to become one of the sponsors of *Monday Night Football* games—this unquestionably a result of being represented by a major advertising agency with network "clout."[32] Other sponsorships included the Seattle Seahawks and Tampa Bay Buccaneers (football), Los Angeles Dodgers (baseball), and all the professional athletic teams in New York City except the Yankees.

=12=

PARTS, SERVICE, AND ENGINEERING

Some of the history of the Parts and Service Departments and to some extent of the Engineering Department has appeared in earlier chapters. It has been pointed out that when Nissan, Ltd., decided to enter the U.S. market a careful study was made of the experience of European imports, especially Volkswagen, and this study showed clearly that adequate provision for service and parts was vital to the success of import cars in the United States. When the imports first began to be a visible factor in the American automobile market, domestic competitors were fond of asking, "What if it breaks down in Dubuque?" The answer, the very effective answer that gave VW its long domination of the American import car market, was to make detailed arrangements to ensure that if the car did break down in Dubuque, it would be taken care of promptly and efficiently.

Nissan digested this lesson thoroughly. After the initial showing of Datsun cars, the first company representatives to be sent to the United States—Kawazoe and Zaitsu—were not sent to sell primarily, but to instruct distributors and dealers in the maintenance and repair of Datsun vehicles. This was the beginning of a long process. Datsuns were almost totally unfamiliar to Americans then, so that dealers and their mechanics had to be taught from scratch how to take care of them. With the deficiencies that these first Datsuns on the American market displayed, there was ample opportunity for on-the-job training. The Parts and Service aspect of the NMC-USA operation makes as fascinating a story as the growth in sales, to say nothing of the fact that without what happened in Parts and Service, the growth in sales would have been considerably less.

Parts

When NMC-USA was founded, it had one parts warehouse in Gardena, California, and another in Newark, New Jersey, with a total dimension of 9400 square feet and year-end inventory for 1960 of $43,000.[1] Parts sales for the year had been $75,000. The beginning of an organized Parts Department can be dated from the appointment of Masataka Usami as Kawazoe's assistant for Parts and Service. Usami is an electrical engineer who joined Nissan in 1949, worked in the Overseas Service Department, and arrived in the Eastern Division of NMC-USA in January 1961—early enough to qualify him as a charter member of the organization.[2] He found himself with a very skeletal staff. His first steps were to hire three mechanics and three typists, working for both Parts and Service, and set up an inventory control system. Then he decided that the division needed an experienced Parts Manager and in 1965 brought in Robert K. Scott, who asked for a year to straighten out the Eastern Division's parts system. The Western Division, with Masahiko Zaitsu in a somewhat comparable role to Usami's, went through a similar process, with a trained Parts Manager in Tom Yasumi being appointed in 1963.

In this early period the Parts operation consisted simply of supplying parts to dealers as needed, but even so it could get complicated. The catalogs in those days were fairly elementary, updates were by bulletin, and the flow of information was not as smooth and efficient as it has since become, so that the NMC-USA parts people frequently discovered parts on cars that were not in inventory or listed in their catalogs.[3] When that happened, company policy was to do whatever was needed to satisfy the customer. Scott said,

> Many times Mr. Kawazoe when I first worked for him said, "Spare no expense. Whatever it costs us to get that thing for the customer, whether we have to take it off a car that we are driving or off a car that is down there at the port or fly it in from Tokyo, do it." Well, since the day I first started for the company, no one has ever told me—you can't do that anymore.[4]

With the growth of Datsun sales, the Parts operation expanded correspondingly. By July 1968, NMC-USA's warehouse space was 141,000 square feet, representing expansion at Gardena, a new warehouse in Secaucus to replace the Newark installation, and warehouses in Houston (1964) and Jacksonville (1968).[5] By this time it was obvious that a centrally controlled parts supply system was needed, so Scott went to California to become National Parts Manager in 1968, with Yasumi as Assistant National Parts Manager. A year later, Katayama and Kawazoe concurred in transferring Usami to National Headquarters to supervise a reorganization of both Parts and Service.

When Scott became National Parts Manager, his staff at National Headquarters consisted of himself, Yasumi, and a secretary, all housed in a trailer at the Gardena office. There were another fifty to sixty people employed in the various parts depots. Ten years later, there were more people in Parts than in National Headquarters alone, and just about that many in the Master Parts Depot. Scott and Usami had ambitions for the Parts Department, specifically to make it not only a supply organization but a sales organization in its own right, contributing to the profits of the company. This they achieved. The Parts Department now accounts for a respectable share of the gross profits for NMC-USA.[6] This objective was part of the "Alliance for Progress" between Parts and Service in 1969, mentioned in Chapter 5, Coping with Expansion, 1966 to 1970. It involved a process of upgrading parts requirements for dealerships, insisting on well-balanced inventories and well-trained parts personnel, with adequate and neat-appearing Parts Departments capable of providing courteous, prompt, and efficient service.[7] As part of the process, both the Gardena and Secaucus offices were equipped with EDP systems using IBM 360 computers, not just for parts but for more effective control of all of the company's fast-growing activities.

The Parts Department was also responsible for a time for construction and lease contracts on all NMC-USA facilities, a responsibility that lasted until the creation of the Corporate Services Department (now called National Corporate Administration Department) in 1971. Usami, Scott, and Wylie, the National Service Manager, traveled together examining potential sites for regional offices. They also made the decision that there should be a central Master Parts Depot, because reliance entirely on regional warehouses would have required more total space and a larger staff. The Master Parts Depot was built on Artesia Boulevard in Compton, California, close to the present National Headquarters complex, and opened in 1970.

The Parts warehouses as they existed in mid-1978 are shown in Table 12.1. There has been no major change since then. They are linked by computer and all inventory records are on-line at the Master Parts Depot. About 80 to 85 percent of all Datsun dealers can get any part within 24 hours.[8] If it is not in the regional warehouse, the EDP system immediately searches the Master Parts Depot and if necessary the other regional warehouses. About 80 percent of all parts orders are filled from the regions, the rest from the Master Parts Depot. Air freight is used when the need is urgent and on occasion the Parts Department has chartered planes to ship parts direct from Japan. The Master Parts Depot also carries an estimated lifetime supply of parts for Datsun models that are no longer in production, all the way back to 1960.

The selling structure for Datsun parts is in Figure 12.1, The Parts Department has achieved the goal of being a sales operation in it own right. It has not only filled orders from Datsun dealers, it has encouraged the dealers to build up their own parts sales and it has gone after sales to parts distributors and jobbers. All this took effort and organization. Standards and guidelines were established for Datsun dealers' Parts Departments, and a Parts Manager was required for all except the smallest dealerships. Parts inventories were expected to be maintained at a ninety-day supply of active parts. In addition, the market for import automobile parts has changed dramatically over the years. As the number of import cars on the roads of the United States has increased sharply, so has the need for replacement parts—with this result, as the Parts Department of NMC-USA puts it:

> In the area of import automotive parts the market has become dynamically competitive. Major retailers such as Sears Roebuck & Co., Penneys, and Montgomery Ward have begun selling import auto parts. In addition, numerous auto parts stores that ten years ago sold exclusively

TABLE 12.1   *Nissan Motor Corporation In U.S.A.*
             Master Depot and Regional
             Warehouses

	Square feet
Master Depot	337,800
Regions:	
Boston, Massachusetts	71,146
Chicago, Illinois	76,640
Dallas, Texas	93,150
Denver, Colorado	65,490
Jacksonville, Florida	69,523
Los Angeles, California	200,000
New York (New Jersey)	117,096
Norfolk, Virginia	81,400
Sacramento, California (June 8, 1978)*	151,550
Total	1,263,795

SOURCE: National Parts Department, *Nissan Motor Corp. in U.S.A.*, 1978.
*Sacramento replaces depots in San Francisco and Portland.

domestic auto parts are now selling import auto parts. Nearly everyone is after a share of the import auto parts market.

Along with the rise in sales and competition has come consumer awareness. This is especially true in the automotive import parts industry. More and more consumers are now repairing their own cars. This is particularly true with regards to women. With this increase in consumer awareness comes an increase in over-the-counter sales. More and more parts are being sold to consumers with the intent that they will be self-installed.[9]

To help meet this challenge, the company created a National Parts Training Department on May 21, 1971, for the purpose of further professionalizing company and dealer Parts personnel. This organization has developed elaborate training programs extending through the whole network of Parts activities—Dealership Parts personnel, Regional Parts personnel, National Headquarters Parts personnel. It produces videotapes and manuals and holds a variety of seminars and workshops.[10]

District Parts Sales Managers (DPSM's), for instance, have an intensive seminar in business management, dealer develop-

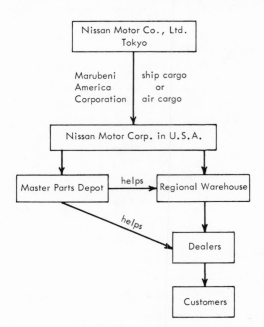

FIG. 12.1 *Parts-selling organization. (Source: Parts Department, NMC-USA.)*

ment, and sales training, designed to enable them to assist Datsun dealers in implementing the company's concept of Parts Departments as profit centers. The DPSM's are expected to spend one day a month with each of their dealers, analyzing their Parts operations, giving advice where needed, and introducing promotional programs. All dealer Parts personnel must attend training programs provided by the National Parts Training Department.

The rapid expansion of the Parts Department was recognized in the 1974 administrative reorganization of NMC-USA by the appointment of a Vice President and General Manager, Parts (Kenjiro Tamaki, who had been Export Parts Sales Manager for Nissan, Ltd.) and the promotion of Scott to be Vice President, Parts. Following this change the Parts Department took further steps to improve its functioning and promote sales: a Microfiche Catalog System; Achievement in Excellence Awards for Regional Parts Departments, DPSM's, and Datsun dealers' Parts Managers; field manuals, and a monthly newsletter for DPSM's.

Parts and accessories go together. In the special situation of NMC-USA, the parts normally come from Japan, even though a number of them are bought in the United States for installation on Datsun assembly lines. The accessories are the extra amenities that can be added at the customer's option after the car has arrived in the United States, before or after purchase. These are predominantly of American manufacture and amount to a substantial volume of business (see Table 12.2). The Parts Department has charge of accessory as well as parts sales.

Service

The Service Department started at the same time and on the same modest level as Parts. It began as very much a "seat-of-the-pants" operation. Most of the people who were selling Datsuns—the used car lots, the service stations, the "supermarkets"—knew little or nothing about the vehicle, and few of them had adequate facilities for service or the mechanical talent

of Ray Lemke. At that period the Service Department consisted
in effect of everyone in the company. We have seen how on
occasion Vice President Kawazoe had to go and repair a Datsun
himself. His assistant Usami had the same experience. He
relates how he became accustomed to being called at any time
of the day or night to answer a customer's complaint. He would
go, frequently with his wife accompanying him, and sometimes
they would end by exchanging cars with the customer.[11]

Jean LaPlant was the first Service Manager in the Western
Division, essentially a stopgap arrangement, and William Renz
in the Eastern, with Zaitsu and Usami supervising and filling in
when they were needed. Their work at the outset consisted
mainly of appointing Service Representatives to visit dealers,
help them with their service problems, try to bring their service
facilities up to acceptable standards, and train their mechanics.
Usami frequently visited dealers himself for this purpose.[12] As
with Parts, Service training programs were established.

In 1964, Leland R. Wylie became Service Manager for the
Western Division. Two years later, Franz Donck replaced Renz
as Service Manager, Eastern Division. Renz went into the office
that Kawazoe had set up to support his work on government
regulations and later joined the Engineering Department of
NMC-USA. Both Wylie and Donck were experienced service

TABLE 12.2 *Purchases of
Parts and
Accessories in
the United States
1973–1979*

Fiscal year (Oct. 1–Sept. 30)	Amount of purchases ($)
1973–74	$18,522
1974–75	13,529
1975–76	23,538
1976–77	26,273
1977–78	38,722
1978–79	34,853

SOURCE: Parts Department, NMC-USA.

men. Wylie's introduction to NMC-USA has already been described. When he decided to stay, his first steps were to get more room and more personnel to handle the backlog (most of it warranty claims) and the work load that he found. Two of those appointees are still working for NMC-USA: Franklin Johnson, Technical Publications Manager, and Mary Dunton, Administrative Secretary to the Director, Corporate Administration. Next he had to add more field staff. Following that was the establishment of Service operations in the regional offices, and there, says Wylie,

> It became quite apparent that we had a two-forked program in existence or demanding attention. One was to develop a Service operation to assist our dealers in becoming more independent and autonomous in their own right as Service operations on a retail basis; and two, we wanted in conjunction with that, to train our Dealer personnel and Dealer Service Managers and so forth in the technicalities involved in servicing a Datsun.[13]

Doing these things took time and hard work, but gradually the desired results were obtained.

There has always been a naturally close relationship between Service and Parts, so that when conditions made a single National Parts Department necessary, it followed that Service had to take the same course. It was, in fact, even more imperative for Service by the late 1960s, not only because the number of Datsun cars on the road was growing rapidly but because Datsun use was spreading geographically. There was a real possibility of a breakdown in Dubuque, so that it was essential for NMC-USA's Service policies and standards to be uniform across the country. The outcome was that Wylie was promoted to National Service Manager in 1969, while Donck became head of the newly created Technical Engineering Department a year later.

This was the year when Usami moved to California to become Assistant to the President and the Service and Parts Departments were launched on a program directed toward increasing their contribution to the profitability of NMC-USA and its dealers as well as to sustain the reputation Datsun vehicles had established for long life and reliability. This reputation, it was accurately stated "has been honestly earned and the people behind the cars are the real heroes of a never ending battle to make sure that there is a part for every need and a well trained mechanic to install those parts and carefully maintain the vehicle."[14]

Continued improvement of this record called for intensification of training programs all the way from the Regional Service Managers to the dealers, improvement in service manuals and bulletins, and better contact with customers and market needs. For this last-named purpose, Service added a Consumer Relations Division, and for the market needs the Technical Engineering Department was created, to be discussed later in this chapter.

These developments were confirmed in the 1971 reorganization, when Usami was promoted to Vice President, Parts, Service, and Technical Engineering and the regions were given a semiautonomous operating status. There was some confusion over this arrangement at first and even some opposition because Regional Service and Parts Managers did not see why they should report in the first instance to the Regional Sales Manager and only after that to their national departments.[15] However, this was a temporary and minor difficulty that cleared itself once the new organization went into operation.

The Service Training Programs have been continuous and constantly expanding. There is simply no point at which any Datsun service person can be said to have completed his training. The accumulating numbers of Datsuns on the roads of the United States produced increased demands on Service and Parts, even more than the rise in annual sales, and there were always new models coming along to be incorporated into the training requirements. Wylie described the problem in this way:

> You have to get out there and teach how many thousand mechanics? Say, 5,000 or 6,000 mechanics, the needs of our new models. That doesn't mean do it a year down the road or two years down the road; that means as close to immediately as you can possibly get it, which is

a huge challenge, which requires the program, number one; and the Regional Service Managers to carry out that program, number two, through the training operations and the District Service Managers. [16]

A comprehensive Service Training Program began in 1968 when Frederick M. Abbott was appointed to organize the programs and develop curricula for them. He is still with NMC-USA as Tool and Equipment Coordinator in the Service Department. As part of the development of Service training facilities, he helped to design NMC-USA's first mobile training unit in 1973, along with Calvin B. Smith, Reprographics Supervisor of the National Service Department.[17] These training units are elaborately equipped vans, including videotape, projection screens, etc., for the Service Training Instructors in the various regions. They have been steadily improved on the basis of input from the Service Training Instructors who use them. The fourth generation of these units came out in 1979. Dick Williams, a Service Training Instructor in the Jacksonville Region, picked up the first one in Los Angeles in September to drive it back to Jacksonville and said of it:

> We're staying out in front of the industry in the area of Service Training. I don't know of anyone else who has a unit or program comparable to ours. To the technicians who work in the dealerships, this van is a sign of professionalism. We are putting forth a big effort to train our dealership technicians to keep them updated on the latest innovations. No one else in the industry is in any closer touch with their technicians than we are. And mobile training is our closest tie-in with the technician in his environment.[18]

The objective of these intensive Service Training Programs is twofold. First and foremost is the maintaining of the Nissan principle that responsibility to the customer continues after the sale, in fact as long as the vehicle continues to run, and this responsibility includes access to prompt and high-quality service. Second came the goal of building up Service as a profit center in its own right for Datsun dealers. The ideal is to have a dealer's Service operations carry all the overhead of the business and yield a profit in addition. As a major step toward this end, NMC-USA introduced its "Much More" Program. It called for reorganizing a dealer's Service personnel into four-man teams, in which the more experienced technicians could help and train the others. Charges are based on the average hourly wage rate of the group. The system gets work done faster and usually at lower prices than the conventional one-job, one-mechanic system.[19] Dealers are left to set their own prices, depending on their local market conditions, but it was expected that this system would let them compete more effectively with the mass merchandisers and the independent repair shops.

Dealer participation in "Much More" is optional. It is obviously practical only for Datsun dealers with at least four Service Technicians, and the Service Department has focused the program on the larger dealerships and the major market areas.

For all Datsun dealers, the Dealer Service Development Department has a group of Service Consultants who are available to analyze dealer Service operations and advise on the directions the dealer should take to improve profitability and efficiency. The nature of their work is well summed up in this statement: "While the work they perform is both complex and demanding, it always comes down to the color of the ink on the bottom line."[20] To be successful, this kind of consultation has to be done in close cooperation with NMC-USA's Regional and District Service Managers.

The Service Department lists its basic programs as:

1. Consumer Relations—handling consumer comments to provide customer satisfaction.

2. Technical Compliance—providing information to and liaison with governmental regulatory agencies; handling modification and recall activities.

3. Dealer Service Development—analysis and consultations toward profit maximization through the "Much More" Program.

4. Service Merchandising and Management Training—providing personnel and management training for dealerships through S.T.A.M.P. (Service Training Applied Management Program).

5. Facilities Design—gives direction and advice to dealers on design of service facilities. A program named Tech Mate enables dealers to buy tools and equipment through the Service Department at discounts.

6. Service Technical Training—regional and mobile training programs for dealership technicians. There are awards for technician incentive through a rigorous program called SCOPE (Service Career Opportunities for Professional Enrichment).

7. Warranty Department—computer processing of warranty and recall claims.

The department's current long-range plans call for:

1. Improving dealer total service capability so as to reach 65 percent of aftermarket penetration and have 45 percent of the dealers in the "Much More" Program.

2. Overall strengthening of Service personnel by further training and formalized education programs.

3. Improved management information on overall Service operations.

4. Raising the consumer comments percent to 5 percent of average sales by more effective utilization of the dealer Customer Relations guidebook, fuller management participation in Customer Relations, and a computerized Customer Relations retrieval system.

5. Improving the Datsun Warranty/Service image by expanding Service point-of-sale, direct-mail, advertising, and merchandising programs.[21]

Engineering

The Engineering Department of NMC-USA began in 1970 as an offshoot of the Service Department, called the Technical Service Department. It had two divisions, Product Support and Emission Control.[22] This step was a product of the growth of Datsun sales, already in six figures and going up rapidly; the greater variety of Datsun models on the U.S. market, which in 1970 took 11 percent of Nissan's total production and 39 percent of its exports; and the increasing complexity of governmental regulations. The tasks of the new organization were to study the technical problems associated with Datsun vehicles in the American market; to ensure that cars, parts, and accessories met all federal, state, and local standards; and to improve the flow of technical information to Nissan Motor Co., Ltd. This last function had to be carried beyond merely providing technical information. NMC-USA was now operating under conditions that required some of the product evaluation to be done in the United States; it could no longer all be done in Japan.[23]

The importance of this activity was recognized in 1971 when the Technical Service Department was separated from the Service Department to become the National Technical Engineering Department, with Franz Donck as Manager reporting to Usami as Vice President, Parts, Service, and Technical Engineering. The new department had five divisions: Technical Research, which took over Product Support and Emission Control; Government Regulations; Technical Communication; Competition (rallies and racing); and Equipment Approval.

Donck left NMC-USA in 1972 and was replaced as National Technical Engineering Manager by Robert J. Whitehead, who held the position until he became National Service Manager in 1975, when Lee Wylie's failing eyesight compelled him to give up active management. During Whitehead's term as head of Technical Engineering the Technical Research division was renamed Technical Operations as a more accurate designation of what it did. Its Quality Control Division has the responsibility of monitoring Datsun products, cars and parts shipped from Japan as well as parts and accessories made in the United States to ensure that they meet the standards required by government authority. Still more important, it sees that cars and parts arrive at the dealers in the condition that Nissan standards require.[24] This is done in part through Port of Entry inspections by a roving mobile unit and by quality checks on the products made in the United States.

After the vehicle is sold the Product Support Group takes

over. It uses information from the field—warranty status reports, analyses of the number and type of parts sold, consumer complaints, and technical reports from the regions—to identify and evaluate problem areas. These problems are turned over to Vehicle Specialists, who are available on call to go into the field to evaluate specific points.

When Technical Research became Technical Operations, the Government Regulations and Equipment Approval Departments were consolidated into a single Legislative Affairs Department. This change was designed to make for tighter control by having the entire area of governmental regulations affecting Datsun products come within the scope of a single organization. Legislative Affairs was transferred to the Service Department in 1975. The Competition Department was moved to Marketing Services a year later, and in 1977 Technical Communications became Technical Publications and went into the Service Department.

These changes represented a clarification of the Engineering Department's functions. Its true role was recognized in 1977, when the redundant "Technical" was dropped from its title. The development of the department's activities from what had initially been a troubleshooting function is graphically described by Richard G. Hoffman, Director of the Engineering Development, in a recent interview for the magazine *Automotive Design and Development*. Hoffman makes the point that because of the size and uniqueness of the U.S. market it became necessary to pay special attention to Nissan products destined for it; therefore, NMC-USA's Engineering Department functions like a satellite organization of the Engineering Department of NMC, Ltd. He states:

> We are following trends in consumer preferences, following trends in changing statutory requirements from the EPA, NHTSA, and ARB and following trends of the competitive manufacturers. Given this information, the Japanese design staff is able to keep our products current in the world market. Naturally our products on a worldwide basis are as similar as possible except where you have a major departure in standards or customer preferences. In that case the U.S. product becomes unique.[25]

He adds that the NMC-USA Engineering Department cooperates in testing Nissan designs intended for the American market because the United States offers a different set of conditions for motor vehicles. The extremes of climate are greater than those in Japan, and driving patterns are markedly different. Because of high traffic density and generally narrow roads, vehicle speeds in Japan average about 30 miles per hour (50 kilometers per hour), and for the most part the Japanese family car is used only on weekends where its American counterpart is most likely to be in service seven days a week. Consequently, the kind of performance the customer expects from his car in each country is likely to differ substantially.

The Technical Engineering Department started with twenty-five employees; the Engineering Department of today has three times that many. It lists its current programs as:

1. Conducting objective engineering evaluations of current and proposed Datsun vehicles, parts, and accessories.
2. Presenting test results and recommendations that will aid in the manufacture and service of current and future vehicles.
3. Conducting a continuous program of research aimed at maintaining improvement of product quality.
4. Continuously evaluating the product from the standpoint of consumer protection (safety, antipollution, and other regulations).
5. Assisting dealer personnel to resolve technical problems involving Datsun vehicles and parts.

The department's long-range goals are:

1. Improving its capability to provide early product information to the factory.
2. Improving its flexibility in responding to changing emphases from the factory and from other NMC-USA departments.
3. Increasing support to other NMC-USA departments, especially Service.

Personnel changes have accompanied the organizational changes, not necessarily in direct relationship but to the extent that few of the men who built Parts, Service, and Engineering for NMC-USA are still active with the company. Usami returned to Nissan, Ltd., in 1976 after a term of service with NMC-USA surpassed only by Katayama and Kawazoe. He was succeeded by Tatsuo Ozaki at that time Parts, Service, and Engineering were again brought together with Ozaki as Vice President and General Manager of all three. Scott, after fifteen years in Parts, became President of DAS in 1980. Wylie, as stated before, was disabled by failing eyesight in 1976, although he remained as a consultant for the company. Of the pioneering appointees, only Yasumi is active. Donck, Whitehead, and Renz left NMC-USA, and Benny Ackermann died on July 7, 1980, after almost twenty years of service to the company.

=13=

TRANSPORTATION AND DISTRIBUTION

The description in the introduction of the movement from factory to customer of the two-millionth Datsun to be sold in the United States gives some idea of the organization required to transport large numbers of Datsun vehicles from Japan to the United States and then to see that they get to where they are supposed to go at the right time and in the condition demanded by Datsun standards. Achieving such an organization was a long evolutionary process, developing as the company grew and Datsun sales increased. There are three distinct but closely related stages in this process. First is the transportation of the vehicles from Japan to the United States. During this stage the cars are officially the property of the importer, the Marubeni America Corporation, and remain so until they have been landed and cleared customs. Second, on arrival the cars are inspected, cleaned, and transit damages are repaired. Third comes the orderly distribution of the vehicles to their assigned

destinations. As NMC-USA's business expanded, this organization of necessity became more complex. In particular, stage two,
the port operations, acquired two additional functions: the truck
assembly previously referred to, and the installation of accessories of various kinds.

This complex process of transportation and distribution is distinctive to the import car segment of the automobile industry.
The U.S. producers have a considerably simpler situation. Their
vehicles are normally shipped direct from assembly plant to
dealer in a single line haul, so that the risk of transit damage is
much reduced and necessary repairs can usually be made at the
dealers'. There is no need for the elaborate structure that an
import company such as NMC-USA has to have in order to get
the right cars into the hands of the right customers.

Transportation

When Datsuns were first imported into the United States and
for some years thereafter, they came over in ordinary ocean
freighters, as part of the cargo at first and usually all of it later,
but always in ships without special facilities for carrying motor
vehicles. It was the only possible way to go under the circumstances. Datsun sales in the United States, and for that matter
Nissan's total motor vehicle exports, were hardly large enough
to justify investment in special provisions for overseas transportation during the first half of the 1960s.

It was not a satisfactory arrangement by Nissan standards.
The incidence of damage to cars from poor stowage, dirty holds,
and carelessness was high. Kawazoe has described some of his
early experiences in this regard:

> Nissan then did not have its own fleet of transports so freighters were
> chartered to bring the cars from Japan. Some of the tramps were noto-
> rious for damages to the cars. Once a long awaited load of sports cars
> arrived in Jacksonville. Fifty of them had to be sent to the repair shop.
> Someone had walked across the hood of all fifty with hob-nailed boots.
> Another time in Baltimore, some 180 cars were wrecked. All the tem-

porary floors in one hold collapsed and the cars just piled up on each
other. The mess was so bad that the longshoremen refused to go down
the hatch to attach steel cables to pull the cars up. I had to send a vol-
unteer from my Service Shop to do the dangerous work. Some of the
tramps leaked so badly through the hatch covers that once more than
200 sedans got soaked in saltwater up to the steering wheel. Some of
them were dirty too. A ship carried fertilizer to Japan and although the
hold was supposed to have been cleaned, the rain soaked through the
hatch, mixed with the fertilizer and poured down on all the cars, leaving discolored streaks all over the paint. All 600 had to be repainted
completely. We had endless fights with the insurance company and the
rate went up sky high.[1]

Many of the tramp steamers that brought Datsun cars to Los
Angeles hauled scrap metal back to Japan. They had subdecking
installed to handle the vehicles, and after unloading the cars
this was knocked down and the holds filled with scrap metal in
small chunks about two inches square.[2] The unhappy result of
this procedure was that the holds were always full of rust.

Conditions at the ports were no more satisfactory, since neither Nissan, Ltd., nor NMC-USA had complete control over the
loading and unloading of their vehicles. In Los Angeles, Datsun
cars would be brought into one of the docks in the Wilmington/
San Pedro area of Los Angeles Harbor, unloaded, and then
trucked some 15 miles to Santa Fe Springs by an organization
called Vehicle Maintenance and Painting (VMP), which was
responsible for cleaning, repairing in-transit damage, and otherwise preparing the vehicles for shipment to Datsun dealers in
the southwest. The extra road haul, of course, was an additional
hazard. There was constant bickering between NMC-USA and
VMP over responsibility for costs, especially the extra charge
for such things as excessive dirt, or alleged excessive dirt, coat-
ings of coal dust, lime dust, copra, and so on, on the cars; irreg-
ularities in shipping schedules that necessitated overtime work;
even questions of recharging batteries and repairing tires.[3]

The growth of Datsun business made it both possible and
necessary to improve the shipping arrangements, and it was
done. The first major step was the organization by Nissan Motor
Company, Ltd., of a transportation subsidiary, Nissan Motor Car

Carrier Company, Ltd., on June 12, 1965, for the purpose of transporting Datsun vehicles smoothly from Japan to North America.[4]

This company operates a fleet of specially designed car-carrying vessels, equipped with ramps so that vehicles can be driven on and off. The first vessel, the Oppama Maru, was built late in 1965; in 1979 the Nissan fleet came to twenty-five such ships. With one or two exceptions these ships are not owned by Nissan Motor Car Carrier Co. They are built and owned by shipping companies such as Mitsui O.S.K. and Showa Shipping Co., Ltd., and operated under long-term, cargo guarantee charter by Nissan Motor Car Carrier Co. The first of these vessels were built as combined automobile/bulk carriers so as to be able to carry backhaul loads on the return trip, but the later ones have been exclusively car carriers. Mounting Datsun sales in the United States and Canada have resulted in the volume of business outpacing the growth of the Nissan fleet (see Figure 13.1) so that it has been necessary to charter car carriers from other

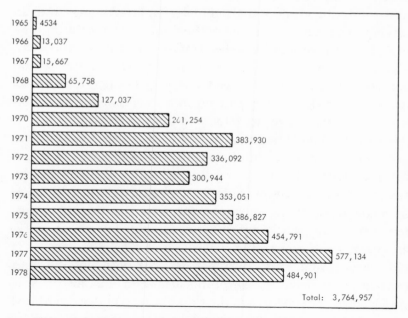

FIG. 13.1 *Annual shipments to North America by Nissan Motor Car Carrier Company, 1965 to 1978. (Source: Nissan Carrier, p. 9.)*

shipping companies. As of June 1979, Nissan Motor Car Carrier Co., was operating as many as fifty-one of these vessels and about three times that number of ships altogether. The earliest of the Nissan car carriers had a capacity of 1900 vehicles; the latest, completed in 1979 and 1980, can transport 5000 Datsuns at a time.

Use of these ships resulted in reduced vehicle damage. In contrast to the "rust-buckets" of earlier years, the Nissan car carriers, as Wylie observed, were so clean you could eat off the decks, and the roll-on/roll-off feature effectively cut down the handling risks in loading and unloading.

Improvement of port facilities accompanied the development of the car carrier fleet. The first, and probably the most important single step, was the opening of Hommoku Wharf in Yokohama in 1967, the first wharf in Asia built exclusively for the purpose of shipping motor vehicles. It covers 330,000 square meters, approximately 3.5 million square feet, on reclaimed land bought from the city of Oppama.[5] The main berth can accommodate two large car-carrying ships simultaneously. There are three storage buildings for finished vehicles, plus workshops for predelivery processing of cars (cleaning, rustproofing) and similarly processing and packaging knock-down (KD) parts. The wharf can handle 100,000 vehicles and 20,000 KD parts sets a month. The parts are shipped by container, in container ships or ordinary freighters. Sometimes the containers are sent on car carriers, but this is unusual. At present Nissan has about 500 employees, all administrative, at Hommoku Wharf, and there are some 1700 others working there for twenty affiliated companies engaged in transport, loading, packaging, and all the other activities required to send thirty shiploads of vehicles and parts to the United States every month.

Like the Nissan car carrier fleet, Hommoku Wharf is no longer big enough. Some shipments have to go from adjoining public wharves in Yokohama. A new and even larger wharf is being built just to the south in Yokosuka, also on reclaimed land.

At the other end of the transpacific voyage, NMC-USA has

steadily improved its port arrangements. Datsuns were initially brought into Los Angeles, Newark, New Jersey, and Houston, and these are still among the Datsun Ports of Entry. As more regional offices were added and business expanded, other ports were added to the list until by 1972 there were nine Datsun Ports of Entry (see Table 13.1). Since then the list of ports has been revised. Portland and Baton Rouge have been dropped and Providence, Rhode Island, added to take care of expanding sales in the Boston Region. This was an especially welcome choice, since Providence had been losing its traditional industries and was eager to have new business locate there.[6] Shipping coming from the south, from the Panama Canal for instance, has a shorter trip to Providence than around Cape Cod to Boston, and Providence is as close to the Datsun regional office in Mansfield, Massachusetts, as is Boston. The San Francisco port operation is now located across the bay in Benicia, certainly a better location for distributing Datsun products through the San Francisco Region. A Datsun first in motor vehicle transportation was the shipment of 308 cars direct from Yokohama to Anchorage, Alaska, in May 1972.[7] It was the first time that any automobile manufacturer had sent cars to Alaska in this way;

TABLE 13.1   *Datsun Ports of Entry, 1972*

Unloading ports:	Los Angeles, California
	San Francisco, California
	Portland, Oregon
	Seattle, Washington
	Houston, Texas
	Baton Rouge, Louisiana
	Jacksonville, Florida
	Newark, New Jersey
	Baltimore, Maryland

Note: Listed are the ports used at that time for receiving automobiles, parts, and printed matter. Ship voyages take fourteen days to the West Coast and forty days to the East Coast.
SOURCE: Distribution Department, NMC-USA.

the usual practice was to barge them in small quantities from Seattle.

The most marked improvement in port operations was to eliminate the unsatisfactory situation in Los Angeles. The relationship with VMP ended in 1968, and NMC-USA made a new warehousing arrangement with an organization named Consolidated Dock and Storage Company in Long Beach.[8] This was strictly an interim operation, because NMC-USA was already involved in the planning for its own port facilities, which produced Distribution and Auto Service, Inc. (DAS). This was a project that NMC-USA undertook jointly with Marubeni and the Towa Warehouse Company, an American subsidiary of Mabuchi Kensetsu, a warehousing company in Japan.[9]

A site for the terminal was found in the port area on 22 acres of Port of Los Angeles land in Wilmington, California, then used by the Sun Lumber Company. The finding was the result of a careful search; Leland Wylie relates how he and his wife gave up a number of Sundays to tramp through weeds and brambles looking at prospective locations and taking pictures— the Service Department still had charge of distribution. DAS reached an agreement with the Port of Los Angeles in mid-1969. The agreement gave DAS a lease on the property, with the port authorities agreeing to move Sun Lumber's material elsewhere and, more important, to keep two berths available for Datsun shipments. This agreement was confirmed by the Los Angeles City Council at the beginning of January 1970. As completed early in 1970, the facility had storage space for 7000 cars, including a 68,000-square-foot warehouse, and a shop for preparing cars for delivery to dealers and repairing damage incurred in transit. A railroad spur, one of the attractions of the site, permits long-distance shipments to go directly from the terminal. The facility has expanded to 111 acres and now receives 10,000 cars a month, as compared to the 3000 originally planned for. Thus the unloading and processing of Datsun vehicles landed at Los Angeles are done in the same compact area, without the intervening 15-mile road haul of the earlier years and under the supervision of a company affiliated with the Nissan organization. The result has been a substantial saving in the time required to send the vehicles on to their destinations and a lesser risk of damage in transit.[10] On October 15, 1978, DAS also took over Datsun port operations in Houston.

The other Datsun Ports of Entry have their own warehousing and port agencies. They operate in the same way as DAS in receiving and processing the vehicles, but they are independent firms, without the structural relationship that DAS has to NMC-USA. The position of the various Ports of Entry in the Datsun transportation system can be judged by the number of Datsun vehicles landed at each in 1978: Los Angeles—83,267; Benicia—39,442; Seattle—90,521; Newark—37,564; Providence—23,331; Baltimore—71,821; Jacksonville—67,090; Houston—29,914.[11]

Distribution

Getting Datsun vehicles safely and efficiently to U.S. ports is the important first step. After that they have to be distributed to the dealers who are going to sell them, in as nearly as possible the right numbers and models; with almost 1100 Datsun dealers located in every part of the United States, this has become an elaborate operation demanding careful planning and accurate execution.

It was different at the beginning. NMC-USA's distribution system started at an elementary level—primitive might be a more accurate description. We know how Katayama drove cars to Datsun dealers himself, as did the company's treasurer, Tadayuki Ide.[12] We have also seen how dealers in the Western Division used to drive to Los Angeles to pick up cars and tow them back, often with hitches improvised by Jean LaPlant. Or, like the Dailys in National City, they would take a carload of drivers to return the cars. Distribution depended very much on what was available, not necessarily what was wanted; sometimes distribution was unexpected. One of the early Datsun dealers was Earl Hughes of Fort Worth, Texas, a garage owner who had a Datsun brought in for repair after an accident. He was so impressed by the car's sturdy construction that he inquired about becoming a dealer. The company responded, some months later, by sending him a truck with eight new Datsuns.

Growth necessarily demanded more system. The organization of DAS was part of the change, and the 1971 reorganization provided for a Department of Import and Distribution, with a Vice President in charge. This at first was Kimio Namba, but he died after a short illness, and for a time Ryunosuki Miyakoda ran this department as well as his own Marketing Department.[13] Then Kazutoshi Hagiwara took over as Vice President, Import and Distribution, and set out to

> ... strengthen the department's operations at the regions and the National Headquarters by reviewing and making the appropriate changes in organization, staffing, policies, and systems and procedures; improving the coordination with the factory and with other NMC-USA departments; lowering distribution and transportation costs; and improving inventory control and service to dealers.[14]

Hagiwara brought Charles P. King from the Chrysler Corporation, where he had been director of marketing for Chrysler Australia, to be National Import and Distribution Manager. King, now Vice President and General Manager, Sales, explained the responsibilities of Import and Distribution in the following way:

> It all starts with the Sales Department telling us what vehicles they need and when and where they want them. Then we order the vehicles three months ahead of delivery; specifying proper model and color mix, and making sure they are scheduled into the necessary ports. We are then responsible for getting the vehicles from the ships to the docks, checking them into our inventory, repairing damage if necessary, and advising the Sales Department of their availability. Then we accept the sales order and ship the cars to the ordering dealers.[15]

He set out to improve his department through better control of inventory and of ordering and forecasting procedures, analysis of the existing distribution pattern, and tighter control over billing. To this end he appointed Gene Quinn, who had been national distribution and purchasing director for Saab, as Distribution and Port Manager and Gary Holland, formerly Los

Angeles regional distribution manager for the Dodge Car and Truck Division of Chrysler, as Import and Administration Manager.

The Introduction has illustrated how the distribution system functions by following one car through it. The process really begins on Hommoku Wharf. Vehicles are assembled there for shipment to the United States according to which of four zones they are going to, and the car carriers normally serve two or three ports on each trip. The zones have differences in the type and styling of the vehicles they want; the northeast, for instance, prefers dark colors on its Datsuns, and California requires a special emission control system.[16] Each vehicle and each parts package carries a sticker designating the regional office it is destined for, and the regional office takes charge of distribution to the individual dealers.

On arrival in the United States the vehicles go through a four-phase operation, illustrated by the DAS activity in Los Angeles:

1. Cars are inspected upon arrival by a DAS representative and an insurance adjuster.

2. Cars are then driven to their storage areas, where they are sorted according to color and model. Damaged vehicles go to the body shop for repair and are then reinspected and returned to inventory. "Damage" includes everything from minor scratches to major injuries—all are repaired.

3. Cars are cleaned in preparation for shipment to dealers.

4. Cars are then taken to the delivery zone for loading aboard auto transporters or railroad rack cars for the longer hauls and are then shipped directly to the dealers in the Los Angeles Region, or the inland regional offices served by the Los Angeles port operation.[17]

On August 21 to 24, 1973, executives of over thirty-five of NMC-USA's major carriers were given recognition at a meeting organized by the company's National Transportation Manager, during a National Transportation Meeting in San Diego.[18] They were hailed as the essential "middle men" in the company-dealer relation. Besides discussions on traffic operations, there were talks by Katayama, Link, and Hagiwara.

This whole operation, from factory to dealer, has to be controlled with the utmost precision. The basic control is through the EDP (Electronic Data Processing) system, but in our computerized world we can easily forget that a computer is only as accurate as the data that is fed into it. Reaching and maintaining the needed degree of precision calls for close cooperation and accurate exchange of information between National Headquarters, regional offices, and dealers. Since 1974, the allocation of vehicles to Datsun dealers has been made by the Equitable Distribution System, which uses carefully worked-out formulas to distribute Datsuns fairly on the basis of available supplies and as nearly as possible in response to dealer requests.

Port Programs

The facilities that were developed at the Ports of Entry for taking care of arriving Datsun vehicles opened up opportunities to add other activities. The first of these, described earlier, was the assembly of truck chassis and beds. DAS began this operation at its Los Angeles port installation in January 1973.[19] Subsequently truck assembly was extended to Seattle and Jacksonville. The cab and chassis are shipped in the regular car carriers, while the truck beds are packed in containers, nine to a container, and sent in container ships. At the beginning DAS was assembling 2000 to 3000 trucks a month; the truck assembly now accounts for the majority of Datsun trucks sold in the United States.

The future of this operation has become somewhat uncertain. As previously noted, the U.S. Customs Bureau changed its policy in the spring of 1980 by ruling that the truck cab and chassis constitutes an unfinished automobile truck and is no longer to be classified as a chassis. This ruling meant that Datsun trucks became subject to the 25 percent Chicken War tariff whether partially assembled in the United States or not, whereas previously the cab and chassis was subject to a 4 percent duty as a chassis. The ruling became effective on August 21, 1980, and since January 1981, Datsun trucks have been shipped completely assembled. Beyond that, when Nissan opens its truck assembly plant in Tennessee, then obviously the import situation for Datsun trucks will be drastically changed.

In the meantime, the port facilities have been found valuable for other purposes. To express it briefly, they have become modification centers. This is an ingenious method of reconciling the difficulty that it is not economical for Nissan, Ltd., to build cars designed and styled exclusively for the tastes of the American consumer, and yet the U.S. market is too important for these consumer preferences to be disregarded. Richard Hoffman, Director of Engineering Development, describes the system: "Many of our models are imported into the country in a

TABLE 13.2   *Distribution of vehicles from planning stage through retail selling.*

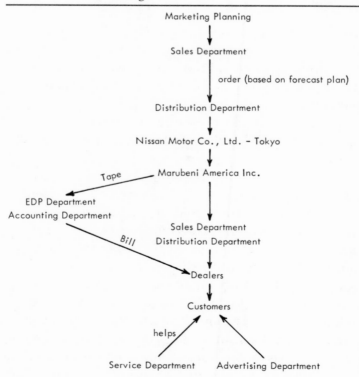

'vanilla' form. They're just a basic car. A lot of the identity is given to the car in the small production line operation at the port where a station wagon may get a roof rack and air conditioner, stereo radio and woodgrain trim on the side. So the car is kind of personalized there and goes into the distribution system to the dealer."[20]

Curtis Bartsch, Product Planning Director, further explains:

> Port installation is basically an extension of the factory. By removing some of the product options from the factory and moving them to our POE's, we are able to better tailor our models to the needs of the U.S. market. For example, by installing a certain number of air conditioner units at the port we can try to insure that cool-climate regions don't receive more air conditioned cars than they have a demand for, while hot-weather regions are asking for more. Port installation allows quick reaction to specific demands of the market. A change in port installation rates can be effected almost immediately. If that change were to be applied in Japan, it would be months before it would be reflected in actual delivery of equipped units, and that could mean lost sales.[21]

In 1979, 12,000 air conditioners were installed on Datsuns at the Ports of Entry—the climate of Japan creates a very limited demand for automobile air conditioners—and the 1980 figure was expected to be double that.[22] Other modifications done at the ports include styling for American tastes, such as adding molding and accent stripes.

These three activites—transportation, distribution, and port programs—have been discussed separately as a matter of convenience, but they should properly be looked at as parts of a highly integrated operation whose objective is to ensure a smooth flow of Datsun vehicles from the assembly plants in Japan to the customers in the United States. The total process is very neatly encapsulated in Table 13.2. It puts Marubeni America, still the legal importer, into the picture but omits the auto and rail carriers, the "middle men." These, of course, are separate business firms, not part of the actual Nissan organization. In any event the flow chart makes the focus point of all the planning and effort unmistakably clear. The arrows all point to the customer.

═14═

RACING, RALLIES, AND
SPORTS CARS

Nissan, both Nissan, Ltd. and NMC-USA, has been committed to racing and rallies for many years. Datsun cars, in fact, began winning races in Japan in 1936. The first appearance in international competition was the highly successful Datsun entry, at Katayama's instigation, in the Round Australia Mobil Gas Trial in 1958; since then Datsuns have achieved distinction in races and rallies all over the world. The company's position on competition is summed up in this simple and straightforward statement: "Automotive manufacturers enter rallies and races for several reasons: to create a strong company image for engineering excellence, to test the new technology developed for rally vehicles and so possibly to incorporate that technology in mass production vehicles, and to provide engineers and mechanics with specialized on-the-job study and training."[1]

There is also an important public relations and advertising element. Automobile racing is a popular sport in the United

States and draws large crowds. Major events such as the Indianapolis 500 attract nationwide attention. There was a brief restriction of racing and rally activities during the oil embargo of 1973 to 1974; otherwise, it has gone on unimpeded. Consequently, the successful racing makes become well known, and this reputation carries over into sales.

The NMC-USA Start

Given the Nissan commitment to competition and Katayama's enthusiasm, it was inevitable that NMC-USA should be involved in racing from its founding, just as given the size of the company in its early years, the racing effort was necessarily small-scale and informal. It began when Jean LaPlant, with Benny Ackermann's assistance, modified an early Datsun sports car, an SPL212 with a 1300cc engine, and won a race with it at the Palm Springs Airport.[2] LaPlant and Ackermann continued to work on racing cars, doing everything themselves. They did their own modifications, took the cars to the track themselves, and raced them without the help of a pit crew. This was done with Katayama's approval and encouragement, but at the same time with a strict injunction that all racing work must be done after hours.

Then as more and better Datsuns arrived on the market, the racing record began to grow. In 1964, Paul Jaremko, who was not only a race driver but also a Datsun dealer in Spokane, Washington, completed fourteen successive victories in a Datsun SPL310 sports car.[3] The record accumulated steadily. Here are a few examples:

- June 19 and 20, 1965—A Datsun SPL310 won the G Production race at the Los Angeles County Fair, Pomona, California, and also outran the Class H Modified cars.
- April 17, 1966—In the SCCA (Sports Car Club of America) National Championships at Vineland, New Jersey, Bob Sharp won the G Production race in a Datsun 1500 sports car and the

F Production race in a Datsun 1600 sports car. Sharp is a Datsun dealer from Wilton, Connecticut, who has been racing Datsuns and winning championships with them since 1964.

• February 10 to 12, 1967—A Datsun Sports Sedan won the Canadian Winter Rally in Toronto, a difficult 1200-mile course covered with snow and ice. Of the 101 cars entered, 59 finished.[4]

Besides the sports cars, the 510 Datsun sedan, suitably modified, compiled an excellent record as a production racing car, and it was a source of great pride to NMC-USA that a 510 was selected as the pace car for the California 500 at the Ontario Motor Speedway in August 1971. Mr. K said of this event:

> The selection of the Datsun 510 as official pace car for Ontario Motor Speedway for the 500 and the other races during the next twelve months is truly a milestone. Naturally, we're proud that the car will be seen by millions of television race fans as well as the thousands of spectators that are going to attend the California 500 and the other Ontario races. To us, this participation in a great sporting event means that auto enthusiasts (as well as the general public) will see Datsun in a completely new light. They are going to recognize that the Datsun 510 is much more than just another small car. They're going to see the Datsun 510 in a position of authority and leadership. This is what a pace car should be on the track, but it is also a position that Datsun has honestly earned after eleven years and countless miles on American highways.
>
> I have said before, and it certainly is worth repeating, that we are participating in Trans Am racing, SCCA amateur sports car racing, and promotions like the California 500 mile race because we're proud of the products we sell. We sincerely hope that all Datsun dealers and all Datsun owners share our pride. Datsun has truly found a home in the U.S. marketplace and now has found another home as part of a truly unique American sporting event.[5]

He also told how at the lunch where this was announced, the driver of the pace car was asked by the press about the ability of the 510 to stay ahead of the race cars and replied that he thought he could hold them off for a lap or two.

Through the 1960s, company involvement in racing was enthusiastic but small-scale. In 1966, NMC-USA awarded $11,-000 to a small group of Datsun racers; a year later, $22,000 to 37 people; and, in 1969, $43,000 to 118 drivers and rally teams.[6] The

rally support was a 1969 innovation. Rallies do not get anywhere near the same attention in the United States, and elsewhere in the world, as races do, but they are in some ways
superior to races as a test of a car's qualities. Datsuns have compiled an impressive record in the major international rally
events. The company support in the United States helped Datsun drivers to move from eleventh to second in the SCCA Manufacturer's Championship, another achievement for the 510.[7]

The Competition Department

By this time, 1969, the company had committed itself to encouraging and supporting Datsun participation in races and rallies
as something much more than an off-hours occupation. In 1967,
Lee Wylie brought Dick Roberts into the company, a mechanical engineer from Colorado with an enthusiasm for automobile
racing. Roberts began racing Datsuns in 1966 when he was
sponsored by a Datsun dealer in Colorado Springs.[8] During this
phase of his career he towed his racer 70,000 miles in one year
to compete in thirty-four race weekends. When he was first
hired by NMC-USA he was classified as a District Service Manager, but the bulk of his work from the outset was in Competition; the Service Department in those days seems to have been
a convenient catchall for otherwise unassigned company activities. Roberts organized a Competition Department, which was
subsequently and more appropriately assigned to Marketing
Services several years later.

It is a small department, six people including the Manager.
One of its principal responsibilities, obviously, is to see that
Datsuns are entered in the important racing and rally events,
but Roberts does not view this as the top priority in NMC-USA's
competition program.

> Our philosophy ... is different than that of any other manufacturer.
> Most of them pump a lot of money into the factory teams but they for-
> get about all the good little guys out there. I'd rather have Datsuns win-
> ning in all parts of the country. I feel we've done a good job whenever

a private individual wins a race, and if he can beat the factory team, then that's even better.[9]

To this end the Competition Department provides support, mainly in the form of information and advice. The department handles over a hundred telephone calls a day on questions of racing car parts, engine modification, and all the innumerable details of adapting stock cars for racing. There are also some financial supports in the form of awards to winning drivers and some contingency funds. As visible results of this help and encouragement, there are more than 800 independent racing and rally teams driving Datsuns in the United States,[10] as well as thousands of other enthusiasts whose involvement in competition consists of weekend meets on local drag strips or rallies pursuing a route through side streets and back roads.

There has been a return on the investment in competition. Enough specialized parts business has been generated to justify creating a Competition Parts Department; sales of such parts totaled $4.5 million in 1978. The Competition Department puts out its own catalog of racing car parts and takes orders for them, but sales are normally expected to go through regular Datsun dealer channels. In an emergency the part will be shipped directly; at times a part ordered from a race track during a morning crisis has been installed and is in service that afternoon.

One interesting feature is that many of these parts are made in the United States. Roberts has explained: "We take a basic car and throw everything away and all we take is the bare body shell and we start from there: roll cage, fuel cells, special suspensions."[11]

The engines are also very highly modified. Making these modifications is exacting hand labor, most of it done by the owner or his crew, and the parts and components that are needed are unlikely to come off a production line; they are custom-made, and one of the Competition Department's jobs is to be able to tell its clients where to get what for their cars.

Promoting competition this vigorously has a direct sales consequence in racing car parts, although these parts are often sold at cost. Besides the Datsun owners actively involved in competition, innumerable others who just like to tinker with their cars turn to the competition parts catalog when they want to put some extra performance into their Datsuns. For one Datsun dealer in 1976, the competition parts business meant four full-time employees doing $15,000 a month in sales; for another, a tripling of overall parts business through sales of performance parts and accessories.

Are Datsun vehicle sales similarly stimulated? The Competition Department believes that they are, although it admits that there are no hard-and-fast figures to show as proof. It can cite demographic studies showing that 44 percent of all car buyers believe that a company that races builds better cars, and that racing appeals to the same group of people that have histori-cally been Datsun purchasers.[12] The same sources contain sev-eral dealer inputs on the subject. One from New York and another from California can be cited:

■ New York—"Nissan's competition support program in the U.S. has a great impact on Datsun's reputation for quality, dura-bility, and dependability and has consequently been a very pos-itive factor in the growth of Datsun sales in this country."

■ California—"The excellent job Datsun has done in racing has been one of the reasons we have been able to sell as many cars, parts, and services as we have. And since no other manufacturer is as active as Datsun in promoting its success, that helps us sell cars."

The New York dealer also pointed out that every time a Datsun won an event there were reports in the media, free advertising of a kind that could not be bought; also, because this reporting came as a news story, it carried greater believability in the eyes of the public.

The Datsun Competition Record

The proof of the pudding, says the proverb, is in the eating. By this criterion the effectiveness of NMC-USA's competition pro-gram has been proved abundantly and repeatedly. Table 14.1

TABLE **14.1** *Major Datsun Championship Record*

C/Production:				*Trans-Am Championship*
John Morton	240-Z	1970		1971, 1972
John Morton	240-Z	1971		
Bob Sharp	240-Z	1972		
Bob Sharp	240-Z	1973		*National Rally Manufacturers Championship*
Walt Maas	260-Z	1974		
Bob Sharp	280-Z	1975		1971, 1972, 1973, 1974, 1975,
Elliott Forbes-Robinson	280-Z	1976		
Logan Blackburn	280-Z	1977		1976, 1977, 1978, 1979, 1980.
Frank Leary	280-Z	1978		
Paul Newman	280-Z	1979		
				PRO Rally Manufacturers Championship
SSA:*				1975, 1976, 1977 (tie), 1978, 1979
D. J. Fazekas		1977		
D. J. Fazekas		1978		
				North American Rally Cup Championship
D/Production:				1977, 1978, 1979
Jack Scolville	SRL2000	1969		
Jim Fitzgerald	SRL2000	1970		
Bob McQueen	SRL2000	1971		*IMSA GTU Manufacturers Championship*
Bob McQueen	SRL2000	1972		
Tom Brennan	SRL2000	1978		1975, 1976, 1979
B/Sedan:				*IMSA Racing Stock Manufacturers*
Bob Sharp	510	1971		*Championship*
Bob Sharp	510	1972		
Dave Frellsen	510	1973		1977
Dave Frellsen	710	1974		
Dave Frellsen	710	1975		
Elliott Forbes-Robinson	610	1976		*IMSA GTU† Drivers Championship*
Dave Frellsen	510	1978		
Bill Coykendall	200-SX	1979		1974, 1975, 1976, 1979
Dave Frellsen	510	1980		
C/Sedan:				*IMSA Racing Stock Drivers Championship*
Don Devendorf	1200	1973		1977, 1980
Don Devendorf	B210	1974		
Don Devendorf	B210	1975		
Damon Pleasant	B210	1976		*SCORE Off-Road Mini Truck*
Dick Davenport	B210	1977		*Manufacturer of the Year*
Dick Davenport	B210	1978		
Dick Davenport	B210	1979		1975, 1976, 1977, 1978
G/Production:				*SCORE Off-Road Sedan*
Joe Hauser	SPL1600	1976		*Manufacturer of the Year*
F/Production:				1979
Bob Sharp	SPL1600	1967		

*Showroom stock.
**International Motor Sports Association.
†Under 2.5 liters.
SOURCE: Competition Department, NMC-USA.

lists the major achievements over a ten-year span. Another summation puts the record in a slightly different perspective: "Datsun racing teams hold 34 Sports Car Club of America (SCCA) national championships—a record no other manufacturer can match. Add International Motor Sports Association (IMSA) titles, SCCA Pro Rally championships and off-road racing titles, and Datsun has won 66 major championships, amounting to more than 4,000 checkered flags during the last dozen years."[13]

These are the first-place finishes. An equally important index of Datsun racing achievement is suggested by Table 14.2. In the American Road Race of Champions at the Road Atlanta race in 1972, Datsuns not only finished first in three of the four events but had four out of the first six places in two of them and five in the third. The same pattern was repeated in 1975, except that

TABLE 14.2   *1972 ARRC Results*

B Sedan (same as 2.5 Trans-Am cars)	
1st—Bob Sharp, Wilton, Conn.	510
2d—Walt Maas, Mountain View, Calif.	510
3d—Jim Fitzgerald, Clemmons, N.C.	510
4th—Carl Fredericks, Redondo Beach, Calif.	BMW
5th—Lothar Stahlberg, Utica, N.Y.	510
6th—Loren St. Lawrence, Salem, Ore.	BMW
C Sedan	
1st—William Fox, Studio City, Calif.	Austin-C
2d—Jim Boffo, Rochester, Pa.	Austin-C
3d—Ed Spreen, Hackensack, N.J.	Austin-C
4th—Jim Hensel, Redwood City, Calif.	1200
C Production	
1st—Bob Sharp, Wilton, Conn.	240-Z
2d—Bob Tullius, Falls Church, Va.	Triumph
3d—Jim Fitzgerald, Clemmons, N.C.	240-Z
4th—Al Holbert, Warrington, Pa.	Porsche
5th—Jim Gammon, Miami, Fla.	240-Z
6th—Ron McFarlin, Los Altos, Calif.	240-Z
D Production	
1st—Robert McQueen, Smyrna, Ga.	2000
2d—B. Fuerstenau, Falls Church, Va.	Triumph
3d—Dan Parkinson, La Canada, Va.	2000
4th—Kirk Allegro, Manhattan Beach, Calif.	2000
5th—Tom Costello, Benton Harbor, Mich.	2000
6th—Don Herman, Mayfield Hts., Ohio	2000

SOURCE: *Datsun News*, February 1973, p. 8.

this time the Datsun B210 swept the C Sedan class, taking the first five places with Don Devendorf, one of the top Datsun racing drivers, well out in front. In B Sedan, a Datsun 710 was first and a 610 second, than an all-Datsun parade from fourth place to eighth. Bob Sharp won C Production in a 280-Z, followed by three others.

A description of Sharp's IMSA GTU car gives a good illustration of what has to be done to make a championship racer out of a production model:

> The engine is the same basic engine found in all Datsun Z cars, but, for racing, the displacement has been reduced to 2450cc to keep it just under the class limit of 2.5 liters. It is fed by three 50 mm Mikuni-Solex carburetors. The compression ratio, which started out at 8.3:1 has been raised to 11.8:1. Horsepower, of course, is also up at 275, compared to the stock version's 150. Top speed of the race car is 150 mph, and that with a 4.11:1 final drive. Although it can't be found in a showroom Z car, Sharp's racing car has a 5-speed racing transmission developed by the factory. The 4-wheel disc brakes were designed by the Datsun Competition Department and are manufactured by Hearst/Airheart.[14]

One achievement recorded in 1974 deserves special mention. A team of NMC-USA employees built up a stock B210 to enter in the I Production class speed trials at the Bonneville Salt Flats in Utah. Most of them raced cars individually, but this was the first combined employee effort to race a Datsun. Their project received company approval and the work was done at the Technical Engineering Center, after hours and on weekends. NMC-USA helped with tools and materials. They had ten weeks to prepare the car for the trials, which were held August 18 to 24. Their efforts were rewarded. The Datsun B210 set a new world record in its class—121.871 miles per hour.[15]

The Datsun racing and rally record has carried on consistently. The national championship victories won in 1979 have two very interesting features. One, in the International Motor Sports Association contests, Mazda (Toyo Kogyo) brought over their top factory driver. He should have been racing for NMC-USA; his name was Katayama. He lost two close races to Don Devendorf in a 280-ZX, the car that in fact dominated the IMSA series. Second, actor Paul Newman, who is an enthusiastic racing driver, made his debut as a professional Datsun race driver in 1979, driving for Bob Sharp in a 280-ZX in IMSA and SCCA competition and in a 200-SX in B Sedan races, where he registered eight successive wins.[16]

A review of the worldwide Nissan-Datsun racing and rally record for 1979 contains a description of the working arrangement between the Competition Department of NMC-USA and Datsun racing and rally teams. It is worth giving some excerpts that tell how they combine for mutual improvement of Datsun performance:

> One of the main Datsun teams involved in developing these competition parts, along with building championship race cars, is the Electramotive team headed by John Knepp and Don Devendorf. Knepp is a long-time Datsun performance specialist whose success goes back to the Datsun 510. Devendorf, the 1979 IMSA GTU champion, has won five SCCA national championships and two IMSA championships in his 12 years as a road racer.
>
> Electramotive's value as a race car developer to work with the competition department was displayed in 1979 when building the Datsun 280ZX race car for the IMSA circuit. Although the 240Z powerplant remained the same, the aerodynamics of the new ZX were completely different from the old 280Z. Working under the direction of the competition department, Devendorf and Knepp designed test equipment to determine an accurate drag coefficient, along with equipment to measure lift or downforce created by various fender flares, spoilers or wings. True tire size specifications were pinpointed using a fifth wheel and speed radar. As a result, correct fender flair shape and rear wing size were determined.
>
> Further ZX development came through the shop of Bob Sharp Racing in conjunction with the competition department. Sharp's Connecticut-based race shop is one of the prime reasons for Datsun's racing success in America. Sharp as a driver was responsible for six national championships plus countless trips to the winner's circle for Datsun. His first victories came in a Datsun 1500 roadster in 1964. These were also the first wins for Datsun racing in the United States.
>
> Today, Sharp, along with team manager Peter Slater and Chief mechanic Gene Crowe, runs one of Datsun's most successful racing programs. Sharp and Crowe took the chassis of the new 280ZX and concentrated their efforts on building a C Production SCCA racer for their driver, motion picture star Paul Newman. The 280ZX won at its first race at Summit Point, West Virginia, before Newman proceeded to win six of the eight races he ran in the car, and then swept to victory in the

national championship event, breaking the Road Atlanta track record that Sharp himself had set.

The Sharp team also prepared a Datsun 200SX for Newman to drive in 1979, giving Newman an even better record, winning all eight of the races he entered and breaking the qualifying and race lap records in each. He finished third in the B Sedan national championships, behind a Datsun 200SX and a Datsun 510.

The 280ZX is the latest race car developed in this fashion, following other national championship-winning cars in the past. They include the Datsun 240, 260, and 280Z, the 210, 510, 610, and 710, the 200SX, 1600 and 2000 sports cars and the King Cab pickup in off-road racing.

The result puts American Datsun racers among the most sophisticated racing sedans in the world. Racing teams across the country are building complicated suspension and engine components with technical help from the competition department of Nissan U.S.A. and sharing their test results so this information can be passed along to other Datsun racers with similar projects. This way, instead of having a few factory-prepared race cars, there are more than 800 superbly prepared active racers—all of whom have the benefit of input from Roberts, his department, Sharp, Devendorf, and the other Datsun teams. The success of the Datsun racing program is supported by the Marketing Services Department in its advertising, public relations, sales promotion and merchandising programs. And, as Vice President Bob Kent quickly points out, "All that sells Datsuns."[17]

It does still more. All the testing of aerodynamic properties and the experiments with suspensions and engine components feed back through the Nissan organization; what is useful in due course appears in the Datsun cars and trucks that people use in their daily lives.

Tests on racing cars contributed to the development of the NAPS-Z engine and to the turbo engine that Nissan introduced in 1981. Improved braking systems and more efficient body designs have also resulted from racing experience.

The Z-Cars

In January 1952, Nissan Motor Co., Ltd., brought out for its domestic market a model named Datsun Sports, the first sports car to be produced in Japan since World War II. It was a little thing, with a 20-horsepower four-cylinder engine and a maximum speed of 43 miles per hour (70 kilometers per hour), but it was the pioneer of a long and increasingly distinguished line of Datsun sports cars. Sports car activity then lagged until the appearance of the S211 in 1959. This model had two important features; it had a fiber-glass body and it paved the way for the SPL212 of 1960, which was the first Datsun sports car designed for mass production.

These cars attracted little attention in the United States, but Nissan persisted, in part under the constant urging of Katayama. The SPL310, introduced in 1961 and the SPL311 of 1965 showed definite improvement in design, especially for sales appeal in the United States. This series reached its peak with the SRL311 of 1967, a 2000-pound vehicle with a 1595cc, 96-horsepower four-cyclinder engine.

By that time it was becoming apparent that customer demand in sports cars favored a combination of racing car performance with the utility and comfort of a personal vehicle.[19] To meet this challenge, Nissan developed the Z series, which has built an enviable reputation both in racing and in popularity as a sports car. It is very appropriate, in fact, that NMC-USA's twentieth anniversary should coincide with the tenth anniversary of the Z line in the United States. The 240-Z made its appearance on the American market in the 1970 model year, proudly presented by President Katayama in these words:

> With the introduction of the Datsun 240-Z, Nissan will have enjoyed the accomplishment of covering the American market from the Pickup to the Personal Sports Car.
>
> We are proud to have been able to cover all purposes of motor car use, and for our Datsun dealer network, the new 240-Z affords an opportunity to create an exciting new image.
>
> 240-Z represents the imaginative spirit of Nissan, and was designed to please a demanding taste that is strictly American. It meets all the requirements of sports minded drivers, fulfilling their desire for superb styling, power, safety and providing them with the most thrilling, and enjoyable ride available in any car.
>
> Our new product reflects the rapid advancement of our company, and its development will be unique in automobile history. We have studied the memorable artistry of European coachmakers and engine

builders and combined our knowledge with Japanese craftsmanship. The result is an exotic, high performance car exclusively for America. It will be the beginning of a new romance for true car lovers who believe that motoring is more than just a commute.

We adopt this new 240-Z as an aggressive innovation in automobile building and take pride in having been totally responsible for its concept.

Nissan offers this spirited car with affection—its heart is Japan and its soul is America.[20]

The company described the car as "a personalized two-passenger fastback. Power from a new 2.4-liter single overhead cam six-cylinder engine produces 150 horsepower and speeds up to 125 miles per hour. Blending race-proven features with contemporary styling and luxurious appointments, the all new 240-Z is Datsun's answer to the high-performance personal car market." The vital statistics of the Z series and other Datsun sports cars are given in Table 14.3.

These claims were fully validated. The 240-Z was an immediate and sensational success. Datsun dealers found themselves with an accumulating backlog of orders so that some buyers had to wait almost a year for delivery. Some customers, indeed, were so eager that they bypassed the waiting period by going into the used car market and paying more for a used 240-Z than they would have had to pay for a new one. The 240-Z was designed for the U.S. sports car market rather than primarily for racing, although its designers must have realized that its efficient power plant and aerodynamic lines made it a natural for the racetrack.

The first 240-Z to reach the United States became a racing car somewhat unintentionally. While it was being displayed in automobile shows, a model who was having her picture taken with it sat on the roof and left a dent in it that took the vehicle off the show circuit and out of the new car market. Bob Sharp bought it and entered it in SCCA C Production class races, where it won several national championships. The record does not tell whether the dent in the roof was ever repaired or if the public relations people elected to employ somewhat more slender models.

TABLE **14.3** *Specifications of Datsun Sports Cars*

Model SPL212:
  Dimensions
    Length: 158.5 in.
    Width: 58.1 in.
    Height: 54.3 in.
    Wheelbase: 87.4 in.
    Tread-front: 46.7 in.
        -rear: 46.3 in.
  Seating capacity: 4 persons
  Engine
    4-cylinder in-line water-cooled
    Bore & stroke 2.875 in. × 2.796 in.
    Displacement (1,189cc) 72.5 cu. in.
    Compression ratio:
    Max hp: 48/4800 rpm
    Max torque 60.7 ft·lb/2400 rpm

Model SP(L)311-U:
  Dimensions
    Length: 155.7 in.
    Width: 58.9 in.
    Height: 52.2 in.
    Wheelbase: 89.8 in.
    Tread-front: 50.2 in.
        -rear: 47.2 in.
  Seating capacity: 2 persons
  Engine
    4-cylinder in-line water-cooled
    Bore & stroke 3.43 in. × 2.63 in.
    Displacement (1,595cc) 97.3 cu. in.
    Compression ratio: 9.0:1
    Max hp: 96/6000 rpm
    Max torque 103.0 ft·lb/4000 rpm

Model 260-Z & 260-Z 2 + 2:
  Dimensions
    Length: 173.2 & 185.4 in.
    Width: 64.2 & 65.0 in.
    Height: 51.0 & 51.2 in.
    Wheelbase: 90.7 & 102.6 in.
    Tread-front: 53.3 & 53.3 in.
        -rear: 53.0 & 53.0 in.
  Seating capacity: 2 & 4 persons
  Engine
    6-cylinder in-line water-cooled
    Bore & stroke 3.27 in. × 3.11 in.
    Displacement (2,565cc) 156.5 cu. in.
    Compression ratio: 8.8:1

Model SP310-U:
  Dimensions
    Length: 155.6 in.
    Width: 58.9 in.
    Height: 50.2 in.
    Wheelbase: 89.8 in.
    Tread-front: 47.8 in.
        -rear: 47.1 in.
  Seating capacity: 3 persons
  Engine
    4-cylinder in-line water-cooled
    Bore & stroke 3.15 in. × 2.91 in.
    Displacement (1,488cc) 90.7 cu. in.
    Compression ratio: 9.0:1
    Max hp: 85/5600 rpm
    Max torque 92 ft·lb/4400 rpm

Model 240-Z Sports:
  Dimensions
    Length: 162.8 in.
    Width: 64.1 in.
    Height: 50.6 in.
    Wheelbase: 90.7 in.
    Tread-front: 53.3 in.
        -rear: 53.0 in.
  Seating capacity: 2 persons
  Engine
    6-cylinder in-line water-cooled
    Bore & stroke 3.26 in. × 2.90 in.
    Displacement (2,393cc) 146 cu. in.
    Compression ratio: 9.0:1
    Max hp: 151/5600 rpm
    Max torque 145.7 ft·lb/4400 rpm

Model 280-Z & 280-Z 2 + 2:
  Dimensions
    Length: 173.2 & 185.4 in.
    Width: 64.2 & 65.0 in.
    Height: 51.0 & 51.2 in.
    Wheelbase: 90.7 & 102.6 in.
    Tread-front: 53.3 & 53.3 in.
        -rear: 53.0 & 53.0 in.
  Seating capacity: 2 & 4 persons
  Engine
    6-cylinder in-line water-cooled
    Bore & stroke 3.39 in. × 3.11 in.
    Displacement (2,753cc) 168 cu. in.
    Compression ratio: 8.3:1

NOTE: Dimensions featured in the specifications charts are based on the United States model.
SOURCE: NMC, Ltd., *280ZX*

The 260-Z replaced the 240-Z in the 1974 model year, differing from its predecessor mainly in having a somewhat larger engine. A year later the 260-Z 2+2 came along, offering a sports car with accommodation for four people instead of just two. It had a longer chassis and a slightly different roof line but otherwise was very similar to the two-seater Z. The 260-Z continued the successful racing tradition of the family, but it had a fairly short life span—effectively the 1974 and 1975 model years. Then it was withdrawn in favor of something still better, the 280-Z and later (1978), the 280-ZX, proudly hailed as "the flagship of the Datsun line."[21] In the 280-ZX, the engine displacement went up to almost 2800cc; more important, electronically controlled fuel injection replaced the twin carburetors of the previous Z models. Nissan, Ltd., presented the car as "a totally new Fairlady Z series" (the name by which the Z-cars are known on the Japanese market) and explained:

> An all-out effort was made to create a mass-produced sporty personal car that would offer superior safety and handling characteristics as well as a combination of luxury, comfort and performance. At the same time, Nissan wanted to come up with a car that fully conforms to today's energy and environmental requirements. The goal was not just to make changes in the existing model, but to incorporate the latest technology and ideas to anticipate and meet future market trends and give the owner a refined sporty car with greater comfort and elegance while retaining the proven high performance of the previous model.[22]

The American publication *Motor Trend* carried its enthusiasm even farther:

> The 280ZX is totally new and probably the most innovative thing to ever come from Nissan steel . . . Nissan designed the ZX to satisfy a number of requirements. The car of the 80's incorporates things that will help the driver to avoid or survive accidents, give him superior braking and visibility and extend to him necessary maneuverability through the car's handling and acceleration capability.
>
> They (Nissan) built this car because they had to: they collected their input from magazines, papers, and what the car maker bigshots got caught saying. They studied the corporate strategy of others and watched the market and the amalgamation of trends, and five years later they are sitting smiling with a car that has everything built in, not merely added on.[23]

Year and Model	U.S.	Canada	Australia	Great Britain	West Germany	France
1970 2 seater	16,215	1,201	319	2		
1971 2 seater	33,684	3,440	894	264		82
1972 2 seater	52,628	4,020	362	549		402
1973 2 seater	45,588	2,537	783	1,114	112	188
1974 2 seater	40,172	1,370	442	129		
2 + 2	9,499	766	599	320	40	74
1975 2 seater	40,216	1,153	198	20	22	1
2 + 2	11,594	329	742	139	372	100
1976 2 seater	45,766	876	385			
2 + 2	13,792	351	1,615	444	417	184
1977 2 seater	54,954	1,005	98	312	1	1
2 + 2	16,065	237	990	513	519	71

FIG. **14.1** *Sales record of Datsun Z series. (Source: NMC, Ltd.,* Datsun 280-ZX, p. 153.)

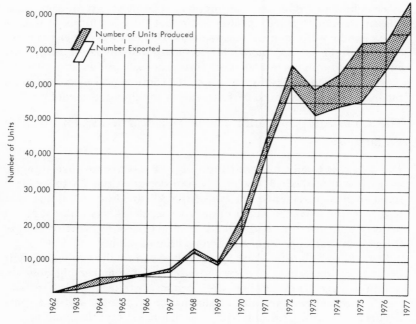

FIG. **14.2** *Export sales, Datsun Z series. (Source: NMC, Ltd.,* Datsun 280-ZX, p. 152.)

The magazine observed that Nissan expected to sell 70 percent of its ZX output in the United States. This was hardly news. The Z series had always been designed predominantly for export and primarily for the American market (see Figures 14.1 and 14.2). As of 1980, at the end of the first ten years of Z-cars, they had sold over half a million units in the United States, making the Z the most popular sports car ever to be offered for sale in this country.

=15=

ADMINISTRATIVE
ORGANIZATION

This chapter is concerned with the multitudinous activities that have to be performed in order to ensure the smooth operation of any organization. They include the management of finance and personnel, government and community relations, and all the variety of administrative services required to care for the physical plant and, to borrow a famous phrase, promote the general welfare of the organization in question. These activities do not show directly in sales statistics or balance sheets. They normally remain unpublicized. They are likely to appear in the limelight only if they are done badly; in that case the effects will be felt through the entire organization.

As with the other aspects of its operations, the development of this kind of administrative organization at NMC-USA has been a process of evolutionary growth. When the company was first organized all these activities, what little there was of them, were carried out directly from the offices of the two Vice Presidents, Katayama and Kawazoe. The one exception was finance, which was supervised by Tadayuki Ide as Controller from 1960 to 1970. Later, when the expansion of the company made a somewhat more structured administrative system desirable, the Service Department became a convenient repository for various housekeeping duties.

By the end of the 1960s, it was evident that Finance and Administration must be included in the sweeping reorganization contemplated for NMC-USA—a reorganization, it must be emphasized, that was designed not merely as a response to present growth but still more as a foundation for planned future expansion. Consequently a department of Finance and Administration was created as part of the 1971 reorganization. This arrangement lasted for five years.

Finance

The Finance Department's area of responsibility is self-explanatory. Its duties are described as:

- Provides the company with a competent staff of accounting personnel for the maintenance of day-to-day accounting functions.
- Institutes controls within the accounting procedures to safeguard company assets.
- Develops a reliable body of historical financial information available for use in planning the company's future, as well as reporting to management and governmental agencies.
- Evaluates economic trends as they relate to the company's financial goals.
- Provides guidance and assistance in profit planning, cost control programs, and cost reduction plans.[1]

This description represents a substantial advance from the days when Tadayuki Ide had as one of his major concerns getting Datsun dealer's notes accepted by the banks. The Bank of Tokyo and the Bank of America were his principal recourses in

California; the latter in fact established a system for providing credit for small dealers, which at that time meant practically all Datsun dealers.[2] In establishing the financial relationship between NMC-USA and its dealers, Ide did what Nissan had done in other matters—carefully studied the Volkswagen system.

While Ide was setting up his financial and accounting system, he, like other NMC-USA executives, periodically took time off to deliver cars to dealers and do other odd jobs for the company. This activity ended for him in 1963, when the growth of Datsun business required his full time for his regular duties. That was the year when the Western Division first showed a profit; the Eastern Division did so three years later. As part of the management of finances, Haskins and Sells became the company's auditors.

From this beginning the Finance Department has grown into a multifaceted organization. The variety of its activities is well described in a special issue of *Datsun Employees Echo* at the time Finance and Administration were made separate departments.[3] Some illustrative excerpts follow:

> The Finance Department is mainly concerned about our future financial strength. By helping departments to establish realistic budgets and by providing top management with analytic information used to establish overall company objectives, our Finance Department can then provide us with the necessary funds that will operate Nissan U.S.A. at a profit.
>
> The company's budget is built around our planned sales projection and expected company expenses for a year. It is a guide to help make things happen as we originally planned. It is a reasonable pre-planned and coordinated course of action in which all departments within Nissan U.S.A. participate in establishing.
>
> Almost as fast as the money is collected (most money is collected and recorded in our bank accounts throughout the country within 24 hours), our bills are paid. Once the bills are paid, the money that is left over is invested on a daily basis in order to keep that money working for us. Invested capital, our savings account so to speak, is used along with money borrowed to purchase vehicles and parts from Japan to sell to our dealers. The borrowed money is obtained at the best interest rates possible from the three largest banks in the world; Bank of America; City Bank; or the Chase Manhattan Bank.

The careful management of money extends to paying taxes, a chore that is no more agreeable for a corporation than it is for an individual. The policy of the NMC-USA Finance Department is to see that taxes are paid on time—not late so that penalties are incurred, but not early either, because then the corporation loses interest on its money.

Corporate Administration

While the Finance Department has its functions explained in its title, Corporate Administration is less definite. Jack Bukaty, formerly head of the department, has described it as, "We're everything that everybody else isn't."[4] To put it more formally, Corporate Administration includes the following responsibilities:

1. Administration of Policy, Systems, and Procedures Management: Provides and assists in policy making and systems and procedures analysis at the request of management.
2. Records Management and Corporate Library: Assists other departments in records management and provides records retention storage. Maintains Corporate Library.
3. Administrative Services: Develops and administers services such as telecommunications, mail, printing, company vehicle management.
4. Procurement: Administers procurement of supplies, equipment, fixed assets, and services for operating departments.
5. Facility Management: Administers construction, purchase, lease, and maintenance of buildings.
6. Insurance: Administers programs for Risk Management.[5]

These functions fell among the miscellaneous duties of the Service Department when the company was small, but here, as elsewhere, growth made a more formal organization necessary. The result was the creation of what was at first called the Corporate Services Department when the Finance and Administration division was formed in 1970 as part of the overall process of company reorganization. At that time the Administration side of the division supervised Personnel, Data Processing, and Corporate Services. Then in 1971 a department entitled National Administrative Operations was organized, its function was to apply to the regional offices the financial and administrative systems that were being adopted in the national office.[6] A year later (1972), the first head of Corporate Services left the company and this department and National Administrative Operations were merged. The combined department was renamed Corporate Administration in 1974.

Corporate Administration's records and information function deserves some special attention. In 1972, it established both a Records Center and a Corporate Library. The Records Center is for more than storage; it is organized to make information promptly available when it is needed. In the middle 1970s, the records storage area contained over 7000 legal-size file boxes, but since then the records have been gradually converted to microfilm. The Library is a general purpose business library with a trained librarian in charge. It has several thousand books and magazines, with an emphasis on the automotive industry and international trade. The department also administers the company's printing operations. A study of these initiated in 1972 produced a report recommending that facilities be improved so that most of the company's printing requirements could be performed in-house.[7] As of 1975, the proportion of in-house printing was 70 percent, including all the company magazines.

The department also has charge of all procurement and purchasing, other than motor vehicles and parts. Add to this list management of the telephone, telex, and mail systems, and of the acquisition and use of company-owned vehicles, and it becomes evident that "everything that everybody else isn't" is a very apt description of Corporate Administration. What it really means was spelled out for NMC-USA personnel in the *Datsun Employees Echo:*

> If you are reading this article at work and are sitting down, you can thank them for the chair you're sitting in. If you're reading this article away from work, you can thank them for the "Echo" itself. They

printed it. While you're in a thanking mood, you might as well thank them for your mail, telephone, and telex service at Nissan, the pens and pencils you write with, the paper you write on, the stapler and tape you use, the company car you drive, and the coffee and tea you drink. In fact, you can thank them for almost everything around you at Nissan, including the building you work in and the ground it sits on, as well as the upkeep on both. This is what Corporate Administration does for you. They are the suppliers of your work tools, the providers of many of the systems you rely on to get your job done, and the maintainers of the facilities where most of us spend eight hours a day, five days a week. In many cases, they are even responsible for providing the food you eat at a company-sponsored party, including the peanuts.[8]

Personnel

The story of the Personnel Department follows the familiar NMC-USA pattern. In the company's early days employee relations consisted of the two Vice Presidents hiring most of the staff personally and everyone in each division knowing everyone else. Old timers in the company still look back at that period with fond recollection but this state of affairs was bound to end, and actually it applied just to the divisional offices. Katayama and Kawazoe could not be everywhere, and in the company's parts depots and warehouses and regional offices as they were added, employee relations took a more conventional course.

During the 1960s some of the parts warehouses were organized by the Teamsters Union and the International Association of Machinists, but labor problems within the company were minor; such negotiations as were necessary were among the miscellaneous responsibilities handled by Reid Briggs and Lee Wylie.

The disputes that bothered NMC-USA were external: longshoremen's, seamen's, or railroad strikes. In other personnel matters, until 1970 each department handled its own, with, as the Employee Relations Department observes, varying degrees of success.

This haphazard system, like so much else, vanished in the reorganization of NMC-USA that ushered in the 1970s. The present Employee Relations Department was established in 1970 as part of Finance and Administration. It was then called the Industrial Relations Department. This Department's history is well told in its own words:

Nissan Motor Corporation in U.S.A. had been operational for 10 years when the personnel function was first organized into a centralized department, in 1970, as a part of Finance and Administration. Prior to the establishment of this department, each department conducted its own personnel activities with varying degrees of success.

A personnel staff was assembled with people recruited to assume responsibility for recruiting, compensation, security and clerical duties. Two major events occurred in mid-1971. In June of that year, a standardized benefit program was established by the Department and then in July, the first formalized approach to compensation at Nissan was put into effect. Prior to that time, there were no formal salary structures or definite administrative policies in the area of compensation. In addition to the wage and salary structure, the department also began establishing formal corporate personnel policies for the first time in the Company's history. In 1973, the NMC Employees' Federal Credit Union was started as an additional benefit for Nissan employees. The Department began to take its current shape in April, 1974, when Ron Cabibi joined Nissan as National Industrial Relations Manager. A few weeks later, Bob Walpole joined the Company to administer our compensation and benefit programs, and during 1974 our employee benefit package was dramatically improved. By the end of 1974, employee benefits included group life, medical and dental insurance, short term disability insurance, maternity benefits and a retirement plan. Long term disability insurance was added to the package a year later.

It was in 1974, when there were about 17 employees in Industrial Relations, that work was begun on "Nissan Today," the first employee handbook in the company's history. This handbook, which included inserts explaining benefits, was completed in 1975 and updated in 1977. "Nissan Today," which provides new employees with strong Company identification, is continually being reviewed to assure that it contains current information for Nissan employees.

In the area of Labor Relations, Nissan U.S.A. experienced its first strike in January, 1975, when union employees in several locations walked off their jobs. The Industrial Relations Department played a dominant role in the negotiations that settled this dispute and helped establish a strong, positive and fair image for Nissan U.S.A. in its labor-management relations program. The communications section of Industrial Relations, which had been responsible for development of the "Nissan Today" handbook, created the Company's first orientation program in October, 1975. "The Beginning," an award winning audio/visual presentation provides new employees with information about the Company's history and benefits, and it was designed to complement the "Nissan Today" handbook.

In March, 1976, a major change was made in retirement benefits. The new plan stated that benefits would be calculated based on total annual earnings of the highest five years of the last 10 years of employment. This marked a significant improvement in the retirement plan offered to Nissan employees.

Consolidation of employee publications also took place during 1976. Two magazines (Employee's Echo and Nissan People) were replaced by a monthly magazine, Datsun Profile. The twice-monthly newsletter (Datsun Dateline) which has been published since 1974 at National, was expanded to cover the regional offices in 1977.

The Department's title was changed in 1977 from Industrial Relations to Employee Relations and Cabibi became Director, Employee Relations. The Manpower Services Department, under Employee Relations, was formed in 1977, and Dave Gaffney was brought aboard as National Manpower Services Manager. Manpower Services coordinates the training, communications, employment and recreation functions of Employee Relations. At the same time, the benefits, compensation and personnel records functions were consolidated.

Employee training, which has been part of Employee Relation's responsibilities since the early 1970's, began to take a more professional posture under Manpower Services. Equal Employment Opportunity compliance training, which had begun on a formal basis in 1976, was updated and continued for all supervisory employees. The major advance in training, however, came with the developments of the STEP (Success Training for Effective Performance) Program in 1977. This management training program was based on direct input from management level employees and it became Nissan's first on-going, credible management training program.

Another program that will have long-range impact on Nissan's future is the Corporate Management Trainee Program developed in 1977. Participants are exposed to all phases of Nissan's operation in preparation for a management career with the Company.

Employee Relation's 1978 contributions include the issuance of the Employee Complaint Procedure, the development of an Employee Suggestion System and a Job Posting Program. These programs are in line with Employee Relations' desire to have all Nissan employees treated fairly and equitably. The future calls for continual review of existing

employee benefits and programs to refine and improve them. The goals
of these programs are to assist in making Nissan U.S.A. a profitable,
growth oriented company, while providing an outstanding work environment for all employees.[9]

Legal

The Legal Department is part of Administration. In the 1960s
the company's legal affairs could be handled by an outside law
firm, with Reid Briggs acting as a part-time general counsel. But
the rapid expansion of NMC-USA in the 1970s along with the
increasingly complex regulatory atmosphere in which the automobile business lived made it necessary for the company to
have its own legal staff. This was done, and Michael A. Cornelius became its head as General Counsel in 1975.

The new organization inherited the antitrust suit discussed in
Chapter 6, but its duties extend far beyond that. It has to handle
questions of dealer sales agreements, product liability, all the
mass of federal and state law and regulations affecting motor
vehicles—in short, all the broad range of law-related matters
that arise in the day-to-day conduct of business. One of Cornelius's first steps was to emphasize what he called "preventive
law"—educating NMC-USA employees in the legal implica-
tions of problem situations that they were liable to encounter
in the normal course of business dealings.[10]

This was effectively accomplished, and then the Legal
Department went on to provide strong professional assistance
to each department and to NMC-USA itself in corporate matters
in such areas as corporate business law, litigation, and product-
related laws. The success of the Legal Department in defending
motor vehicle imports before the International Trade Commission proceedings in 1980 (see Chapter 16, Past to Future) exem-
plifies the unique role it has in coordinating all departments of
NMC-USA and the outside law firms retained by the company
to achieve a common corporate goal.

External Relations

The External Relations Department dates back to the time when Mr. Kawazoe established a separate office in Englewood Cliffs, New Jersey, to handle his growing responsibilities in dealing with the U.S. government. (This office later became the Nissan's Engineering Office of North America.) His principal assistant in this office was Yasuhiko Suzuki. They worked together on this basis until 1975, when Suzuki was transferred to National Headquarters as Assistant to the President, obviously in preparation for Kawazoe's retirement. When that event occurred in 1976, the External Relations Department was formed with Suzuki at its head as Vice President. The department was organized in two divisions: International Trade and Public Affairs and Technical Legislative Affairs.

Suzuki's description of his department's mission is worth quoting:

> Our doing business without knowing what is happening on Capitol Hill is like sailing the ocean in the dark without a compass. Therefore, it is our goal to maintain a high degree of awareness of government and political trends, issues, and legislation; to determine the effect of public and governmental issues in light of dollar costs and management decisions; and to perceive and anticipate the need for action as a result of government administrative legislation or agency action, or political, economic or social changes; and develop corporative measures to cope with them.[11]

The document that contains this statement goes on to explain how the External Relations Department functions:

> In order to carry out their duties, the External Relations Department has established contact and maintains effective communications with governmental departments and agencies important to Nissan; i.e., Department of State, Treasury, Commerce, Transportation, Office of Special Trade Representative (STR), Environmental Protection Agency (EPA) and National Highway Traffic Safety Administration (NHTSA), key congressional members and their staff; congressional committees (i.e., Senate Finance and House Ways and Means Trade Subcommittees); Washington-based members of the press; and industry and trade oriented associations (Motor Vehicle Manufacturers Association,

National Automobile Dealers Association, American International Automobile Dealers Association, and U.S./Japan Trade Council).

However, their contact is not one-way. They provide pertinent data to members of these groups in an effort to present an accurate picture of Nissan sales efforts in the U.S. In addition to these activities, the External Relations Department represents Nissan in the A.I.A. Mr. Suzuki was elected to the position of Second Vice Chairman in October, 1977. In this capacity, he takes a responsible role in A.I.A. decision making.

The Department's goals are to increase its effectiveness through continued and expanded contacts with members of Congress, government departments and agencies, the press, and trade associations. The Department will strive to refine its information gathering and interpreting capabilities to better project future political problems and their solution.

The External Relations Department therefore has two basic responsibilities. One is to collect full and accurate information about activities in government, legislative and administrative, that affect NMC-USA's business. The other is to interpret and transmit this information in a form that will enable the company's management to make intelligent decisions about it.

Community Relations

It has always been a policy of NMC-USA to be a good neighbor. This is a policy that does not fit neatly into an organization chart; it has been expressed in numerous ways throughout the company. For instance, the "Plant a Tree" and "Send a Kid to Camp" advertising campaigns were a contribution to the community. Admittedly their ultimate objective was to sell Datsuns, but that is an indispensable part of the package. If NMC-USA were not selling Datsuns, it would not be making contributions to the community either.

There are other examples of NMC-USA's good-neighbor policy. Beginning with a program for Indians in the southwest in the late 1960s, NMC-USA has periodically offered special training programs for members of minority groups for the purpose of enabling them to become Datsun service technicians. These have been very successful because the graduates are promptly snapped up by Datsun dealers. In 1973 the company sponsored a traffic safety film featuring racing driver Bobby Allison and Jurate Kazichas, a wire service feature writer.[12] They were shown driving a Datsun B210 on California freeways, in the Rocky Mountains, on Interstates, and in New York City. The film was shown on television and prints were given to the American Driver and Traffic Safety Education Association, an affiliate of the National Education Association. In addition, Datsun dealers were encouraged to use the film in their communities.

Another ongoing program was launched in this same year (1973), when the company presented a Datsun 510 Sedan to Cypress College, a community college in southern California. The vehicle was mechanically sound, but it had been salt-damaged on the voyage across the Pacific so that it was deemed "not of acceptable quality to be saleable."[13] It was, however, perfectly suitable as a live model for students in the college's automotive training program. A complete set of tools and a collection of service manuals went with the car. Similarly damaged vehicles have since been given to other educational institutions, although such vehicles have become increasingly rare with the growth of the Nissan car carrier fleet.

One piece of community service has been unpublicized. In 1977, NMC-USA contributed generously to Honeycomb House at Stanford University.[14] This is a building donated to Stanford for use in accommodating distinguished scholars from other countries who are visiting the university. Many of these visitors, especially those from Asia, have special requirements— diet, for example—and Honeycomb House is organized to meet such needs. NMC-USA became one of the important supporters of this establishment, without fanfare and certainly with no visible relationship to selling Datsuns.

These are just samples of NMC-USA's involvement in community and charitable activities. A complete list for any one year would run to several pages. The company contributes generously to a large number of health and welfare organizations; to education—universities, colleges, and schools; to culture and art; to a variety of civic activities; and many other causes not readily categorized. NMC-USA is proud of its substantial support to the Los Angeles Music Center and to Youth for Understanding, an organization that conducts international exchange programs for young people of high school age. Moreover, the company's corporate giving is supplemented by regional offices and Datsun dealers, who have their own programs for the support of charitable and community organizations in their localities.

16

PAST TO FUTURE

An anniversary, it has previously been observed, is a twofold occasion: a time to look back at what has been achieved in the past and to look forward to what may be achieved in the future. Nissan Motor Corporation in U.S.A. completed its twentieth year under very special, indeed unique conditions. In 1980 Japan became, for the time being, the world's leading producer of motor vehicles, after three-quarters of a century in which the United States had so completely dominated the industry that its position must have seemed unassailable. The automobile industry in the United States was in a state of flux, and whatever changes emerged were certain to affect both the domestic and the import firms. For several reasons the anniversary year for NMC-USA was going to be one to be remembered. There was the company's career over the past twenty years to contemplate; there were ample grounds there for celebration. It was also a record year for Datsun sales in the United States, and there was a prospectively exciting but highly unpredictable future to plan for.

Twenty Years of Growth

The story of Datsun growth over the past twenty years has been told. There is no need to repeat the factual record, but some analysis of it may help to clarify the nature of the Datsun achievement.

The first and perhaps the most important point that has to be made is that for most of its existence NMC-USA has had to face unfavorable rather than favorable market conditions. The small-car market in the United States has been growing steadily during these twenty years, but until very recently it has been a minority segment of the total U.S. motor vehicle market, and it was not necessarily a market for import cars. Nissan calculated at the beginning that its most promising prospect in the United States was the market for second cars, and from the time NMC-USA was founded, commentators on the automobile industry kept announcing at frequent intervals that the import car boom had reached its peak and was about to decline.

The oil embargo of 1973 to 1974 gave a boost to small-car sales, but under conditions that gave the imports little advantage over the domestic products. In any event this situation lasted only a few months, and when it ended the majority of American car buyers returned to their big-car habits. It was not until 1979 that consumer preference finally turned away from the gas guzzlers. This appears to be a lasting change and it came upon the domestic automobile manufacturers at a time when they were still unprepared to meet it, so that the imports found themselves temporarily in a favorable market position.

To sum it up, NMC-USA does *not* owe its long-term success to luck or to circumstances especially favorable to the sale of Japanese motor vehicles in the United States. On the contrary, the company had to make its way in face of some severe handicaps. The import car market was and is fiercely competitive. In 1960 it was dominated by European models, with Volkswagen far in the lead. Japanese cars at that time were not well designed for American tastes and driving conditions, and they acquired an undeservedly poor reputation. In Datsun's case this was offset by the manifest sturdy qualities of its pickup truck, but it still took effort and patience to establish a foothold in the American automobile market.

The Datsun had to make its way in the face of competition from European import cars whose names were far better known to the American public—MG, Fiat, Renault, Hillman, and above all Volkswagen. The astonishing feature of Datsun's performance is that in less than ten years it was outselling all the European makes except VW, and within fifteen years it had surpassed that also. What lies behind this achievement?

There is no simple or single answer to this question. Price can be ruled out as secondary. Datsuns have sold competitively with other small cars, domestic and import, but at generally similar price levels, and they have certainly never been pushed as "cheap" cars. Quality has definitely been a factor in Datsun's success. There has been a remarkable transformation in the attitude of the American buying public over these twenty years, from alleging that Japanese cars were made out of melted-down beer cans to a widespread belief that they are better built and more dependable than their American counterparts. For Datsun this particular accomplishment is the product of close cooperation between NMC-USA and the parent company in Japan. The company's policy of "responsible marketing" has also played its part by assuring the buyer of a Datsun prompt and efficient service.

The question of management necessarily comes into the picture. The success of Japanese companies in competing in the U.S. market has attracted a considerable amount of attention to Japanese management and comparison with American management. Japanese management prefers to operate by consensus, whether in arriving at policy decisions on business matters or in dealing with labor. The advantage, according to President Arakawa, is that while this procedure may require more time to reach decisions than in the average American business firm, it tends to produce wholehearted support for the decision once it has been made.[1]

One country's ways of doing things does not transplant readily to another, and NMC-USA is after all an American company doing business in the United States with predominantly American personnel and using American business methods. Naofumi Uchiyama, who had an important role in giving the company its present structure, describes NMC-USA as (italics by author) "one of the top 200 companies in the U.S.A. (sales amount basis)—a novel and progressive type company which has a nationwide business organization and management system *based on typical contemporary American management theories and practices."*[2]

The management structure that he was instrumental in creating has been modified but not drastically changed. Before that, NMC-USA had its two-division arrangement. The rivalry that developed between the Eastern and Western Divisions has tended to obscure the fact that it was a reasonable system for a situation when Datsun sales were heavily concentrated on the Atlantic and Pacific Coasts and were virtually nonexistent in the interior. In any case, the divisions were really not planned in advance. They were inherited from the period when Marubeni on the West Coast and Mitsubishi on the East appointed their own separate distributors. The 1971 reorganization made NMC-USA a single, integrated, national company.

The current management structure could be the organization chart of any number of American businesses, allowing for the fact that NMC-USA is a subsidiary of Nissan Motor Company, Ltd., and its top executives have normally come from Japan. Under these circumstances it could be expected that some evidence of the Japanese managerial style would appear in the way that NMC-USA functions. It does, discernibly but not obtrusively, and largely in intangibles such as interpersonal relationships. One of President Arakawa's goals is to strengthen this influence where it can benefit the company, as in promoting greater coordination and better communication between departments at all levels of management and encouraging consensus in arriving at decisions.

Actually too much can be made of the differences between Japanese and American management; they are not that far apart in either theory or practice. The family atmosphere that is noticeable in NMC-USA was implanted when it was just a small company and it was encouraged by the personal relationships that Katayama and Kawazoe maintained with their staffs. But this situation was neither Japanese nor American. Any small organization is likely to be less structured and formal than a large one, and Mr. K would have been a paternal figure anywhere in the world. On the record, Nissan, Ltd., has chosen well in recommending executives for NMC-USA; it has also had the wisdom to understand that a company organized and doing business in the United States would be well advised to operate by American methods, with some qualifications. It is particularly noticeable in the organization structure that Sales, the area where NMC-USA is most directly in contact with the American public, is staffed by American executives, and this has been the situation since Ray Hoen became National Sales Manager in 1965. There is always room for improvement in any organization, but it can be honestly claimed for NMC-USA that in its twenty years of existence it has successfully combined the best features of both American and Japanese management practices.

The key element is NMC-USA's story, however, has been neither organizational structure nor managerial technique but people. When the company was founded just about 3000 Datsuns had been sold in the entire United States, including Hawaii, which has a separate distributorship. When the twentieth anniversary year began this total had risen to 3.5 million; it would pass 4 million by the time the year ended. Certainly it takes efficient organization and sound methods to achieve this kind of success, but it takes something more. The best organization chart in the world can do nothing by itself; it needs the right people to give it life and accomplish the ends the organization aims for. NMC-USA has been well served in this respect. In its early years it was able to find dedicated people who were willing to accept the risk of joining a company whose prospects were at best uncertain and who possessed the talent to give Datsun a secure place in the U.S. import car market. Later, when it had risen to be one of the country's leaders in the import car field, NMC-USA's staff—including a number of the people who had helped to build the organization—had the ability and the continuing dedication to keep the company growing in the face of constantly fiercer competition from domestic and import automobile firms alike. None of the Datsun growth was inevitable or happened automatically. It was all the result of accurate foresight, careful planning, and above all unremitting effort.

A Changing Automobile Market

It was not planned that Nissan Motor Corporation in U.S.A. should celebrate its twentieth birthday at a watershed point in the history of the motor vehicle industry in the United States. That was just happenstance, but nevertheless it made the anniversary an unusually crucial occasion in the life of the company, because the situation called for skillful and careful planning of the company's future course. NMC-USA was not alone in this respect. Every motor vehicle company that was concerned with selling its products in the United States—for practical purposes the entire world automotive industry—was facing the same situation. Actually the automotive crisis that began in 1979 was worldwide in scope, but the giant American motor vehicle industry was at its center. It had been hard hit by the combination of the sudden shift of customer preference to small cars and the onset of the 1980 recession, so that even General Motors had a deficit in 1980, its first in almost sixty years.[3] The industry would recover; that has never been seriously in question. However, this time the recovery will not be simply a return to "business as usual," as has been the pattern for previous recessions. The most obvious change will be that the average size of U.S.-built automobiles will be markedly smaller than it has been for the past thirty years. Some large passenger automobiles will continue to be built and used because there will be a demand for them from people who can afford them or require them for some special reason, but they are extremely unlikely to dominate the American market again.

These problems had been anticipated. American automobile manufacturers were working on reducing car weights and dimensions, partly because of the need to meet CAFE requirements. A study by General Motors in 1977 even forecast that the Japanese automobile industry would be competing with the American for world leadership in the 1980s.[4] To repeat what was said in Chapter 10, what Detroit did not anticipate, and could hardly be expected to have anticipated, was that the motor vehicle market would make a radical change of course almost overnight. It is easy to point to mistakes in product planning, but since it takes a minimum of four years for a new model to go from concept to dealer's showroom, it is difficult not to be mistaken when consumer preferences shift drastically in about four weeks. Unlike the 1973 to 1974 oil crisis, the 1979 one, which was actually less acute, seems to have convinced the American public that the world oil supply is in fact limited. The emphasis on fuel economy is not only a response to rising prices but also to concern about supply. Motorists do not want long waits at the service stations and possibly empty pumps again. This may be an even stronger contributor than price to reducing gasoline consumption by about 1.6 percent since early 1979.[5] To put it another way, "It's a Long Way to Empty," the ability to go long distances without having to stop for gas, is more important to motorists than the cost of filling the tank.

As a result of plans now in progress, the average weight of American passenger cars will be less than 3000 pounds by the latter half of the 1980s, 600 pounds less than in 1979, and about half a ton less than in 1969[6]—evidence that "downsizing" was on the way before the 1979 crisis struck. By the same time, as many as half the passenger automobiles made in the United States may be powered by four-cylinder engines, as compared with less than a fifth in 1979; certainly a radical transformation since 1970, when almost 90 percent of all American-built passenger cars had V-8 engines. These forecasts are naturally contingent on a reasonable degree of political and economic stability. A change in the world situation that cut off or even severely restricted Middle Eastern oil supplies or a major economic depression would drastically affect the world automotive scene. So, too, would a dramatic technological breakthrough that produced a radically different automotive powerplant—a solution to the limitations of the electric car, for instance—or a new and plentiful source of automotive fuel. All that can be said is that no such breakthrough is immediately in sight.

This transition involves far more than the restyling and redesigning of American passenger automobiles. It may well produce major readjustments in the structure of the U.S. automobile industry and from that to the world automobile industry (excluding the Communist countries, where the industry is entirely state owned and operated and has not so far been a significant element in the world market for motor vehicles). The changes that the U.S. firms are making demand enormous investment in plant, equipment, and tooling. The models that come from them will have to sell in large quantities to justify the cost—very large quantities because the unit profit is less as the size of the car declines, and profit is essential if a company is to stay in business, even for a state-owned organization.[7] Since this process will work out more successfully for some of the domestic producers than for others, it is likely to result in a restructuring of the American motor vehicle industry, although it is not possible to predict just what will emerge.

Whatever changes do occur will necessarily affect the rest of the world's automotive industry. The size of the American firms and their extensive international operations would be enough to ensure that, and there is a new factor in the situation. In the past the United States has pretty well monopolized the production of large-size passenger automobiles while the Europeans and the Japanese have emphasized medium-size and small cars. Within a matter of just two or three years all the world's major motor vehicle producers will be competing with the same basic type of passenger automobile—small, lightweight, fuel-efficient. This is a field in which the enormous productive capacity of the American automobile industry has never been fully employed until now. The consequences of this shift cannot be forecast, but they will certainly be far-reaching. For example,

European motor vehicle manufacturers (BL, Peugeot, Mercedes-Benz) who had a profitable market in medium-size passenger cars have also been affected by a customer shift to smaller vehicles; as they face readjustment they look with alarm at the prospect of a revived Detroit challenging them with small cars not only in the United States but in their own home markets as well.[8] So the world automotive industry is at present in the anomalous situation that while deep concern is being expressed in the United States about the adverse effect of imports on the domestic automobile industry, the makers of those imports are bracing themselves for the competition they see coming from a torrent of small, fuel-efficient passenger automobiles produced by the still-dominant giant American firms.

One very probable consequence of this intensified competition is that there will be an increasing concentration of motor vehicle manufacturing in a few very large companies, all worldwide in their operations. Some small, specialized producers with limited markets may survive (Mercedes-Benz, Rolls-Royce), but otherwise the smaller competitors will be absorbed or vanish, as has conspicuously happened already in the United States. This will not happen overnight, but it is a fair guess that by the end of the century there will be not more than ten or twelve motor vehicle manufacturers in the entire free world, all operating on an international scale.

This view is supported by Gerald C. Meyers, chairman of American Motors, who predicts, "The 30 or so independent manufacturers in the world today will narrow to about a dozen by the end of the century. That dozen will be transnational in scope and will compete all over the world, with North America, Europe, and Japan simply being parts of one whole."[9] The head of Fiat, Giovanni Agnelli, is less sanguine. He lists only six sure survivors—his own company, General Motors, Ford, Nissan, Toyota, and Peugeot[10]—although Renault (including American Motors) would seem a likely prospect also. Some allowance has to be made for probable governmental intervention, since the automotive industry represents so great a share of the economy of the industrial world. It has been estimated that if British Leyland went out of business, "major cities such as Birmingham and Coventry would be turned into industrial deserts, regional unemployment could reach 30 percent, and the swing against the United Kingdom's balance of payments could reach $7 billion."[11] The collapse of Chrysler would be equally devastating for the United States, so it can be taken for granted that the large firms at least will be propped up—although the author of the article just cited also makes the point that government support is no substitute for good management.

The automotive industry has always been internationally minded, but now the process is going well beyond a national company selling in the world market or even having affiliates and subsidiaries in other countries. The manufacturing process will be internationalized too. When the motor vehicle of the future is labeled "Made in U.S.A." or "Made in Japan," that will simply identify the country of final assembly; parts and components will be drawn from all over the world.

This estimate is supported from a knowledgeable source, appraising 1980 trends in the U.S. import car business:

> A gray area of cars and trucks that defies description was emerging. Instead of "imports" and "domestics," cars were becoming either mainly-domestic-content, U.S.-built "world" cars; less-domestic-content, U.S.-built "imports" such as Volkswagen; or still less-domestic-content, U.S.-built projects such as that of Renault-AMC, and so on.
>
> One major unresolved question was whether the U.S. Congress would respond to growing demands for protection of the U.S. industry, either through local content laws or quotas. If the Japanese reacted by establishing U.S. assembly plants in significant numbers, the pure import car could become virtually extinct in the U.S., joining that other endangered species—the purely domestic car.[12]

These changes will not occur tomorrow, but the trend is visibly developing. Renault has an interest in Volvo as well as in American Motors. Chrysler remains associated with Peugeot, now Europe's largest car manufacturer by virtue of its acquisition of Citroen and Talbot (Chrysler's European operations renamed), and with Mitsubishi, which makes engines for the K-cars. British Leyland will build Hondas in Britain under license.[13] Toyo Kogyo makes transaxles for Ford, which is also negotiating with Toyota for joint production in the United States. Nissan is a participant in this process. Besides assembly plants in Australia and Mexico and the truck assembly plant projected for the United States, it has a 35 percent interest in the Spanish truck manufacturer Motor Iberica and has just concluded an agreement with Alfa Romeo to build an assembly plant for joint production in Italy. This plant, near Naples, has a planned capacity of 60,000 cars a year.[14] Nissan is to provide the basic design and body panels and suspensions; Alfa Romeo will supply engines and transmissions, and related components. As 1980 came to an end, negotiations were in progress between Nissan and Volkswagen for a possible arrangement whereby Nissan would manufacture and sell VW's in Japan.

The Datsun Prospect

Nissan Motor Corporation in U.S.A. now enters its second twenty years. No one can say now just what they will be like; the one thing that appears certain is that they will be quite different from the first twenty. The company's progress since 1960 can be divided into two very broad stages, each just about ten years long. The first was the highly crucial business of getting Datsun established in the U.S. motor vehicle market. This was accomplished very successfully, so that in its second decade NMC-USA found itself dealing with the problems attendant on rapid growth to the position of the second-largest importer of motor vehicles in the United States—a gratifying position to reach but not necessarily an easy one to hold.

What the next stage will turn out to be remains to be seen. NMC-USA would of course like to see Datsun become number 1 among import cars. It has happened before, and it could happen again; the two leaders are very close in sales totals. However, for the immediate future it appears highly likely that Datsun and Toyota will have more pressing issues to contend with than even their long-standing rivalry with each other. The Nissan organization, both worldwide and in the United States, has to face the changes in the automotive industry that have just been described, and while Nissan is in the forefront of the industry in terms of production techniques and vehicle design, it will still require first-class management to maintain its position in the predicted "volatile and uncertain marketplace" of the 1980s and thereafter.[15] Indeed, the challenge that faces NMC-USA as it looks ahead in 1980 is every bit as great as the challenge it faced twenty years ago when it set out to win a place for the Datsun in the U.S. automotive market.

For a start, it is quite obvious that the spectacular growth in Datsun sales, for that matter all Japanese car sales, that occurred in the United States during the 1970s is not going to be repeated. There may be further gains to be made, but the Japanese automobile companies will be far more deeply concerned with retaining the position they have already attained. The conditions facing them have changed drastically. In the import car market ten years ago, Nissan and Toyota were just beginning to challenge the long Volkswagen domination of the U.S. import car market. They succeeded in dislodging the VW from first place, but in the meantime found new competitors in other Japanese firms.

Now Volkswagen is competing in the small-car market as a domestic product, with Volkswagen of America, Inc., a member of the Motor Vehicle Manufacturers Association. A similar situation could well be in prospect for Renault through its tie-in with American Motors. Thus as NMC-USA goes into the 1980s it can expect continued stiff competition in the small-car market from its accustomed rivals among the import firms—probably stiffer than in the past, because the competition is now made up of the firms that were strong enough to survive a rigorous weeding-out process.

However, this is the lesser of the challenges looming up for NMC-USA. The bigger one—much bigger—is the appearance of the American Big Three in the small-car market on a scale and with an intensity far beyond anything they have done before. Until 1979 small cars were basically peripheral for the Big Three; the larger models were the money makers. But now these larger models have become peripheral; they have become unprofitable because they simply do not sell. The future of the Big Three, as far as it is possible to foresee the future, lies in making and selling smaller vehicles, and this they are doing to the utmost of their capacity. The changeover is a painful process because it requires enormous outlays of capital; outlays must be made in a period of inflationary recession, when motor vehicle sales are down, so that the investment cannot be fully internally financed, and the cost of capital is abnormally high. Yet the changeover is being made; and, when it is completed, NMC-USA and the other import car companies will be facing a challenge in the small-car market on a scale that they have not previously encountered.

The long-range prospect for Nissan therefore is that the passenger automobile market will be primarily one for small, fuel-efficient cars; although Nissan has established a worldwide reputation for manufacturing small cars of high quality, it will encounter more rather than less difficult competitive conditions. This is not necessarily a discouraging outlook. Nissan is used to competition; certainly in the United States there has never been a time when NMC-USA could afford to be complacent about its position. It seems safe to predict that Datsuns will continue to hold a respectable share of the U.S. motor vehicle market, but impossible to forecast just what that share will be. Given the current condition of the motor vehicle industry, there is no way to tell what anyone's share of the market is going to be.

For the short run, NMC-USA has had to be concerned with possible restrictions on motor vehicle imports. The risk that the problem might come to a head during the company's anniversary year was removed by a ruling of the International Trade Commission (ITC) on November 10, 1980. By a majority vote the Commission rejected petitions from the Ford Motor Company and the United Automobile Workers asking for protection from automobile imports from Japan and elsewhere, and it unanimously refused requests for restrictions on imports of light trucks.[16] The Commission ruled that imports were not the major cause of the U.S. automobile industry's current difficulties, so that restrictions are not justified. If the ITC had found that imports were the cause of injury to the domestic industry, the President of the United States could have accepted or rejected the findings; if he had accepted, he could have chosen what action to take. Where there is no finding of injury caused by imports, then there is nothing for the President to act on. The case is not necessarily closed, because it is always possible for Congress to intervene.

The reaction to the Commission's ruling was understandably mixed. Spokesmen for the domestic automobile industry and the UAW expressed disappointment; spokesmen for the import car business were gratified. In Japan, the Minister of International Trade and Industry welcomed the decision but added that his government would urge prudence on exports to the United States by Japanese automobile manufacturers.[17] In fact there was a distinct atmosphere of reserve about the comments, pro or con. None of the parties involved were quite sure what would happen next or what was the best way to proceed.

When the newly elected Congress met in 1981, a measure was introduced seeking to reduce Japanese car imports by twenty percent for three years. However, early in May, 1981, the Japanese government announced a unilateral policy whereby passenger car exports to the United States would be cut by seven to eight percent for the first year of a two-year period, beginning April 1, 1981. The figure for the second year is to be determined by the state of the American passenger car market. The program may be extended for a third year. The limitation does not apply to pickup trucks or special purpose vehicles. The policy is administered by the Japanese Ministry of International Trade and Industry. It is understood that this arrangement does not create problems with the United States antitrust laws.

As with the ITC ruling, this agreement met with mixed responses. Spokesmen on both sides of the Pacific greeted it with a noticeable absence of enthusiasm. There were complaints in the United States that it did not go far enough, and on the other hand objections that the restriction of Japanese imports would reduce the number of low-priced, fuel efficient cars available to American consumers. However, action on the bill before Congress, which the Reagan administration did not want, was suspended and the Japanese announcement averted a conflict on trade policies between two countries who needed each other's goodwill and support in a number of areas possibly even more important than the sales of an indeterminate but finite number of passenger automobiles.

Mention should be made here of the strong backing that the Datsun dealer group gave in the presentation before the ITC. The dealers would naturally support the company's position on import restrictions because they had much at stake too, but the degree of support exceeded expectations. In 1979 and 1980 Datsun dealer membership in the AIADA more than doubled; the AIADA was the body that officially presented the dealers' position to Congress and the ITC. In addition, Datsun dealers campaigned on their own by seeing to it that the case against protectionism was adequately presented to the people of their communities through local news media and otherwise, and as individuals they communicated their views to their congressmen and to the relevant executive agencies.

There are some very critical issues and some highly emotional factors involved in this controversy, with the risk that the latter may becloud the former. A realistic appraisal of several important aspects of the problem comes from Robert B. Reich, director of the Federal Trade Commission's Office of Policy Planning. After enumerating a list of products, including motor vehicles, in which American consumers seem to turn increasingly to imports, he writes:

> Why are we losing this battle? Some lay blame on cheap foreign labor, or on "dumping" at prices below those prevailing in home markets. But foreign wage rates are rapidly catching up with our own; Japan's labor costs are now on a par with ours. And many of these imports sell here at prices comparable to or above those of American-made counterparts. By the mid-1970's Japanese and West German autos had lost any price advantage over their American-made competitors.
>
> Some say regulation is to blame. But imports must meet the same standards as American products in order to be sold here. And in any event health, safety, and environmental regulation is as strict in Japan and Western Europe as it is in the United States, if not stricter.[18]

There is even some evidence that reduction of Japanese imports might occur through normal market forces without any need for governmental intervention. The market share of Japanese automobiles in the United States reached a peak of 26 percent in July 1980, and then declined to 21 percent in October, the last full month before the ITC decision.[19] Part of the decline was due to price increases for Japanese cars made necessary by a 15 percent rise of the yen against the U.S. dollar in the second half of 1980. The rest was a combination of recession conditions and the attraction of the new domestic small-car offerings.

To recapitulate, as NMC-USA observes its twentieth birthday, it has three major challenges to face in its discernible future. The first, just discussed, is the possibility of motor vehicle imports being limited by tariffs, quotas, or otherwise. This is probably a short-term problem. At least the appeals for import curbs have implied that they are needed just for the critical period when the U.S. automobile industry is making its changeover to small-car production and presumably could be dropped after that. The experience of the Chicken War might lead to some skepticism about dropping restrictions on competition once they have been imposed, but it might happen that way.

The second challenge is intensified competition in the import car market, most of it from other Japanese automobile manufacturers. In 1980, the European automobile producers were handicapped by recession conditions and labor troubles but they were certain to provide vigorous competition in the U.S. market also.

The third and by far the greatest challenge that NMC-USA must encounter comes from the U.S. automobile industry. Its transformation is a slow and painful process, but it is taking place and it will be completed in due course. The management of NMC-USA is fully aware that this is going to happen and has no illusions about the competition that will then ensue.

There is confidence that the Datsun can hold its own in a freely competitive market, but at the same time there is a realistic appraisal of what the U.S. motor vehicle market is going to be like over the next several years—reaching the fairly obvious conclusion that even if competition is free, it is still going to be very, very difficult.

It is appropriate that President Arakawa should have the final word on this subject, since he will be steering NMC-USA through these next critical years. These are excerpts from his interview on September 11, 1980, just about two weeks before the company celebrated its twentieth birthday.

In my opinion—not a third party opinion—I hope that imports will still occupy a certain share of the U.S. market. I don't see a big share, but maybe at least a 20 percent share of the market will be occupied by imports. I would like to point out that the American people welcome competition, and import cars give a kind of competition, a kind of stimulus, particularly in these small, efficient cars. We are somewhat of an expert in producing small cars. American industry is now turning to produce small cars. They are full of energy, so soon, within two to three years, they will have the capacity to bring out very competitive products. Sometimes they might be superior to us, but still we are confident of competing with the future American cars with our techniques. We know the American auto industry is catching up in producing quality small cars. If we ourselves are satisfied with current conditions, then maybe sometime the American manufacturers will have passed us.

Our Nissan products should be unique, since everybody is now producing similar cars. Datsun is a unique product in the technical sense. For instance, we are the first Japanese automobile manufacturer to introduce a fuel injection system engine here in the United States. Several manufacturers are planning to have turbo engines, but we shall be the first auto manufacturer among the Japanese to introduce it. An engine which is also in the future is the electronically controlled engine.

This company is an American corporation, but still we are selling Japanese products, so in a sense it is a Japanese company too. If we are a 100% American corporation, there would be nothing unique about us and I insist on being always unique.

This makes a suitable final note. In mid-1981, Nissan Motor Company, Ltd. announced that the Datsun name will be gradually phased out in favor of Nissan, but the change has no bearing on the ability of NMC-USA to remain unique.

APPENDIX A

ARTICLES OF INCORPORATION
OF
NISSAN MOTOR CORPORATION IN U.S.A.

ONE: The name of this corporation is:
NISSAN MOTOR CORPORATION IN U.S.A.

TWO: The purposes for which this corporation is formed are:
(a) to engage primarily in the specific business of importing, distributing and selling automobiles and automotive parts, equipment and accessories;
(b) to engage in any one or more businesses or transactions which the board of directors of this corporation may from time to time authorize or approve, whether related or unrelated to the business described above or to any other business then or theretofore done by this corporation;
(c) to exercise any and all rights and powers which a corporation may now or hereafter exercise;
(d) to act as principal, agent, joint venturer, partner or in any other capacity which may be authorized or approved by the board of directors of this corporation;
(e) to transact business in the State of California or in any other jurisdiction of the United States of America or elsewhere in the world.

The foregoing statement of purposes shall be construed as a statement of both purposes and powers, and the purposes and powers in each clause shall, except where otherwise expressed, be in nowise limited or restricted by reference to or inference from the terms or provisions of any other clause, but shall be regarded as independent purposes and powers.

THREE: The county in the State of California where the principal office for the transaction of the business of this corporation is to be located is Los Angeles County.

FOUR: This corporation is authorized to issue only one class of shares of stock in the total number of 20,000 shares, of the aggregate par value of $2,000,000, and of the par value of $100 per share.

FIVE: The number of directors of this corporation shall be three. The names and addresses of the persons who are appointed to act as the first directors of this corporation are:

Yutaka Katayama
961 South Westmoreland Avenue
Los Angeles 6, California

Masahiko Zaitsu
1803 San Ardo Street
Torrance, California

Takayoshi Sogo
961 South Westmoreland Avenue
Los Angeles 6, California

IN WITNESS WHEREOF, for the purposes of forming this corporation under the laws of the State of California, the undersigned, constituting the incorporators of this corporation, including the persons named hereinabove as the first directors of this corporation, have executed these articles of incorporation this 27th day of September, 1960.

Y. KATAYAMA
Yutaka Katayama

MASAHIKO ZAITSU
Masahiko Zaitsu

TAKAYOSHI SOGO
Takayoshi Sogo

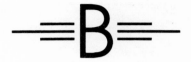

APPENDIX B

Automobile and Truck Sales Statistics (1957–1979)

	Industry*		Import*		Import from Japan		Datsun		Toyota	
	(000) Cars	(000) Trucks	(000) Cars	(000) Trucks	Cars	-0- Trucks	Cars	Trucks	Cars	Trucks
1957	6,033	894	207	16	—	—	—	—	—	—
58	4,668	760	379	29	(E) 400	—	83	—	288	—
59	6,100	965	614	37	(E) 2,300	179	1,131	179	1,028	—
60	6,641	963	499	37	(E) 2,400	346	1,294	346	821	—
61	5,935	937	379	29	(E) 1,800	576	1,157	279	576	—
62	7,092	1,100	339	32	2,629	711	1,812	736	711	—
63	7,720	1,270	386	40	4,707	1,096	2,724	1,983	1,096	—
64	8,101	1,393	484	42	8,816	3,528	6,791	3,524	2,025	4
65	9,332	1,554	569	14	17,851	6,476	13,201	5,514	5,442	962
66	9,028	1,636	651	17	40,183	9,856	21,726	8,431	19,483	1,425
67	8,337	1,544	769	21	69,135	14,429	34,028	12,601	36,245	1,828
68	9,656	1,831	1,031	24	107,300	20,936	40,219	17,712	68,779	2,684
69	9,583	1,977	1,118	34	185,885	31,107	57,543	29,351	128,288	1,756
70	8,405	1,819	1,285	65	312,777	62,534	104,067	50,954	196,750	11,565
71	10,250	2,106	1,568	85	554,247	82,473	185,270	66,655	294, 389	14,974
72	10,950	2,638	1,623	143	615,010	141,171	187,513	73,871	296,407	15,363
73	11,439	3,166	1,763	233	737,811	232,051	231,191	87,816	289,378	37,466
74	8,873	2,704	1,419	176	592,113	175,396	185,162	60,111	238,135	31,243
75	8,632	2,478	1,582	229	817,083	229,518	263,192	72,223	283,909	45,009
76	10,103	3,181	1,497	237	941,698	236,181	270,103	80,300	346,920	49,803
77	11,176	3,675	2,072	323	1,386,810	320,837	388,378	99,839	493,048	83,680
78	11,307	4,114	2,014	337	1,355,968	334,338	338,096	94,604	441,800	94,882
79	10,659	3,480	2,497	469	1,769,674	465,702	472,252	101,914	507,816	130,075
							2,806,933	868,943	3,653,334	522,719
							3,675,876		4,176,053	

* NMC data base.
-0- 1957–1969 Ward's Annual Yearbooks; 1970–1977 NMC data base; Data courtesy Melvin J. Wexler, Market Analyst, NMC-USA.
SOURCES: 1959–1974 MVMA: 1975–1977 NMC data base.

Automotive and Truck Import Sales Analysis (1957–1979)

Year	Import % industry		Japan % industry		Japan % imports	
	Car	Truck	Car	Truck	Car	Truck
1957	3.4	1.8	—	—	—	—
1958	8.1	3.8	—	—	0.1	—
1959	10.1	3.8	—	—	0.4	0.5
1960	7.5	3.8	—	—	0.5	0.9
1961	6.4	3.1	—	—	0.5	1.9
1962	4.8	2.9	—	—	0.8	2.2
1963	5.0	3.1	—	—	1.2	2.7
1964	6.0	3.0	0.1	0.2	1.8	8.4
1965	6.1	0.9	0.2	0.4	3.1	46.3
1966	7.2	1.0	0.4	0.6	6.1	60.0
1967	9.2	1.4	0.8	0.9	9.0	68.7
1968	10.7	1.3	1.1	1.1	10.4	85.0
1969	11.7	1.7	1.9	1.6	16.6	91.5
1970	15.3	3.6	3.7	3.4	24.3	96.2
1971	15.3	4.0	5.4	3.9	35.3	97.0
1972	14.8	5.4	5.6	5.4	37.9	98.7
1973	15.4	7.4	6.4	7.3	41.7	99.6
1974	16.0	6.5	6.7	6.5	41.7	99.7
1975	18.3	9.2	9.5	9.2	51.6	99.9
1976	14.8	7.5	9.3	7.4	62.9	99.7
1977	18.5	8.8	12.4	8.7	66.9	99.3
1978	17.8	8.2	12.0	8.1	67.3	99.2
1979	23.4	13.5	16.6	13.4	70.9	99.4

SOURCES

Company Materials

Most of the information on the history of Nissan Motor Corporation in U.S.A. has come from within the company, from both documentary and published sources and from interviews.

Documents: NMC-USA has not only kept its records, but has kept them in good order so that they can be located readily when wanted. The specific documents that have been used are cited in the footnotes.

In addition to company documents, Soichi Kawazoe made available the chapter of his unpublished memoirs that covers his career with NMC-USA, and Naofumi Uchiyama provided a statement of his career with the company and an analysis of its management structure at the time of the 1971 reorganization.

Publications: There have been several in-house periodicals which provide useful insights into the company's history. The company periodicals I have used are—*Datsun Dashes, Datsun*

Dealer News, Datsun Discovery, Datsun Employees Echo, Datsun News, Datsun Profile, and a weekly newssheet, *Datsun Dateline.* Files of all these are in the Corporate Library in the National Headquarters building.

There are also three very useful booklets published by NMC-USA:

- *Antitrust Compliance Policy* (1978).

- *Nissan Motor Corporation in U.S.A. From Small Beginnings, 1960–1978,* issued by the National Parts Department, May 1978, as a history and description of the Parts Department.

- *National Parts Training Overview, 1978,* also issued by the National Parts Department.

Interviews: The fact that NMC-USA is a young company has made personal interviews an extremely valuable source of information, since it has been possible to talk with employees and others connected with the company whose recollections cover the entire span of the company's history. These interviews have provided information that would have been lost otherwise. The list of participants follows:

Johann B. Ackerman	Hiroshi Majima
William B. Akers	Mayfield Marshall
Tetsuo Arakawa	Ryunosuki Miyakoda
Reid Briggs	Masashi Nagao
William Cushing	Jack Nielsen
Dale R. Finley	Joseph M. Opre
John R. Gladen	Richard Roberts
Karl A. Henning	Robert K. Scott
Tadayuki Ide	LeRoy L. Stubberfield
Yutaka Katayama	Johnnie K. Ueda
Soichi Kawazoe	Naofumi Uchiyama
Robert B. Kent	Masataka Usami
Yukio Kitahora	Gunnel V. Vacha
Jean LaPlant	Leland R. Wylie
Ray Lemke	Takashi T. Yasumi
Robert O. Link	Masahiko Zaitsu
Benjamin Machinist	

Reference Works

Several annual publications have been invaluable as sources of factual data.

A Guide to the Motor Industry of Japan, Japan Motor Industrial Federation, Tokyo.

The Global Datsun Family. A Guide to Nissan Motor Co., Ltd., Nissan Motor Co., Ltd., Tokyo.

Motor Vehicle Facts and Figures (formerly *Automobile Facts and Figures*), Motor Vehicle Manufacturers Association, Detroit.

Ward's Automotive Yearbook, Ward's Communications, Detroit.

Books

Allen, G. C.: *Japan's Economic Expansion*, Oxford University Press, London, 1965.

Bloomfield, Gerald: *The World Automotive Industry*, David and Charles, Newton Abbott, England, 1977.

Drucker, Peter: *Managing in Turbulent Times*, Harper & Row, New York, 1980.

Duncan, William C.: *U.S.—Japan Automobile Diplomacy*, Ballinger Publishing Co., Cambridge, Mass., 1973.

Edwards, Charles E.: *The Dynamics of the American Automobile Industry*, University of South Carolina Press, Columbia, S.C., 1965.

Fukuda, Haraka: *Japan and World Trade: The Years Ahead*, Saxon House, Farmborough, England, 1973.

Hollerman, Leon: *Japan's Dependence on the World Economy*, Princeton, Princeton, N.J., 1967.

Nelson, Walter H.: *Small Wonder. The Amazing Story of the Volkswagen*, Little, Brown, Boston, 1961.

Nissan Motor Co.: *History of Nissan Motor Co., Ltd., 1933–1963*, Nissan Motor Co., Tokyo, 1965.

Rae, John B.: *The American Automobile*, University of Chicago Press, Chicago, 1965.

———: *American Automobile Manufacturers: The First Forty Years*, Chilton, Philadelphia, 1959.

Rosovky, Henry and Patrick, Hugh, eds.: *Asia's New Giant: How the Japanese Economy Works*, Brookings, Washington, 1976.

Schrader, H. and P. J. Vierebl: *The History of Datsun Automobiles*, Schrader and Partner Comb H., Munich, Germany, 1968.

Sedgwick, Michael: *Fiat*, Arco, New York, 1974.

Soutter, Arthur W.: *The American Rolls-Royce*, Mowbray Co., Providence, R.I., 1976.

Toyota. The First Twenty Years in the U.S.A., Toyota Motor Sales, U.S.A., Torrance, California, 1977.

White, Lawrence J. *The Automobile Industry since 1945*, Harvard, Cambridge, Mass., 1971.

Articles

Burck, Charles G: "A Comeback Decade for the American Car," *Fortune,* vol. 101, no. 11, June 2, 1980, pp. 52–65.

Crow, James T.: "Dick Roberts," *Road and Track,* vol. 30, no. 5, February 1979, pp. 4–5.

Hein, John: "The Emu, the Snake in the Tunnel, and Other Financial Fauna," *Across the Board,* vol. 9, no. 9, September 1972, pp. 9–13.

Horrocks, Ray: "Euro-Japanese Collaboration: A New Pattern of Cooperation," *Outlook,* Summer 1980, pp. 35–36.

Kraar, Louis: "The Japanese Are Coming—With Their Own Style of Management," *Fortune,* vol. 91, no. 3, March 1975, pp. 116–121, 160–164.

Mateyka, James A. and Leonard Sherman: "The American Automobile: Facing up to Its Consumer," *Outlook,* Summer 1980, pp. 43–56.

McCosh, Dan: "Imports Chart a Smooth Course in Troubled U.S. Waters," *Ward's Automotive Yearbook, 1980,* pp. 21–23.

Reich, Robert B.: "Made in U.S.A.—A Label for Second-Rate?" *Across the Board,* vol. 17, no. 11, November 1980.

Seeger, Fred: "NAPS-Z," *Datsun Discovery,* vol. 3, no. 3, Fall 1979, pp. 30–32.

Sheehan, Robert: "A Big Year for Small Cars," *Fortune,* vol. 56, no. 2, August 1957, pp. 104–107, 196, 198.

Shields, T. Arthur: "The Automotive Industry: A New Crossroads," *Outlook,* Summer 1980, pp. 19–22.

Snyder, Frank R., "Imports Come Alive. Take Record Share in 1975," *Ward's Automotive Yearbook, 1976,* pp. 25–33.

Wiegner, Kathleen K.: "Down but Very Far from Out," *Forbes,* vol. 122, no. 6, September 18, 1978, pp. 57–62.

Unsigned Articles

"Datsun 280ZX," *Motor Trend,* vol. 30, no. 11, pp. 34–38.

"How Nissan Motor Deals with Competition and Devaluation," *Business Week,* no. 2274, Apr. 7, 1973, pp. 66–70.

"Import Car of the Year," *Motor Trend,* vol. 31, no. 2, March 1979, pp. 42–53.

"A Tried and True Model for GM," *Fortune,* vol. 102, no. 7, Oct. 6, 1980, pp. 15–16.

Other

Extensive use has been made of the following:

Newspapers:
> Los Angeles Times   The Wall Street Journal
> The New York Times

Periodicals:

Across the Board	*Nation's Business*
Automotive Industries	*Newsweek*
Business Week	*Oriental Economist*
Forbes	*Time*
Fortune	*U.S. News & World Report*

REFERENCES

Chapter 1

[1]The information on the early history of Nissan comes from *Nissan Motor Co., Ltd., 1967*, a brochure published by the company.

[2]William C. Duncan, *U.S.-Japan Automobile Diplomacy*, Ballinger Publishing Co., Cambridge, Mass., 1973, pp. 63–66. This a good, brief account of this phase of Japanese automotive history.

[3]This information is from an interview with Mr. Y. Katayama in Los Angeles, California, May 4, 1979. The Manchurian Motor Company was founded before the war and was basically a move to escape heavy Japanese taxation. "Mr. K" also points out that Nissan is a large-scale industrial complex encompassing about 200 companies, including Nissan Motor Co., Ltd.

[4]*History of Nissan Motor Company, Ltd., 1933–1963*, Nissan Motor Co., Tokyo, 1965, p. 226.

[5]G. C. Allen, *Japan's Economic Expansion*, Oxford University Press, London, 1965, p. 146.

[6]*Business Week*, Aug. 2, 1958, p. 69.

[7]*The Oriental Economist*, August 1958, p. 418.

[8]Katsuji Kawamata, "My Dream to be a Multi-National Corporation," speech published by Nissan Motor Co., Ltd., Oct. 31, 1966.

[9]The information on these preliminary steps is contained in a statement entitled "Recollections of the Introduction of Datsun Vehicles into the United States Market," by Mr. Koichi Iwata of the Export Department of Nissan Motor Company, Ltd., who

took the three Datsuns to the Los Angeles Exposition. It was made available to the author by Mr. Hiroyuki Yoshii, Vice President of Administration, Nissan Motor Corp. in U.S.A., on April 10, 1979. Additional information is in a manuscript provided by Nissan Motor Company, Ltd., and translated through the courtesy of Messrs. Toshitaka Enomoto, Hidetoshi Okada, and Takayoshi Yamada of Nissan Motor Corp. in U.S.A.

[10]Kawamata, "My Dream to be a Multi-National Corporation," Oct. 31, 1966.

[11]Katayama interview, May 4, 1979.

[12]Iwata statement.

[13]These cars had an engine modeled on the Austin Seven, with the narrow bore and long stroke the British were still using. This was pointed out by Jean LaPlant, first Service Manager of the Western Division, NMC-USA, in an interview on July 30, 1979.

[14]*Road and Track*, December 1958, p. 22.

[15]*Automotive News*, Nov. 10 and 17, 1958, pp. 2, 10.

[16]Nissan Motor Company manuscript.

[17]*Business Week*, Aug. 2, 1958, p. 77.

[18]*Automotive News*, July 14, 1958, p. 7.

[19]*Datsun Profile*, May 1979, p. 2.

[20]The information on Mr. Lemke comes principally from an interview with him on June 19, 1979, plus a news release from Nissan Motor Corporation in U.S.A., dated October 1978.

[21]"One Person's Opinion," *Datsun Profile*, March 1977, p. 14.

[22]This statement is quoted in "Nissan Motor Corporation in U.S.A.," National Parts Dept., NMC-USA, 1978, p. 4.

Chapter 2

[1]Lawrence J. White, *The Automobile Industry since 1945*, Harvard, Cambridge, Mass., 1971, pp. 71, 180–181. This a thorough analysis of these pricing policies, which White terms "cost-oriented." But none of these producers had the financial strength to risk cutting prices on the uncertain chance of getting greater volume.

[2]Ibid., p. 183.

[3]Ibid., p. 16.

[4]J. B. Rae, *American Automobile Manufacturers: The First Forty Years*, Chilton, Philadelphia, 1959, p. 8.

[5]For this case see Rae, *American Automobile Manufacturers*, pp. 72–79; William Greenleaf, *Monopoly on Wheels*, Wayne State University Press, Detroit, 1961.

[6]Arthur W. Soutter, *The American Rolls Royce*, Mowbray Co., Providence, R.I., 1976.

[7]Robert Sheehan, "A Big Year for Small Cars," *Fortune*, vol. 56, no. 2, August 1957, p. 105.

[8]Ibid., p. 196.

[9]*Ward's Automotive Yearbook, 1969*, p. 177.

[10]Sheehan, pp. 106–107.

Chapter 3

[1]The information on Mr. Kawazoe was provided by him in a letter to the author, August 21, 1979, and in interviews on November 27, and December 6, 1979.

[2]Katayama interview, May 4, 1979. Zaitsu confirmed that this was the primary purpose of the mission in an interview on February 27, 1980.

[3]Data provided by Market Analysis Department, NMC-USA.

[4]*Business Week*, April 7, 1973, p. 67.

[5]*Road and Track*, March 1961, p. 36.

[6]This account is from Mr. Kawazoe's memoirs, still in manuscript form, chap. 21, pp. 1, 2.

[7]Katayama interview, May 4, 1979. The Woolverton situation is also described in an interview with Reid Briggs, Pasadena, California, August 6, 1979, and by Zaitsu. Mr. Briggs was NMC-USA's first legal advisor and served for some years as Secretary of the corporation. Buying back cars from dealers is very unusual in American practice. It was done for Datsun at that time because otherwise it would have been virtually impossible to recruit dealers.

[8]The twentieth anniversary of this event was commemorated in *Toyota. The First Twenty Years in the U.S.A.*, Toyota Motor Sales, U.S.A., Torrance, California, 1977.

[9]*Business Week*, April 23, 1960, p. 26.

[10]Manuscript memoirs of Soichi Kawazoe, chap. 21, p. 9.

[11]The figure is frequently given as thirteen, but this excludes Alaska, which was in the process of becoming a state and was part of the Western Division. Hawaii had a separate distributorship, directly under Nissan Motor Co., Ltd.

[12]*Business Week*, Apr. 7, 1973, p. 66.

[13]Interview with Robert K. Scott, Vice President, Parts, NMC-USA, June 6, 1979. He became President of DAS early in 1980.

[14]*Ward's Automotive Yearbook, 1961*, p. 125.

[15]Ibid., p. 167.

[16]White, *The Automobile Industry since 1945*, p. 185.

[17]Michael Sedgwick, *Fiat*, Arco, New York, 1974, p. 287.

[18]From an interview with Mr. LaPlant (now retired), July 30, 1979.

[19]The information on Hoen comes from interviews with Robert O. Link, Senior Vice President, NMC-USA, and Gunnie Vacha, Secretary to Mr. Link, both on May 1, 1979.

[20]LaPlant interview, July 30, 1979.

[21]These sales totals include Hawaii.

Chapter 4

[1]Address by Robert O. Link, June 3, 1975, National Sales Meeting, NMC-USA, Newport Beach, California, p. 5.

[2]White, *The Automobile Industry since 1945*.

[3]*Ward's Automotive Yearbook, 1963*, p. 186.

[4]*Ward's, 1964*, p. 202.

[5]*Toyota. The First 20 Years in the U.S.A.*, pp. 31–37.

[6]Gerald Bloomfield, *The World Automotive Industry*, David and Charles, Newton Abbott, England, 1978, p. 209.

[7]Datsun's arrival in the top ten was actually announced in October 1964, by *Automotive News* on the basis of monthly sales figures, but the total for the year was not quite high enough.

[8]Interview with Tom Yasumi, National Parts Depot Operations Manager, NMC-USA, May 21, 1979.

[9]Interview with Jack Nielsen, Fleet Sales Manager, Western area, NMC-USA, Aug. 1979.

[10]From *This is Your Life*, sales promotion circular, NMC-USA, no date (about 1970).

[11]Stubberfield interview, May 8, 1979.

[12]Nielsen interview, Aug. 14, 1979.

[13]Stubberfield interview, May 8, 1979.

[14]Cushing interview, May 11, 1979.

[15]Nielsen interview, Aug. 14, 1979.

[16]LaPlant interview, July 30, 1979.

[17]Scott interview, June 6, 1979.

[18]*Datsun Used Car Reporter*, vol. 3, no. 3, April 1975, p. 1.

[19]*Datsun Dashes*, March 1963, February 1964. The information on profits is from an interview with T. Ide, March 12, 1980. The Eastern Division became profitable in 1966.

[20]Interview with Leland (Lee) Wylie, former National Service Manager, NMC-USA, Nov. 6, 1979.

[21]Interview with Reid Briggs, Aug. 6, 1979.

[22]Interview with Soichi Kawazoe, Nov. 7, 1979.

[23]*This Is Your Life*, sales circular.

[24]*Datsun Dashes*, vol. 1, January 1963, p. 1.

[25]These prices are quoted from the *Kelley Automobile Blue Book.*, 1972.

[26]From a company outline compiled in 1972 for internal reference.

[27]This information was provided by John Gladen, Director, Marketing Planning, NMC-USA.

[28]Company outline, 1972.

[29]Yasumi interview, May 21, 1979.

[30]Robert O. Link interview, May 11, 1979.

[31]Link speech to National Sales Meeting, NMC-USA, June 2, 1975.

[32]Bloomfield, *The World Automotive Industry*, p. 227.

Chapter 5

[1] White, *The Automobile Industry since 1945*, p. 188.

[2] *A Guide to the Motor Industry of Japan, 1969*, Japan Motor Industrial Federation, Tokyo, p. 17.

[3] *Nissan News*, September 1979, pp. 3, 4.

[4] *Ward's Automotive Yearbook, 1968*, p. 161; Nissan sales data (Appendix C). The truck statistics have a large variable in that the VW buslike station wagon and the Toyota Land Cruiser were classified as trucks until 1968 and then as passenger cars. However, Datsun's leadership is not affected.

[5] In some tables, British Leyland, just created in 1968 by merging BMC and Leyland Motors, is shown as fourth in 1968 and 1969, but it holds this position only if all British Leyland models are counted together rather than separately.

[6] Kawazoe memoirs, chap. 21, p. 13.

[7] "How Nissan Motor Deals with Competition and Devaluation," *Business Week*, No. 2274, Apr. 7, 1973, p. 68; interview with S. Kawazoe, Dec. 6. 1979.

[8] The information on the founding of DAS comes mainly from an interview with Masashi Nagao, its former President, Sept. 14, 1979.

[9] *Datsun News*, May/June 1969, p. 2.

[10] Scott interview, June 6, 1979.

[11] Interview with Leyland Wylie, Nov. 6, 1979.

[12] This is described by Reid Briggs in his interview, Aug. 6, 1979.

[13] *Datsun News*, May/June 1969, p. 2.

[14] Ibid., p. 3.

[15] *Datsun News*, December 1969, p. 4.

[16] This department's history is summarized in a memorandum from R. D. Cabibi, Director, Employee Relations, to H. Yoshii, Vice President, Administration, Apr. 25, 1978.

[17] Memo, William B. Young, National Manager, Engineering Services to Moon Kim, Librarian, NMC-USA, May 31, 1978.

[18] "Opening Remarks," Organizational Meeting, NMC-USA, National Headquarters, Compton, California, Apr. 12, 1971.

[19] *Datsun Dashes*, November 1970, p. 2.

Chapter 6

[1] This account is based on a presentation to Nissan Motor Co., Ltd., May 23–25, 1977, by the External Relations Department, NMC-USA.

[2] *Datsun News*, April 1973, p. 6.

[3] This is equally true for any other basis of comparison except aggregate totals of highway accidents, injuries, and fatalities. The United States has more of these because

there are a great many more cars on American roads and they are used more intensively than elsewhere. Comparisons on the basis of vehicle miles traveled are definitely the most informative. See J. B. Rae, *The Road and the Car in American Life*, M.I.T. Press, Cambridge, Mass., 1971, pp. 344–349.

[4]The actual figures for 1966 are 877,656 passenger cars out of a total of 2,286,399 four-wheel motor vehicles. A total of 153,090 passenger cars were exported. *A Guide to the Motor Industry of Japan, 1967*, pp. 21, 22.

[5]Katsuji Kawamata, "My Dream to be a Multi-National Corporation," Oct. 31, 1966.

[6]This information comes from manuscript notes by Kawazoe and made available to the author.

[7]Ibid. This was reported at an AIA Technical Committee meeting on January 7, 1966.

[8]Kawazoe memoirs, chap. 21, p. 14.

[9]*Datsun Dashes*, April 1967.

[10] Kawazoe memoirs, chap. 21, p. 21.

[11]Ibid., p. 22.

[12]*Datsun Employees Echo*, vol. 3, no. 1, January 1974, p. 2.

[13]*Datsun Employees Echo*, vol. 2, no. 6, June 1973, p. 1.

Chapter 7

[1]This information was acquired in interviews with Mr. Uchiyama, March 3, 1980, and Mr. Miyakoda, March 13, 1980.

[2]Link interview, May 1, 1979.

[3]This comes from an annual summary compiled by NMC-USA.

[4]*Pick's Currency Yearbook, 1978*, Pick Publishing Co., New York, 1978, p. 325.

[5]John Hein, "The Emu, the Snake in the Tunnel, and Other Financial Fauna," *Across the Board* vol. 9, no. 9, September 1972, pp. 10–11. The participants in the Smithsonian Agreement were Japan, Austria, Belgium, France, Great Britain, Italy, the Netherlands, Sweden, Switzerland, and West Germany.

[6]*Datsun Employees Echo*, vol. 1, no. 3, May 1972, p. 5.

[7]*Kashu Mainichi*, May 12, 1972.

[8]The texts of Kawamata's and Katayama's speeches are in an illustrated commemorative brochure celebrating this occasion.

[9]"How Nissan Motor Deals with Competition and Devaluation," *Business Week*, no. 2274, Apr. 7, 1973, p. 66.

[10]Appendix B gives a higher figure, but the one in the text is given by the Motor Vehicle Manufacturers Association, Detroit, *Motor Vehicle Facts and Figures, 1979*, p. 12.

[11]These particulars are in a notice to all Denver Region Datsun dealers, May 31, 1972, announcing the following day as the release date for PL620 pickup trucks.

[12]*Business Week*, no. 2274, Apr. 7, 1973, pp. 66–70.

[13]*Datsun Employees Echo*, vol. 2, no. 3, March 1973, p. 4.

[14]*Business Week*, no. 2274, Apr. 7, 1973, p. 68.

[15]The information on this litigation is based on interviews with Michael A. Cornelius, General Counsel, NMC-USA, Jan. 9, 1980, and Reid Briggs and David Toy, Jan. 24, 1980. Mr. Toy was a member of Mr. Brigg's firm when the case first came up, before NMC-USA had its own Legal Department.

[16]The texts of the decree and the company's instructions issued under it are in a pamphlet, *Antitrust Compliance Policy*, issued by NMC-USA in 1973.

[17]*P.D.Q., Inc. of Miami v. Nissan Motor Corporation in U.S.A. and Nissan Motor Company, Ltd.*

Chapter 8

[1]*A Guide to the Motor Industry of Japan, 1979*, p. 218.

[2]Harry A. Stark, "A Review and a Preview," *Ward's Automotive Yearbook, 1975*, p. 11.

[3]*Ward's, 1976*, p. 30.

[4]Frank R. Snyder, "Imports Come Alive, Take Record Share in 1975," *Ward's, 1976*, p. 23.

[5]*Datsun News*, July 1974, p. 4.

[6]Ibid., p. 5. The totals at the end of 1974 were cars, 970,000; trucks, 322,000; 1,292,000 Datsuns altogether.

[7]Link address, National Sales Meeting, June 2, 1975, p. 8.

[8]The speeches by Okuma, Katayama, and Link were published in *Datsun News*, July 1974. Quotations are from this source.

[9]The biographical information about Mr. Majima was given in an interview with the author, Jan. 8, 1980.

Chapter 9

[1]Harry A. Stark, "Another Record Year and Not a Dull Month," *Ward's Automotive Record, 1979*, p. 13.

[2]Ibid., p. 15.

[3]Henry Ford II, quoted in *The Wall Street Journal*, Dec. 5, 1977.

[4]Frank R. Snyder, "Imports Come Alive, Take Record Share in 1975," *Ward's, 1976*, p. 23.

[5]*Ward's, 1979*, p. 14.

[6]*Motor Vehicle Facts and Figures, 1979*, p. 3.

[7]Ibid., p. 4.

[8]*U.S. News & World Report*, Apr. 9, 1979, p. 24.

[9]*Money*, May 1977, p. 50.

[10]*Ward's, 1978,* p. 23.

[11]*Money,* May 1977, p. 52.

[12]This description is based on an interview with Mr. Majima, Jan. 8, 1980, and *Datsun Profile,* vol. 5, no. 3. December–January 1979/80.

[13]Interview with John Gladen, March 27, 1980.

[14]Interview with Dale R. Finley, Feb. 5, 1980.

[15]Memo, Robert O. Link to Datsun dealers, Oct. 13, 1976.

[16]Memo, H. Majima to all managers, Sept. 27, 1976.

[17]*Datsun Profile,* March 1977, p. 6.

[18]Memo, H. Majima to all employees, Jan. 5, 1979.

[19]*Datsun Discovery,* vol. 2, no. 1, Spring 1978, p. 20.

[20]*Los Angeles Times,* Apr. 22, 1977.

[21]Kathleen K. Wiegner, "Down but Very Far from Out, *Forbes,* vol. 122, no. 6, Sept. 18, 1978, p. 59.

[22]Ibid.; *Ward's Automotive Yearbook, 1979,* p. 14; *U.S. Industrial Outlook, 1979,* p. 291.

[23]*The Economist,* Sept. 28, 1978.

Chapter 10

[1]These figures are as of March 15, 1980. They were provided by Dennis Fujita, Personnel Department, NMC-USA.

[2]As of Apr. 11, 1980. Information provided by William B. Akers, Director, Dealer Development, NMC-USA.

[3]The results of the study are in a pamphlet, *What Datsun Means to the American Economy,* issued by the External Relations Department, NMC-USA, 1979.

[4]Fred Seeger, "NAPS-Z," *Datsun Discovery,* vol. 3, no. 3, Fall 1979, p. 30.

[5]Ibid.

[6]*Los Angeles Times,* Sept. 12, 1979.

[7]*Business Week,* March 24, 1980, p. 78; *U.S. News & World Report,* Feb. 26, 1980, p. 71. In these figures Volkswagen's United States production is included among the imports, presumably because the VW operation is simply assembly.

[8]*Los Angeles Times,* March 18, 1980.

[9]*Forbes,* Sept. 18, 1978, p. 69.

[10]Nissan's production forecast for 1980 was 2,745,000 units, of which 1,234,000 were for export. The totals include 186,000 KD (knocked- down) parts sets. Letter to author from Shoji Kato, Manager, Business Management, Export Dept., North America, Nissan Motor Co., Ltd., Apr. 25, 1980.

[11]*Business Week,* March 24, 1980, p. 79.

[12]Charles G. Burck, "A Comeback Decade for the American Car," *Fortune,* vol. 101, no. 11, June 2, 1980, p. 63.

[13]Ibid., p. 78.

[14]Ibid., p. 79.

[15]*Business Week*, Jan. 28, 1980, p. 112.

[16]Excellent analyses of this subject can be found in Charles E. Edwards, *The Dynamics of the United States Automobile Industry*, University of South Carolina Press, Columbia, S.C., 1965, Chap. 7, and Lawrence J. White, *The Automobile Industry Since 1945*, Chap. 4.

[17]*Los Angeles Times*, Apr. 19, 1980.

[18]*Automotive News*, Jan. 21, 1980.

[19]Address to meeting of American Imported Car Dealers Association, Feb. 11, 1980.

[20]*Los Angeles Times*, Feb. 14, 1980.

[21]*Detroit News*, Nov. 30, 1980.

[22]*The Wall Street Journal*, Oct. 31, 1980; *Datsun Dateline*, Nov. 14, 1980.

[23]NMC-USA protested this change in a document that describes the issues at stake in detail; Michael Cornelius, General Counsel, NMC-USA, to Robert E. Chasen, Commissioner, U. S. Customs Service, Jan. 28, 1980.

[24]From conversations with Mr. Zaitsu, NMC-USA Headquarters, Feb. 27, 1980, and Nissan, Ltd., Headquarters, Tokyo, March 13, 1980.

[25]Interview with Yukio Kitahora, Assistant to the Vice President and General Manager, Sales, NMC-USA, March 20, 1980; *Datsun Profile*, Aug. 1979, p. 4.

[26]*Los Angeles Herald Examiner*, March 17, 1980.

Chapter 11

[1]Professor Koichi Shimokawa of the faculty of business administration, Hosei University, Tokyo, has an excellent comparison of automobile sales methods in the United States and Japan in a paper entitled, "Marketing History in the Automobile Industry: The United States and Japan," presented at the Fuji International Business History Conference, sponsored by the Japan Business History Society, Tokyo, January 5 to 8, 1980. Former Vice President Uchiyama stated categorically in an interview with the author, March 3, 1980, that NMC-USA adopted a Detroit-type sales organization.

[2]The information on dealer relations comes from three interviews: William B. Akers, Director of Dealer Development, NMC-USA, Feb. 8, 1980; Dale Finley, Feb. 5, 1980; and Benjamin A. Machinist, National Dealer Organization Manager, Jan. 29, 1980.

[3]Machinist interview, Jan. 29, 1980.

[4]Akers interview, Feb. 8, 1980.

[5]NSA-014-71, Nov. 5, 1971; Benjamin A. Machinist, National Sales Administration Manager, to Datsun dealers in the New York, Boston, Norfolk, Jacksonville, and Dallas Regions.

[6]Memo, Phil Stearns, National Business Management Manager, NMC-USA to Robert O. Link, Jan. 28, 1975.

[7]Gladen interview, March 27, 1980.

[8]The information on this organization is based on the Akers, Finley, Gladen, and Machinist interviews.

[9]Minutes of First Executive Committee Meeting, p. 4.

[10]This is from the transcript of Mr. Machinist's interview as edited and corrected by him, Apr. 11, 1980.

[11]*Datsun Dashes*, vol. 2, no. 7, August 1973, pp. 1, 10; *Datsun News*, April 1974, pp. 3, 8.

[12]Kawazoe interview, Dec. 6, 1979.

[13]This account is in the Gladen interview.

[14]A description of this program appears in *Datsun Employees Echo*, vol. 1, no. 5, July/ August 1972, pp. 1, 15.

[15]*Datsun Employees Echo*, vol. 2, no. 6, June 1973, pp. 3, 9.

[16]*The Wall Street Journal*, Aug. 16, 1972.

[17]This information was brought out in an interview with Robert B. Kent, Vice President, Marketing Services, and Joseph M. Opre, Director of Advertising, May 28, 1980.

[18]*Advertising Age*, June 17, 1974. The campaign enabled some 5000 underprivileged youngsters to go to summer camps.

[19]*Datsun News*, April 1974, p. 2.

[20]*Advertising Age*, Apr. 1, 1974; *Datsun News*, April 1974.

[21]Mayfield Marshall interview, Aug. 14, 1979.

[22]*Datsun News*, March 1979, p. 4.

[23]Marshall interview, Aug. 14, 1979. Mr. Marshall is still with the company as a consultant to the President.

[24]Robert O. Link to all Datsun dealers, NS-003-75, Aug. 5, 1975.

[25]*Datsun Dealer News*, July/August 1977, has a description of these associations.

[26]Finley interview, Feb. 5, 1980.

[27]*Advertising Age*, June 20, 1977; *Automotive News*, June 29, 1977. The selection committee was composed of President Majima, Vice Presidents Link, King, and Kent, and Joseph M. Opre, Director of Advertising.

[28]*Automotive News*, Oct. 31, 1977.

[29]*Advertising Age*, Apr. 5, 1976.

[30]Finley interview, Feb. 5, 1980.

[31]See *Sports Illustrated*, Aug. 21, 1972.

[32]Kent/Opre interview, May 28, 1980.

Chapter 12

[1]*Nissan Motor Corporation in U.S.A. From Small Beginnings. 1960 to 1978*, National Parts Department, May 1978, p. 2.

[2]The information about Usami is based on an interview with him in Tokyo, March 11, 1980.

[3]Yasumi interview, May 21, 1979.

[4]Scott interview, June 6, 1979.

[5]National Parts Department, *Nissan Motor Corp.*, p. 2.

[6]Scott interview, June 6, 1979.

[7]*Datsun News*, May/June 1969, p. 2.

[8]Scott interview, June 6, 1979.

[9]*National Parts Training. Overview, 1978*, NMC-USA, 1978, p. 1. This publication has a detailed description of the Parts Training Program.

[10]*Nissan Motor Corp.*, p. 26.

[11]Masataka Usami interview, March 11, 1980.

[12]Zaitsu did not visit dealers. His principal responsibility was liaison between NMC-USA and NMC, Ltd. He helped the Service and Parts Managers, but he believed that direct relations with Datsun dealers should be in the hands of the American staff.

[13]Wylie interview, Feb. 8, 1980.

[14]*Datsun News*, May/June 1969, p. 2.

[15]Usami interview, March 11, 1980.

[16]Wylie interview, Feb. 8, 1980.

[17]*Datsun Profile*, September/October 1979, pp. 4, 4.5.

[18]Ibid., p. 4.

[19]*Automotive News*, June 27, 1977.

[20] *Datsun Profile*, September/October 1979, p. 6.

[21]This listing of programs and goals is in the memo, "History of Nissan Motor Corporation—Service."

[22]A summary history of the Engineering Department is provided in a memo from William B. Young, National Engineering Services Manager, to Moon Kim, May 31, 1978.

[23]Mr. Usami made this point in his interview.

[24]*Datsun Employees Echo*, vol. 2, no. 3, March 1973, p. 4.

[25]*Automotive Design and Development*, March 1980, pp. 16–17.

[26]Young memo, May 31, 1978.

Chapter 13

[1]Kawazoe memoirs, chap. 21, p. 11.

[2]Wylie interview, Nov. 6, 1979.

[3]This description comes from an undated document in the NMC-USA company library, evidently written in 1968, itemizing VMP's complaints. Further information was given by Karl Henning, Manager, Port Programs, NMC-USA, Nov. 16, 1979.

[4]There are two brochures describing this company, one issued in 1972 and the other in 1979.

[5]The information on the wharf is from descriptive brochures issued by Nissan, Ltd., and a visit to it by the author, March 7, 1980.

[6]Henning interview, Nov. 16, 1979.

[7]*Kelly Blue Book Reporter,* vol. 21, no. 6, June 1972, p. 11.

[8]Henning interview, Nov. 16, 1979.

[9]This account of the founding and functioning of DAS is based on an interview with Masashi Nagao, President of DAS until 1977, given on Aug. 22, 1979; the Henning and Wylie interviews; and *Datsun News,* October 1970, p. 2.

[10]Nagao interview, Aug. 22, 1979.

[11]*Nissan Carrier,* pamphlet, Nissan Motor Co., Ltd., 1979.

[12]Interview with Mr. Ide, Tokyo, March 12, 1980.

[13]Interview with Mr. Miyakoda, Tokyo, March 13, 1980.

[14]*Datsun Employees Echo,* September/October 1972, p. 9.

[15]Ibid., p. 11.

[16]This information was provided by officials of Hommoku Wharf when the author visited there on March 7, 1980.

[17]*Datsun News,* October 1979, p. 2.

[18]*Datsun Employees Echo,* October 1973, p. 7.

[19]Henning and Nagao interviews; *Datsun News,* April 1973, p. 6.

[20]*Automotive Design and Development,* March 1980, p. 17.

[21]*Datsun Dealer News,* May/June 1977, p. 11.

[22]Henning interview, Nov. 16, 1979.

Chapter 14

[1]*Toward New Horizons with Datsun. A Guide to Nissan Motor Co., Ltd.* Tokyo, 1980, p. 8.

[2]LaPlant interview, July 30, 1979.

[3]*Datsun Dashes,* vol. 2, no. 3, August 1964.

[4]Ibid., September 1965; July 1966; April 1967.

[5]*Datsun News,* August 1971, pp. 5, 12.

[6]Ibid., April 1970, p. 3.

[7]Ibid., pp. 5-6.

[8]Much of the information on the Competition Department and its activities is based on an interview with Richard Roberts, March 20, 1980. There is also a profile of Roberts in *Sports Car,* March 1979, pp. 21-23.

[9]James T. Crow, "Dick Roberts," *Road and Track,* vol. 30, no. 5, February 1979, pp. 4-5.

[10]Roberts interview, March 20, 1980; *Nissan—Datsun Rally and Race Digest,* no. 3, July–December 1979, p. 17.

[11]Roberts interview, March 20, 1980, p. 18.

[12]*Datsun News,* January 1976, p. 2. The figures on parts sales are here also.

[13]*Nissan—Datsun Rally and Race Digest,* no. 3, July–December 1979.

[14]*Datsun News,* January 1976, pp. 3, 8.

[15]*Datsun Employees Echo,* September 1974, pp. 8–9.

[16]*Nissan—Datsun Rally and Race Digest,* no. 3, July–December 1979, pp. 9–10.

[17]Ibid., pp. 17–18.

[18]NMC, Ltd., *Datsun 280ZX,* Tokyo, 1978, p. 135.

[19]Ibid., p. 138.

[20]*Datsun News,* October–November 1969, p. 3.

[21]*Datsun Profile,* September/October 1979, p. 7.

[22]*Nissan News,* no. 446, Aug. 17, 1978.

[23]*Motor Trend,* November 1978, pp. 34–35.

Chapter 15

[1] NMC-USA Organization Manual, Aug. 1, 1972.

[2]Ide Interview, March 12, 1980.

[3]*Datsun Employees Echo,* Summer 1976, pp. 4–7.

[4]*Datsun News,* October 1975, p. 7.

[5]This information provided by H. Yoshii, Vice President, Administration.

[6]Information provided by Jack Bukaty, Aug. 21, 1980.

[7]*Company Printer Report,* NMC-USA, 1974.

[8]*Datsun Employees Echo,* Summer 1976, p. 15.

[9]Memo, Ronald D. Cabibi, Director, Employee Relations, to H. Yoshii, Apr. 25, 1978, RDC 078-094.

[10]*Datsun Employees Echo,* Summer 1976, p. 16.

[11]Memo, Leslie A. Kelly, Manager, International Trade and Public Affairs, to Moon Kim, May 31, 1978.

[12]*Datsun News,* September 1973, p. 5.

[13]*Datsun Employees Echo,* August 1973, p. 5.

[14]Reid Briggs interview, Aug. 6, 1979.

Chapter 16

[1]This view was stated by Mr. Arakawa in an interview on Sept. 11, 1980. On this general subject a good, brief study is Louis Kraar, "The Japanese Are Coming—With Their Own Style of Management," *Fortune,* vol. 91, no. 3, March -1975, pp. 116–121, 160–161; 164.

[2]N. Uchiyama, "Four Years with Nissan U.S.A.," manuscript statement given to author, March 3, 1980.

[3]"A Tried and True Model for G.M.," *Fortune,* vol. 102, no. 7, Oct. 6, 1980, p. 15.

[4]Lawrence R. Gustin, "General Motors vs, the Japanese," *Grand Rapids Press*, Sept. 14, 1980.

[5]*Motor Vehicle Facts and Figures, 1980*, p. 2.

[6]Ibid., p. 3.

[7]Peter Drucker expresses it as "profit is the cost of staying in business," *Managing in Turbulent Times*, Harper & Row, New York, 1980, pp. 30–31.

[8]*Business Week*, Nov. 10, 1980, p. 49.

[9]*U.S. News & World Report*, Oct. 13, 1980, p. 54.

[10]Quoted by Mr. Arakawa in his interview, Sept. 16, 1980. He believes that this consolidation process will be most pronounced in Japan, which has the largest number of small firms in the automotive industry among the chief producing nations.

[11]T. Arthur Shields, "The Automotive Industry: A New Crossroads," *Outlook*, Summer 1980, p. 20.

[12]Dan McCosh, "Imports Chart a Smooth Course in Troubled U.S. Waters," *Ward's Automotive Yearbook, 1980*, p. 23.

[13]*U.S. News & World Report*, Oct. 13, 1980, p. 55.

[14]*The Wall Street Journal*, Sept. 22, 1980.

[15]James A. Mateyka and Leonard Sherman, "The American Automobile: Facing up to Its Consumer," *Outlook*, Summer 1980, p. 45.

[16]*The Wall Street Journal*, Nov. 11, 1980.

[17]*Los Angeles Times*, Nov. 11, 1980.

[18]Robert B. Reich, "Made in U.S.A.—a Label for Second-Rate?" *Across the Board*, vol. 17, no. 11, November 1980, pp. 3–4.

[19]*The Wall Street Journal*, Nov. 11, 1980.

INDEX

About the Author

John B. Rae has been called "the dean of automotive historians" and is listed in *Who's Who in America* as the leading historian of automotive history. Professor emeritus of Harvey Mudd College, Claremont, California, he was awarded the Leonardo Da Vinci Medal from the Society for the History of Technology and the Thomas McKean Memorial Award for Automotive History. He is the author of ten previous books, including *The Road and the Car in American Life, The American Automobile,* and *The United States in World History* (McGraw-Hill).